Lecture Notes of the Institute for Computer Sciences, Social Informatics and Telecommunications Engineering

506

The LNICST series publishes ICST's conferences, symposia and workshops.

LNICST reports state-of-the-art results in areas related to the scope of the Institute. The type of material published includes

- Proceedings (published in time for the respective event)
- Other edited monographs (such as project reports or invited volumes)

LNICST topics span the following areas:

- General Computer Science
- E-Economy
- E-Medicine
- Knowledge Management
- Multimedia
- Operations, Management and Policy
- Social Informatics
- Systems

Khaled Rabie · Rupak Kharel · Lina Mohjazi ·
Taissir Elganimi · Wali Ullah Khan
Editors

IoT as a Service

8th EAI International Conference, IoTaaS 2022
Virtual Event, November 17–18, 2022
Proceedings

Springer

Editors
Khaled Rabie
Manchester Metropolitan University
Manchester, UK

Rupak Kharel
University of Central Lancashire
Preston, UK

Lina Mohjazi
University of Glasgow
Glasgow, UK

Taissir Elganimi
City University
Tripoli, Libya

Wali Ullah Khan
University of Luxembourg
Luxembourg, Luxembourg

ISSN 1867-8211   ISSN 1867-822X (electronic)
Lecture Notes of the Institute for Computer Sciences, Social Informatics
and Telecommunications Engineering
ISBN 978-3-031-37138-7   ISBN 978-3-031-37139-4 (eBook)
https://doi.org/10.1007/978-3-031-37139-4

This Springer imprint is published by the registered company Springer Nature Switzerland AG
The registered company address is: Gewerbestrasse 11, 6330 Cham, Switzerland

Preface

We are delighted to introduce the proceedings of the 8th edition of the European Alliance for Innovation (EAI) International Conference on IoT as a Service (IoTaaS 2022). This conference brought together researchers, developers and practitioners around the world who are leveraging and developing IoT technology.

The technical program of IoTaaS 2022 consisted of 17 full papers. The conference tracks were: Main track, Workshop track and Fast track. Aside from the high-quality technical paper presentations, the technical program also featured three keynote speeches. These keynote speakers were Prof. Mohamed-Slim Alouini from King Abdullah University of Science and Technology (KAUST), KSA, Charles Paumelle from Microshar, Inc., UK and Prof. Cheng Li from Memorial University, Canada. The workshop organized was Edge Intelligence and Mobile Computing for 5G and Beyond Communications and Applications.

Coordination with the steering chair Imrich Chlamtac was essential for the success of the conference. We sincerely appreciate his constant support and guidance. It was also a great pleasure to work with such an excellent organizing committee team for their hard work in organizing and supporting the conference. In particular, the Technical Program Committee, led by our TPC Co-Chairs, Mostafa Fouda, Xingwang Li, Dinh-Yhuan Do, Galymzhan Naurzbayev and A. F. M. Shahen Shah, completed the peer-review process of technical papers and made a high-quality technical program. We are also grateful to all the authors who submitted their papers to the IoTaaS 2022 conference and workshops.

We strongly believe that the IoTaaS conference provides a good forum for all researchers, developers and practitioners to discuss all science and technology aspects that are relevant to IoT technology. We also expect that future IoTaaS conferences will be as successful and stimulating, as indicated by the contributions presented in this volume.

Khaled Rabie
Rupak Kharel
Lina Mohjazi
Taissir Elganimi
Wali Ullah Khan

Organization

Steering Committee

Imrich Chlamtac   University of Trento, Italy

Organizing Committee

General Chair

Khaled Rabie   Manchester Metropolitan University, UK

General Co-chair

Rupak Kharel   University of Central Lancashire, UK

TPC Chair and Co-chairs

Zubair Fadlullah   Lakehead University, Canada
Noushin Karimian   Manchester Metropolitan University, UK
Mostafa Fouda   Idaho State University, USA
Xingwang Li   Henan Polytechnic University, China
Dinh-Thuan Do   University of Texas, Austin, USA
Galymzhan Nauryzbayev   Nazarbayev University, Kazakhstan
A. F. M. Shahen Shah   Yildiz Technical University, Turkey

Sponsorship and Exhibit Chairs

Thokozani Shongwe   University of Johannesburg, South Africa
Moaad Benjabir   University of Oxford, UK

Local Chairs

Aris Christos Alexoulis   Manchester Metropolitan University, UK
  Chrysovergis
Noushin Karimian   Manchester Metropolitan University, UK

Workshops Chairs

Berk Canberk   Istanbul Technical University, Turkey
Belal Alsinglawi   Western Sydney University, Australia

Publicity and Social Media Chairs

Lina Mohjazi   University of Glasgow, UK
Abdelhak Bentaleb   National University of Singapore (NUS),
                                        Singapore
Taissir Elganimi   University of Tripoli, Libya
Tien Anh Tran   Vietnam Maritime University, Vietnam

Publications Chair

Waliullah Khan   University of Luxembourg, Luxembourg

Technical Program Committee

Technical Program Committee Chairs

Zubair Fadlullah   Lakehead University, Canada
Noushin Karimian   Manchester Metropolitan University, UK

Technical Program Committee Co-chairs

Mostafa Fouda   Idaho State University, USA
Xingwang Li   Henan Polytechnic University, China
Dinh-Thuan Do   University of Texas, Austin, USA
Galymzhan Nauryzbayev   Nazarbayev University, Kazakhstan
A. F. M. Shahen Shah   Yildiz Technical University, Turkey

Technical Program Committee Members

Mian Ahmad Jan   Abdul Wali Khan University Mardan, Pakistan
Chinmay Chakraborty   Birla Institute of Technology, Jharkhand, India
Haotong Cao   Hong Kong Polytechnic University, China
Gaoyuan Zhang   Henan University of Science and Technology,
                                        China
Gaojian Huang   Henan Polytechnic University, China

Dan Deng	Guangzhou Panyu Polytechnic, China
Han Wang	Yichun University, Yichun, China
Wael Abd Alaziz	University of Sumer, Iraq
Ziad Alabbasi	Middle Technical University, Iraq
Taissir Elganimi	University of Tripoli, Libya
Khaled Rabie	Manchester Met University, UK
Shubham Mahajan	Shri Mata Vaishno Devi University, India
Gökhan Seçinti	Istanbul Technical University, Turkey
Müge Erel Özçevik	Celal Bayar University, Turkey
Elif Bozkaya	National Defense University, Turkey
Lina Mohjazi	University of Glasgow, UK
Abdelhak Bentaleb	National University of Singapore (NUS), Singapore
Tien Anh Tran	Vietnam Maritime University, Vietnam
Rupak Kharel	University of Central Lancashire, UK
Gad Mohamed	Lakehead University, Canada
Aya Farrag	Lakehead University, Canada
Khaled Bedda	Lakehead University, Canada
Mohamed Elshafei	Lakehead University, Canada
Ahmed Aboulfotouh	Lakehead University, Canada
Bushra Mughal	Lakehead University, Canada

Contents

Next Generation Wireless Networks, Internet of Things, Artificial Intelligence

Home Energy Management System to Reduce Unconscious Electricity
Consumption 3
    Nurkhat Zhakiyev, Yerasyl Amanbek, Aidana Kalakova,
    and Didar Yedilkhan

An IoT Monitoring System for Dairy Products 12
    Evangelos Syrmos, Dimitrios Bechtsis, Dimitrios Vlachos,
    Georgios Papapanagiotakis, Theodora Todi, Maria Papaspyropoulou,
    Konstantinos Georgakidis, and Nikolaos Sfitis

A Review of Emerging Low Power Networks in Internet of Medical
Things (IoMT) 23
    Zahraa Zakariya Saleh

Design of Performance Enhanced Metamaterial-Enabled Absorber
for Low-Power IoT Networks 38
    Kozhakhmet Abdugapbar, Kassen Dautov, Mohammad Hashmi,
    and Galymzhan Nauryzbayev

Effective Exploitation of Ambient EM Energy for Driving Emerging IoT
Devices: Case Study 48
    Kamila Shalpeneyeva, Kassen Dautov, Mohammad Hashmi,
    and Galymzhan Nauryzbayev

Evaluating Direct Link IoT-LoRa Communication via LEO Nanosatellite:
DEWASAT-1 58
    Reem Al-Ali, Sidi Ahmed. Bendoukha, Zineddine N. Haitaamar,
    Mireya Arora, Jayakumar V. Karunamurthy, and Tareg Ghaoud

**Wireless Communications, Vehicular Networks, Resource
Optimization, Satellite communications and Machine Learning**

Bit Error Rate Performance of Wireless Communication Systems
with Passive Intermodulation Interference 73
    Lu Tian, Zhan Xu, Chenrui Shi, Lele Guan, and Yuming Shi

User-Oriented Dynamic MEC Application Deployment in Edge Cloud
Network 82
 Yinan Guo, Yanzhao Hou, Jiaxiang Geng, Hao Chen, and Whai-En Chen

Joint Design of Caching and Offloading for Mobile Edge Computing
in 5G Heterogenous Networks 94
 Jianxiong Xiao, Jing Liu, Xiang Chen, Yuhan Dong, and Terng-Yin Hsu

A Percolation-Based DTNs Routing Using Fountain Coding 106
 Ruxin Zhi, Bilei Zhou, and Zhigang Tian

Bandwidth Allocation for eMBB and mMTC Slices Based on AI-Aided
Traffic Prediction 117
 Xiaoli Zhang, Kai Liang, Jen-Jee Chen, and Jiaxin Liu

A Coded Modulation Scheme for IoT System 127
 Yamei Zou, Dengsheng Lin, and Zhiyuan Jiang

A Resource- and Power-Efficient Implementation of PSS Synchronization
on FPGA in Vehicular Networks 135
 Chengxiang Ge, Fei Peng, Shan Cao, Zhiyuan Jiang, and Terng-Yin Hsu

Cooperative Hybrid-Caching for Long-Tail Distribution Request
with Deep Reinforcement Learning 148
 Weibao He, Fasheng Zhou, and Dong Tang

Distributed Routing Algorithm for LEO Satellite Network Based on Deep
Reinforcement Learning 161
 Yudie Chen, Lan Wang, Houze Liang, Dong Lv, Weizhi Wu, Xiang Chen,
 and Terngyin Hsu

An Intelligent Wireless Signal Detection and Recognition Platform 174
 Haoyu Zhao, Yan Zhang, Wancheng Zhang, Guangchuan Cao,
 Jiupeng Song, and Shanping Yu

Network Security

A Novel Approach to Transmit Audio Content Over a Secure
Communication Channel by Using Light Optics Under the Acousto-Optic
Premise 187
 Vijay A. Kanade

Author Index 199

Next Generation Wireless Networks, Internet of Things, Artificial Intelligence

Home Energy Management System to Reduce Unconscious Electricity Consumption

Nurkhat Zhakiyev, Yerasyl Amanbek[✉], Aidana Kalakova, and Didar Yedilkhan

Astana IT University, 55/11 Mangilik Yel Ave., Astana, Kazakhstan
yerasyl.amanbek@astanait.edu.kz

Abstract. The energy consumption in the residential area of Kazakhstan is increasing every year. One of the primary causes of excessive electricity demand is unconscious consumption. Therefore, to reduce the demand in residential area "Home Energy Management System" (HEMS) is introduced. This paper offers low-cost energy management system that will reduce electricity consumption in dormitories, homes, and apartments by notifying residents about excessive and unnecessary loads. The proposed system includes an energy meter to monitor real-time consumption of the house, a microprocessor to read data from energy meter and redirect it to cloud server via Wi-Fi module. The system also includes occupancy sensor that detects when a person leaves the house or arrive at the house. By relating the output of the occupancy sensor and energy meter the system sends electronic notification to the resident when some event occurs. As an example, in case, if person forgets to switch off any of the electronic device (lights, TV or even iron) when leaving the house, the HEMS will send a notification to the phone. The results have shown, that users could save up to 8000tg/year on energy consumption.

This paper aims: the rise of awareness regarding electricity consumption to the end user. State of the art technology – load profiling, demand control, Wi-Fi connection.

Reduction of electricity bills for customers. Reducing risks associated with electricity consumption. The energy management system that collects, process and display load data.

Keywords: Home Energy Management System (HEMS) · IoT · Smart Cities · Energy Savings · Microprocessors · Embedded Systems · Demand Response · Electricity consumption

K. Rabie et al. (Eds.): IoTaaS 2022, LNICST 506, pp. 3–11, 2023.
https://doi.org/10.1007/978-3-031-37139-4_1

1 Introduction

1.1 Related Works

Latest studies on the fields of energy systems are transitioning towards demand side management and optimization. Demand Responses (DRs), Transactive Energy, and HEMS become burning topic in the power and energy systems. The most recent HEMS review in reference [1] has described over 120 articles related to HEMS projects, that includes microprocessor based systems. Recently General Electric presented HEMS that can be controlled via smartphone application [2]. In this work the HEMS is also planned to be controlled via mobile application. Some HEMS projects are integrated with DR that plays essential role in reduction of electricity demand in peak hours [3, 4]. These projects have applied DR model by utilizing load consumption pattern of customers and available distributed energy recourses (DERs). The authors in [5] has presented DR based HEMS for energy management in Hotels. Their system unlike other DR programs do not penalize end-users if they have failed to reduce power consumption. Some HEMS projects reviewed in [6] are designed specifically for smart homes, where household has control over appliances and HEMS optimizes energy consumption. Authors in [7] have presented real-time energy management of residential appliances including air conditioner, electric water heater, and clothes dryer. The authors in [8] have presented similar HEMS architecture for wider variety of appliances including non-schedulable ones. One of the HEMS project uses ZigBee controller to reduce energy consumption in a room via standby power cut-off outlets [9]. The authors in [10] have presented low-cost, user friendly HEMS using microcontroller – server – web interface layout. This work has also presented device recognition theory; however, authors have not implemented it. According to the theory loads have different amplitude (power), and output voltage (resistive, inductive, or capacitive), and due to devices may have different signatures. There are other microprocessor based HEMS that work with wireless communication like Wi-Fi, Bluetooth or ZigBee wireless protocol presented in [11–13]. Only few of related works have demonstrated practical results. This HEMS project will implement state-of-the art methods described in the literature and demonstrate practical results.

The main contributions of the work are to implement an innovative production of home energy management into the residential buildings of Kazakhstan. One of the goals of the project is to reduce risks associated with electricity consumption relate to the human factor, as well as make energy consumption more efficient. More precisely, HEMS product allow customer to track the consumption and reduce his electricity bills. The proposed system sends alert when there is excessive consumption or when user forgets to switch off electronics when leaving house. E.g., if person forgets to turn off the iron while leaving the house, the notification will be sent to his phone. We expect to make a prototype of the system, then test it in Astana IT University dormitory rooms and in case of the success employ system to other residential buildings of Kazakhstan.

2 Methodology

2.1 HEMS Work

Proposed HEMS consists of two parts, that are hardware and software. In the hardware part, the microcontroller with ESP8266 module connects to Wi-Fi network via ssid and pass, then it establishes connection with the remote server by providing "authentication token". The microcontroller continuously read data from energy meter and occupancy sensor, then microcontroller sends API Write Key containing the data to the remote server. User through phone application can monitor consumption and see his load profile. When consumption reaches certain threshold (E^{Max}) set by user, the app sends push notification. In case when occupancy sensor detects that user has left the house and there are some loads greater than E^{Min}, the app sends push notification. In case of two-zone differential electricity tariffs (with peak and off-peak hours) the user can set different energy limits to participate in DR program.

Software: Arduino program (embedded C), iOS/Android application.

Hardware: HEMS hardware, mobile phones with iOS/Android based application.

System Flow Chart

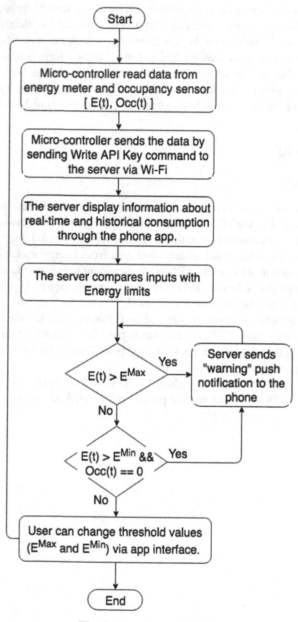

Start

Micro-controller read data from energy meter and occupancy sensor [E(t), Occ(t)]

Micro-controller sends the data by sending Write API Key command to the server via Wi-Fi

The server display information about real-time and historical consumption through the phone app.

The server compares inputs with Energy limits

$E(t) > E^{Max}$ — Yes → Server sends "warning" push notification to the phone

No

$E(t) > E^{Min}$ && $Occ(t) == 0$ — Yes

No

User can change threshold values (E^{Max} and E^{Min}) via app interface.

End

Fig. 1. Flow chart of HEMS

Components. Arduino Uno is used as a hardware that monitors data from the sensors. ESP8266 Wi-Fi module is used for transmitting and receiving data via Internet. Remote server is used to establish communication between hardware (Arduino + ESP) and mobile application.

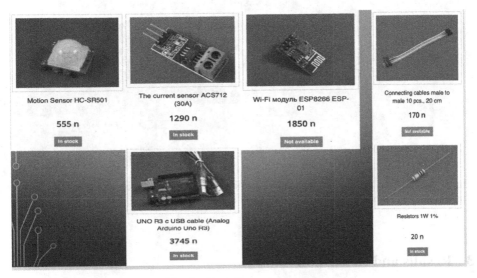

Fig. 2. Hardware components

HEMS project has the iOS/Android app. Unique authorization token was generated for the project. The project was built by utilizing several application widgets. The widgets include chart for power monitoring, several labels and gauges for current, power, occupancy and energy.

The interface has 2 menus: General and Settings. In general menu, all necessary information is displayed. In settings menu, user can choose recommended settings: 221V, pf = 0.85, tariff = 13.5(tg/kWh), $E^{max} = 75$ and $E^{min} = 15$. User can also customize sliders in custom settings.

Application for iOS/Android

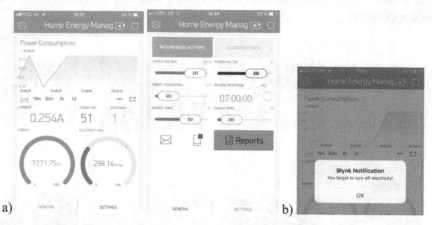

Fig. 3. a) Interface for mobile application. b) Notification system in case of extensive energy consumption and when user forgets to switch off the lights.

3   Results and Discussion

3.1   Building Prototype

The hardware components are packed in the carton box. Inside box there is ESP8266 module for Wi-Fi connection, ASC712 for sensing current, 2x HC-SR501 for motion detection.

Fig. 4. Prototype of HEMS

Cost of the prototype.   The cost of the equipment is estimated for 1 year of operation; it covers expenses for 28 HEMS devises. These devises are planned to be installed for one floor in the Astana IT University dormitory.

Table 1. Prototype cost for 28 pieces

Cathegory	Discription	Amount	Cost ($)	Total cost ($)
Equipment	Arduino board	28	45	1260
	Wi-Fi module	28	15	420
	Occupancy sensor	28	36	1008
	Energy meter	28	139	3892
Electrical Components	Resistors (x20)	20	6	120
	Wires (x20)	10	6	60
	PCB	28	9	252
	LEDs (x5)	90	3	270
	Capasitors (x10)	8	2	16
	Transistors	156	7	1092
Delivery of Equipment	Shipping	4	50	200
Software	Server (yearly subscription)	1	320	320
	Application Interface	1	400	400
Total				**9310**

3.2 Case Study

The price of energy is increasing every year in Kazakhstan [14–16]. Highest consumption level price for electricity has reached to 19.04 tg/kWh. With this tendency more people will be interested in reducing their electricity bills. The product helps to reduce electricity bill by giving user warnings about unnecessary consumption. In case of two-zone differential electricity tariffs (with peak and off-peak hours) the user can set different energy limits to participate in DR program.

The main target is to successfully implement project in the campus and work towards minimizing product cost and sell ready devises in Kazakhstan and outside.

The product is aimed to reduce energy consumption of end-users, since majority of energy sources in Kazakhstan comes from traditional generation like coal the high penetration of product lead to reduction of environmental pollution.

Potential benefits for end-user
For 300kWh consumption per month:
    4635.6 tg/month.
    You can save _6930 tg/year_ if you reduce consumption by 10%
    In case of two-zonal tariffs for 250kWh/50kWh (day/night):
    4333.5 tg/month.
    You can save _7794 tg/year_ if you shift 50kWh to night.
    And _additional 4420.8 tg/year_ if you reduce consumption by 10%
    By the results, potential user without the HEMS could lose up to 8000tg/year.
    Savings are estimated with reference to energy tariffs in Astana [14]:

AstanaEnergoSbyt: September 1, 2022 tariffs (NEW):
the minimum fare (up to 90 kWh) - 10.44 tenge / kWh.
Average rate (from 90 to 180 kWh) - 15.40 tenge / kWh.
the maximum tariff (from 180 kWh and above) - 19.25 tenge / kWh.
AstanaEnergoSbyt: January 1, 2016 tariffs (OLD):
night tariff zone (23:00 to 07:00 h) - 3.62 tenge / kWh.
daily tariff zone (07:00 to 23:00) - 16.61 tenge / kWh.

4 Conclusion and Future Work

The work is suggesting HEMS that can potentially help the problem with unconscious electricity consumption in residential buildings. The hardware IoT prototype were developed that can track energy consumption in households and send push-notifications through app in case of extensive or unconscious energy consumption. The potential monetary benefits for end-users that implements proposed system were estimated.

In the future work, case study on real residential buildings will be conducted, machine learning algorithms to identify type of loads can be implemented. Overall, the data obtained could be carefully analyzed and insights can be obtained from the results.

Acknowledgments. This research was funded by the Science Committee of the Ministry of Science and Higher Education of the Republic of Kazakhstan (BR10965311) and the Frontiers Champions programme of Royal Academy of Engineering (FC-2122–2-39).

References

1. Shareef, H., Ahmed, M.S., Mohamed, A., Al Hassan, E.: Review on home energy management system considering demand responses, smart technologies, and intelligent controllers. IEEE Access **6**, 24498–24509 (2018)
2. "GE Brillion Connected Appliances," General Electric (2018). http://www.geappliances.com/ge/connected-appliances/. Accessed 11 Sep 2018
3. Conejo, A.J., Morales, J.M., Baringo, L.: Real-Time demand response model. IEEE Trans. Smart Grid **1**(3), 236–242 (2010)
4. Nunna, H.S.V.S.K., Doolla, S.: Energy management in microgrids using demand response and distributed storage - a multiagent approach. IEEE Trans. Power Deliv. **28**(2), 939–947 (2013)
5. Tarasak, P., Chai, C.C., Kwok, Y.S., Oh, S.W.: Demand bidding program and its application in hotel energy management. IEEE Trans. Smart Grid **5**(2), 821–828 (2014)
6. Nanda, A.K., Panigrahi, C.K.: Review on smart home energy management. Int. J. Ambient Energy **37**(5), 541–546 (2016)
7. Wu, Z., Zhou, S., Li, J., Zhang, X.: Real-Time scheduling of residential appliances via conditional risk-at-value. IEEE Trans. Smart Grid **5**(3), 1282–1291 (2014)
8. Zhou, B., et al.: Smart home energy management systems: concept, configurations, and scheduling strategies. Renew. Sustain. Energy Rev. **61**, 30–40 (2016)
9. Han, J., Lee, H., Park, K.-R.: Remote-controllable and energy-saving room architecture based on ZigBee communication. In: 2009 Digest of Technical Papers International Conference on Consumer Electronics, pp. 1–2 (2009)

10. Fletcher, J., Malalasekera, W.: Development of a user-friendly, low-cost home energy monitoring and recording system. Energy **111**, 32–46 (2016)
11. Han, J., Choi, C., Park, W., Lee, I., Kim, S.: Smart home energy management system including renewable energy based on ZigBee and PLC. IEEE Trans. Consum. Electron. **60**(2), 198–202 (2014)
12. Babu, V.S., Kumar, U.A., Priyadharshini, R., Premkumar, K., Nithin, S.: An intelligent controller for smart home. In: 2016 International Conference on Advances in Computing, Communications and Informatics (ICACCI), pp. 2654–2657 (2016)
13. Peng, C., Huang, J.: A home energy monitoring and control system based on ZigBee technology. Int. J. green energy **13**(15), 1615–1623 (2016)
14. "Consumer energy tarrifs," astanaenergosbyt (2022). https://astanaenergosbyt.kz/ru/fiz/tarify1.html. Accessed 11 Sep 2022
15. Zhakiyev, N., Otarov, R.: Scheduling and planning for optimal operations of power plants using a unit commitment approach. In: Sustainable Energy in Kazakhstan: Moving to Cleaner Energy in a Resource-Rich Country, pp. 109–115. Taylor and Francis (2017). https://doi.org/10.4324/9781315267302
16. Assembayeva, M.,Egerer, J., Mendelevitch, R., Zhakiyev, N.: Spatial electricity market data for the power system of Kazakhstan. Data in Brief, 103781 (2019).https://doi.org/10.1016/j.dib.2019.103781

An IoT Monitoring System for Dairy Products

Evangelos Syrmos[1]([✉]) [iD], Dimitrios Bechtsis[1] [iD], Dimitrios Vlachos[2],
Georgios Papapanagiotakis[3], Theodora Todi[3], Maria Papaspyropoulou[4],
Konstantinos Georgakidis[5], and Nikolaos Sfitis[6]

[1] International Hellenic University, Thermi, 57001 Thessaloniki, Greece
syrmevag@iem.ihu.gr
[2] Aristotle University of Thessaloniki, 54124 Thessaloniki, Greece
[3] Emphasis DigiWorld, 11136 Athens, Greece
[4] Atlantis Engineering, Thermi, 57001 Thessaloniki, Greece
[5] Mevgal, 57100 Thessaloniki, Greece
[6] Makios Logistics, 54628 Thessaloniki, Greece

Abstract. The inclusion of IoT technologies in smart cities and the industrial domain has drastically influenced the life cycle of processes. The gradual reduction in sensor costs and the ubiquitous connectivity provided by open source, un/licensed networks have sky-rocketed the digital transformation of businesses. Specifically, the distribution of products with a short life cycle, such as dairy products, is a highly important domain that demands consistent monitoring of the product and the surrounding environment to preserve quality and safeguard the consumers' health. Continuous monitoring of vehicle fleets is necessary to safeguard temperature and humidity conditions during delivery from the factory and the distribution center to the retail stores. Due to unpredictable situations that may arise during this process, the conditions of the dairy products are constantly monitored with internal sensors, and GPS location devices mounted on delivery trucks. Additionally, sensors have been placed on dairy crates, thus producing detailed information for prohibiting the quality deterioration of dairy products. An IoT monitoring system has been developed that includes a sensor kit placed on dairy crates to monitor dairy product conditions. Furthermore, a versatile module mounted on each truck is also designed and used to retrieve and broadcast the product's conditions during delivery utilizing Bluetooth Low Energy as the medium for connectivity.

Keywords: IoT · Smart Cities · Bluetooth Low Energy · Last-mile Delivery · Ehealth · Dairy Products · Cold Supply Chain

1 Introduction

The preservation of the quality of dairy products during delivery is a demanding task for producers and transportation companies that is closely linked to multiple environmental and human-oriented factors that can affect the products' quality. It is often observed that

© ICST Institute for Computer Sciences, Social Informatics and Telecommunications Engineering 2023
Published by Springer Nature Switzerland AG 2023. All Rights Reserved
K. Rabie et al. (Eds.): IoTaaS 2022, LNICST 506, pp. 12–22, 2023.
https://doi.org/10.1007/978-3-031-37139-4_2

products could lose their organoleptic properties and even become deteriorated due to inadequate storage and transportation conditions [1]. It is of high importance to provide stakeholders with real-time information systems for monitoring the conditions during the transportation of fast moving perishable goods. Preserving transparency across all aspects of the food supply chain (collecting goods, preprocessing, processing, packaging, delivering from one stage to another) is extremely important for both suppliers and consumers. Although real-time data aggregation has been steadily adopted by the industry it remains a challenge in the transportation domain. In order to address this problem, the incorporation of IoT sensors and vertical applications that track, and monitor the conditions of dairy products has been developed. A substantial number of dairy-oriented companies have included IoT technology in multiple sectors of their production line [2]. Indicatively, deploying sensors for real-time monitoring of the milk tank levels is one of the most common implementations in the dairy supply chain [3]. Sensor-based technologies enhance the workability of the entire dairy industry by providing real-time information and an improved way of providing traceability solutions [4–7]. In this context, the supply chain of the dairy industry is considered extremely complex as it involves numerous internal and external factors such as proper storage availability, temperature, humidity conditions, weather fluctuations, packaging, cold supply chain availability, last-mile logistics, retail store particularities and many others [8]. However, to safeguard secure and on-time delivery of dairy products once crates have departed from their origin (factory storage, distribution center), sensors are placed on crates to monitor the whole process and ensure the proper implementation of the hygiene standards. During the past years, monitoring the cold chain focused on temperature data loggers embedded in trucks and shipping containers to ensure quality temperature handling during delivery. All the collected data had to be processed offline by specialized personnel, to ensure the product's quality. In recent years, real-time data monitoring is the main method for ensuring the product's quality in cold supply chains.

The i-EAT (Intelligent Food Safety & Control) project developed a specialized sensor kit for using it on typical dairy crates named i-EAT Tag. The kit includes RFID tags and sensors for measuring (i) vibration, (ii) acceleration and rotational velocity, (iii) atmospheric pressure (altimeter) and (iv) temperature. Additionally, an IoT module indented to be used by delivery trucks has been designed and engineered to facilitate the connectivity of the crate's sensor kit and provide the medium for forwarding the accumulated data to the cloud named i-EAT Truck kit. The i-EAT Truck kit operates similar to a gateway that communicates with the sensor kits and provides connectivity services. Finally, a comprehensive cloud-based real-time monitoring system has been developed to aggregate all the transmitted information and present information about the vehicle, the crate and the dairy products which is not examined in the current work. Specifically, this paper focuses on the i-EAT Tag and i-EAT Truck kits and their respective operations.

The advent of highly accurate and cost-effective sensors paved the way for the development of a high-quality system that could be easily adopted by many companies as the proposed system (sensor kit and IoT equipment and the cloud software tool) can be easily integrated with the company's proprietary software tools. IoT technologies have transformed logistics activities as they provide effective and added-value solutions to critical business processes [9, 10].

Inside the truck, numerous other sensors are also used for providing complete information about the real-world conditions. For example, there are data streams from the vehicle's proprietary equipment (e.g., the truck's velocity, the condition of the fridge equipment, the vehicle's engine status, sensors located in the truck's doors for monitoring the time they remain open/close and many more. This enables stakeholders to identify the heat exposure periods of the dairy products in the loading and unloading processes and many other incidents that may jeopardize the dairy products.

A sensitivity analysis is also critical as the crates could be placed in many different storing locations inside the truck that could be directly or indirectly connected with the health status of the dairy products. The crate sensor kit could provide enlightening insights by monitoring conditions in specific locations inside the truck during delivery.

To further explain the architecture of the proposed IoT system the remainder of the paper is structured as follows: Sect. 2 presents the related field research focused on a narrow field of supply chain logistics known as cold chain logistics. Section 3 elaborates on the system architecture of each module. Section 4 emphasizes the use case of the proposed system with all the possible cases. Finally, Sect. 5 concludes by presenting the systems' functionality, and the added benefits. Furthermore, future directions of the proposed system are introduced.

2   Related Work

IoT technology has drastically improved many fields of our everyday living by providing real-time information about our surrounding environment and optimizing processes according to environmental conditions. This further strengthens the gradual integration of IoT sensors in the logistics sector and accelerates related research by enabling new ideas to be tested for sustainable operations. In this section, we showcase IoT applications in the supply chain context with a special focus on cold supply chains.

IoT coupled with GPS location services enhances the ability to track real-time vehicles while sensors that monitor state, and conditions can provide insights into daily business processes. Cold Chain Logistics (CCL) is considered a new frontier in the supply chain domain due to the fact that it involves the preservation of products and the delivery of perishable goods using dedicated freezing equipment. Considering the fact that perishable products have a short lifetime and they could lose their organoleptic properties or even become deteriorated due to temperature fluctuations during transportation, it is imperative to follow specific regulations [11]. Standards for controlled temperature in refrigerated delivery services have been widely proposed such as ISO 23412:2020 [12]. Similarly, the ISO/TC 315 ensures the optimal conditions for CCL, for instance, the hygiene conditions during the carriage/storage phases that prevent product contamination, the safety and reliability of the cargo and many more. Additionally, CCL providers integrate sensors in their truck's cabins either for freezing or for refrigeration purposes and expose the information to clients via dashboards. APIs in the application layer or universal connectors are also used for integrating the new solutions with proprietary software tools. This ensures integration to third-party applications and the processing of the accumulated data for monitoring the status during delivery. However, during the transportation of the cargo, several factors are affected as a vehicle is involved in many trips for delivering products. Optimal planning is critical for the lifetime of the products and minimal exposure to external conditions (indicatively temperature) is needed to ensure the cargo's health and safety conditions. Therefore, algorithms are being utilized extensively to identify optimal solutions for the Travelling Salesman Problem [13]. This optimization problem orchestrates deliveries in the logistics domain by highlighting the minimal route for a specific starting and ending point and several loading/unloading places. Several constraints may be imposed making it hard to find an optimal solution. For instance, the fuel consumption, the number of vehicles, the capacity of each vehicle, and the time window for delivery are a handful of constraints to this problem that needs to be analysed.

Comparatively, IoT platforms targeted at the transport and logistics domain have been developed in research projects and tested in pilots [14] to present the accumulated data of the fleet in real-time and facilitate the development of next-generation logistics applications. Although the IoT domain is inherently scattered by different types of devices and data types, several approaches for addressing the heterogeneity factors have been proposed. The incorporation of sensors in the dairy supply chain from the manufacturing to the distribution level must be handled appropriately for the heterogenous data by adopting ontologies and using metadata vocabularies [15]. Interestingly, IoT and blockchain are expected to establish a new architectural approach in the development of IoT applications. The connectivity of a vast number of sensors and actuators generating real-time information about the ambient environment and the use of blockchain for ensuring the immutability of the data can revolutionize the IoT domain. Freight transportation that involves different parties can leverage IoT-enabled blockchain solutions to safely store the temperature, status of shipping containers, position, and arrival times. The immutability of the data provided by the blockchain's fundamental principles helps the parties to trust the data and take actions accordingly. The traceability of the assets specifically in the dairy supply chain was implemented with the use of blockchain technology which can be extended to numerous food supply chain products [16]. Similarly, an IoT with a blockchain-enabled food monitoring application has been developed that tracks the temperature of the cargo and geolocation information [17]. This in fact guarantees the trustfulness, integrity, immutability and traceability of the data from all the involved stakeholders. Moreover, several attempts have been presented in the literature to incorporate IoT and Artificial Intelligence in dairy farms in order to enhance the dairy farmers' ability to monitor and track the livestock and further increase all the by-products [18]. Similar to dairy products that need to be preserved in low temperatures, vaccines must also be kept in extremely low temperatures during transportation while even the slightest temperature fluctuation during transportation must be taken into consideration for the ineffectiveness of the vaccine [19]. Several IoT monitoring systems for the CCL have been proposed with different architectures to provide the backbone of this emerging domain [20].

3 IoT Architecture

The architecture of the proposed system is separated into two distinct sections. A kit (named i-EAT Tag) is integrated with an active RFID tag for the identification and monitoring of a single crate. Off the self, sensors were selected for measuring the conditions of the crate during delivery. An exhaustive market research was conducted prior to the implementation to identify candidate products that could meet the project needs. Due to the fact that harsh conditions would be met on a daily basis by these sensors, we opted for sensors that are able to withstand low temperatures, humidity, and vibrations while maintaining low downtime. An inertial sensor (acceleration, gyroscope, altimeter sensors) was used for identifying the relevant movement of the crate and a temperature sensor for monitoring temperature fluctuations. The purpose of this specialized kit is to be placed on a crate and monitor the product's placement and temperature in order to estimate how this affects the product's lifetime. The second kit (named i-EAT Truck kit) which is deployed on the vehicle level is also integrated with sensors for monitoring the temperature inside the refrigerator and acts as an active logger for storing data about the products and the vehicle's condition. Data could be further analyzed for presenting the results to stakeholders. An overview of the architecture is shown in Fig. 1 where the connectivity of each sub-component is highlighted.

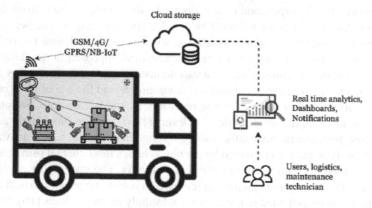

Fig. 1. System architecture

3.1 Crate Kit (i-EAT Tag)

The i-EAT unit is placed on product handling units (typically a plastic crate) that is included in a pallet. Each unit leverages Bluetooth Low Energy (BLE) to connect to the i-EAT truck kit in order to transmit the sensors' measurements. It must be noted that iEAT Tags are going to be reused multiple times as they are mounted and unmounted in numerous crates. Thus, demanding high energy autonomy with minimal power consumption for the onboard computation processes. Having considered the above, the MCU that was selected for the i-EAT Tags is STM32WB55C, which embeds BLE connectivity with low power needs. The RISC architecture is ideal for such projects since it is extensively utilized by mobile devices that need high computing power with minimal energy footprint.

For the identification process of each crate, active RFID tags were selected since minimal effort is needed for integrating them into the system. For the inertial sensor, we selected ISM330DHCXTR since it is tailored for industry applications. Specifically, it employs, a 3D accelerometer with a configurable scale from ($\pm 2/\pm 4/\pm 8/\pm 16$ g), a 3D gyroscope that is able to read values from (± 125 up to ± 4000 degrees per second) that will enable us to measure a broad range of movements since the loading and unloading task is frequently performed manually (by hands). An SPI/I^2C serial interface is also embedded in the inertial sensor enhancing the capabilities, all the while a sensor hub capable of efficient data collection is integrated for connecting additional external sensors. The sensitivity of the inertia sensors enables tracking tilt detection and free-fall with wakeup functionality for low-energy consumption. It also provides a machine learning core that facilitates data cleaning and filtering on the sensor data (false readings, activations, etc.). This is performed by intelligently recognizing patterns in movements during the loading and unloading of each individual unit. Although the inertia sensor is equipped with an internal temperature sensor, we opted to integrate a standalone temperature sensor (NTC Thermistor) connected via the auxiliary serial interface in order to measure the ambient temperature and record the detailed environmental conditions of the handling unit. The selected external temperature sensor was able to identify minimal fluctuation with (± 0.5 degrees of accuracy) compared to the embedded one, thus providing precise measurements for further processing.

Due to the fact that i-EAT Tags are going to be reused for multiple deliveries, energy consumption and battery-related issues were a major concern. After, considering battery life improvements and the autonomy levels of the kit, the research team decided to design the kit to autonomously operate for a month. This decision will enable efficient operation planning while the replacement of the battery will be effectively handled by the stakeholders.

Additionally, an intelligent system for optimal energy management based on the physical movement of the unit was integrated. The main purpose of the system was to intelligently consume energy based on the actions triggered by the loading and unloading activities and exploit the wake-up mode of the MCU whenever this is considered efficient.

Another consideration that had to be taken into account during the development phase was the mounting and unmounting procedure of the i-EAT Tag on dairy crates. On the one hand, a one-step installation phase was the key to enable non-experts to deploy i-EAT Tags. On the other hand, the research team had to consider the harsh

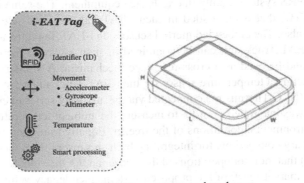

Fig. 2. i-EAT Tag contents and enclosure

conditions of the loading and unloading activities during transportation. Therefore, the i-EAT Tags are enclosed in a tightly sealed container with all the embedded electronics as shown in Fig. 2 and are tolerant to temperature and humidity fluctuations.

3.2 Vehicle Kit (i-EAT Truck)

The development of the i-EAT Truck unit was engineered by embedding several identical parts from the i-EAT Tag. Due to the fact that this kit was going to be deployed on a variety of vehicles with completely different equipment, it had to interoperate with numerous systems. Therefore, the research team focused on modularity and seamless integration with the existing hardware equipment.

The i-EAT Truck kit operates similar to a gateway with additional functionalities for edge processing during transportation. In detail, the unit leverages BLE connectivity in order to detect all i-EAT Tags inside the cargo. After an i-EAT Tag is identified a connection is established and data streams are initiated. Operational processes of every loading and unloading crate equipped with the i-EAT Tag are monitored. The aggregated data streams, either from the i-EAT Tags or the i-EAT Truck unit are sent to the relevant stakeholders, and real-time information about the status of the vehicle and the crate, the duration of the loading and unloading processes are recorded and forwarded to a centralized cloud application for further processing.

To ensure the complete trustfulness transportation of perishable products and the operations that take place during delivery, sensors have been also integrated into the truck's doors in order to extract data for the duration of the loading/unloading processes. These sensors are directly connected to the i-EAT Truck unit and forwarded directly to the cloud application. For instance, in case of an extended period of exposure to high temperature, the health and safety conditions of the dairy products can be significantly affected. This action triggers a process that informs the stakeholders about inconveniences.

The i-EAT Truck unit is equipped with a STM32WB35CE MCU for adequate processing capabilities and future upgradability. Although many transportation vehicles are already equipped with a GPRS system we opted to integrate a dedicated GPRS (SARA-G450) in the i-EAT Truck unit for ensuring reasons: (i) zero downtime in case the vehicle goes out of order, and (ii) plug-and-play solutions to a variety of transportation vehicles that lack GPRS system mainly due to legacy equipment. The same inertial sensor (ISM330DHCXTR) that is embedded in each i-EAT Tag unit was selected for the i-EAT Truck unit also. The embedded inertial sensors on i-EAT Tag units and the inertial sensor of the i-EAT Truck unit can be combined in such a way to increase measurement accuracy and be used as a cross-reference mechanism. A similar approach was taken when selecting a temperature sensor for the i-EAT Truck unit; a standalone temperature sensor (NTC Thermistor) connected via the auxiliary serial interface from the inertial module was integrated in order to measure the ambient temperature and record the detailed environmental conditions of the freezer. Equally important was the ability to provide auxiliary connections for integrating built-in sensors from the truck into the i-EAT Truck unit that monitor operations of the freezer and/or the vehicle. This approach can broaden the market reach of the proposed system since legacy vehicles can utilize the system with minimal modifications.

Since all the accumulated data from the truck's built-in sensors, auxiliary sensors and the transported crates attached to the i-EAT Tag unit are timeseries data, each record includes a timestamp and GPS location information. Finally, the project's team considered the autonomy of the i-EAT Truck unit to be immensely important and included two powering options. A power supply option from the vehicle was considered the main power source, and a backup option with a rechargeable lithium battery is also proposed for redundancy. To provide a robust solution, that can be mounted on any vehicle and have easy access to the embedded electronics, the research team engineered an enclosure with a lid (Fig. 3). Expandability was critical for integrating new sensors, modules and antennas for connectivity.

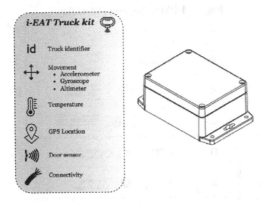

Fig. 3. i-EAT Truck kit contents and enclosure

4 Pilot Use Case Scenarios

Prior to the commercial use of the kits in real-world scenarios, the proposed system was tested in several use cases. The typical workflow in a cold supply chain is considered during the pilot use cases of the project (Fig. 4). In detail, the workflow consists of the pallet accumulation and the loading process from the factory storage to the truck. Followed by the transportation to the branch store, which includes unloading, unpacking, and pallet preparation for preparing the transportation to the retailers. During transportation, several intermediate stops are possible. It must be noted that across the whole process of loading, and delivery, several delays could occur, thus exposing the product to high temperatures. Therefore, temperature sensors are included to monitor the conditions from the factory to the retailer's fridge.

A detailed illustration with several cases is shown in Fig. 5 from the i-EAT Tag placement on the crate to the retailer's store. The purpose of this diagram is to highlight the possible cases that can affect the health and safety conditions of dairy products.

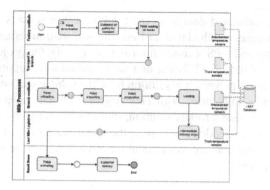

Fig. 4. BPMN diagram (Workflow)

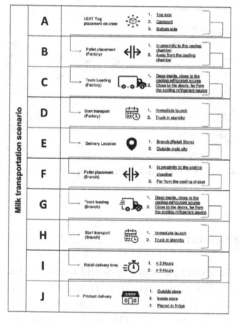

Fig. 5. Use case scenarios for the i-EAT project

5 Discussion and Conclusions

Although the potential of integrating IoT solutions into logistics activities is yet to be explored, the proposed system digitalizes the CCL and provides value-added services to stakeholders. Real-time monitoring of the perishable products' supply chain to determine their health status is a challenging task that could safeguard health and safety in the food industry. The main stakeholders that are being affected by the proposed IoT system are businesses, society and consumers.

The adoption of the proposed system can improve the company's image, and the monitoring of the quality of perishable products while reducing production and distribution costs. The advantages include:

- Increasing traceability conditions in the food supply chain,
- Monitoring and evaluating critical parameters that can affect the quality and lifespan of the products in real time,
- Limiting the reaction time when health and safety issues arise,
- Reducing food quality losses and food waste.

The evolution of Information and Communication Technologies, along with sensors and IoT devices, provides tools for developing innovative products from a farm-to-fork perspective. The i-EAT (Intelligent Food Safety and Control) project created an innovative tool focusing on dairy products. Our scope is to extend the recommended consumption duration of fresh products by improving the cold supply chain's conditions and, furthermore, reducing the rate of returns in the reverse supply chain. This can maximize added value in economic, environmental and social terms, while at the same time enhancing the competitiveness of the dairy industry at European and International levels.

A contemporary IoT monitoring system is developed for monitoring dairy products in the CCL. The proposed system ensures the effective transportation of dairy products by monitoring the parameters of the surrounding environment (storage conditions, external environmental conditions) and even the conditions on individual crates. This enables real-time evaluation of the dairy products in order to inform stakeholders of any inconveniences in the transportation process. Although the system is fully functional, several features and improvements are still to be committed to improving the overall performance.

In our future work, we will provide all the technicalities of the cloud application and the underlying architecture. Specifically, the cloud application will be responsible for gathering the data from all the i-EAT Truck units that accumulate and forward connected i-EAT Tags on individual crates.

Acknowledgements. This research is part of the «Intelligent Control for Food Safety» project (Project code: T2EDK-02495) and was co-financed by the European Regional Development Fund of the European Union and Greek national funds through the Operational Program Competitiveness, Entrepreneurship and Innovation, under the call RESEARCH – CREATE – INNOVATE.

References

1. Liljestrand, K.: Logistics solutions for reducing food waste. Int. J. Phys. Distrib. Logistics Manag. **47**(4), 318–339 (2017). https://doi.org/10.1108/ijpdlm-03-2016-0085
2. Akbar, M.O., et al.: IoT for development of smart dairy farming. J. Food Qual. **2020**, 1–8 (2020). https://doi.org/10.1155/2020/4242805
3. Han, Y., et al.: IOT-enabled quality management process innovation and analytics in China's dairy industry: a data flow modeling perspective (2015)
4. Khanna, A., Jain, S., Burgio, A., Bolshev, V., Panchenko, V.: Blockchain-enabled supply chain platform for indian dairy industry: safety and traceability. Foods **11**(17), 2716 (2022)

5. Tan, A., Pham, T.N.: A proposed framework model for dairy supply chain traceability. Sustain. Futures **2**, 100034 (2020)
6. Tian, F.: A supply chain traceability system for food safety based on HACCP, blockchain & Internet of things. In: 2017 International Conference on Service Systems and Service Management. IEEE (2017)
7. Casino, F., et al.: Blockchain-based food supply chain traceability: a case study in the dairy sector. Int. J. Prod. Res. **59**(19), 5758–5770 (2021)
8. Biz4intellia: Implementation of IoT technology for dairy industries (2022). https://www.biz4intellia.com/blog/implementation-of-iot-technology-for-dairyindustries/
9. Pervez, H., Irfan, U.H.: Blockchain and IoT based disruption in logistics. In: 2019 2nd International Conference on Communication, Computing and Digital systems (CCODE). IEEE (2019)
10. Hopkins, J., Paul, H.: Big data analytics and IoT in logistics: a case study. Int. J. Logistics Manage. **29**(6), 109 (2018)
11. Naden, C.: Cold Chain Logistics. New expert committee to develop standards for transporting temperature-controlled goods (2021). https://www.iso.org/news/ref2661.html
12. Indirect, temperature-controlled refrigerated delivery services – Land transport of parcels with intermediate transfer, ISO standard 23412:2020 (2020)
13. Jünger, M., Reinelt, G., Rinaldi, G.: Chapter 4 The traveling salesman problem, Handbooks in Operations Research and Management Science, vol. 7, pp. 225–330 (1995). https://doi.org/10.1016/S0927-0507(05)80121-5
14. Yacchirema et al.: Interoperability of IoT Platforms applied to the transport and logistics domain, www.scipedia.com, vol. 2018 (2018). https://doi.org/10.5281/zenodo.1451427
15. Jachimczyk, B., Tkaczyk, R., Piotrowski, T., Johansson, S., Kulesza, W.: IoT-based dairy supply chain - an ontological approach. Elektronika ir Elektrotechnika **27**(1), 71–83 (2021). https://doi.org/10.5755/j02.eie.27612
16. Jayasena, K.P.N., Madhunamali, P.M.N.R.: Blockchain and IoT-based diary supply chain management system for Sri Lanka. Advances in Data Mining and Database Management, pp. 246–273 (2021). https://doi.org/10.4018/978-1-7998-6694-7.ch015
17. Wisessing, K., Vichaidis, N.: IoT based cold chain logistics with blockchain for food monitoring application. In: 2022 7th International Conference on Business and Industrial Research (ICBIR), May (2022). https://doi.org/10.1109/icbir54589.2022.9786493
18. Amin, R., Rahman, M.: Artificial intelligence and IoT in dairy farm. Malays. J. Med. Biol. Res. **5**(2), 131–140 (2018). https://doi.org/10.18034/mjmbr.v5i2.516
19. Hasanat, R.T., Arifur Rahman, M.D., Mansoor, N., Mohammed, N., Rahman, M.S., Rasheduzzaman, M.: An IoT based Real-time data-centric Monitoring System for Vaccine cold chain. In: 2020 IEEE East-West Design & Test Symposium (EWDTS) (2020). https://doi.org/10.1109/ewdts50664.2020.9225047
20. Mohsin, A., Yellampalli, S.S.: IoT based cold chain logistics monitoring. In: 2017 IEEE International Conference on Power, Control, Signals and Instrumentation Engineering (ICPCSI) (2017). https://doi.org/10.1109/icpcsi.2017.8392059

A Review of Emerging Low Power Networks in Internet of Medical Things (IoMT)

Zahraa Zakariya Saleh[✉]

Department of Computer Science and Engineering, School of Science and Engineering,
University of Kurdistan Hewler, Erbil, Kurdistan Region, Iraq
zahraa.zsaleh@ukh.edu.krd

Abstract. The future IoT healthcare insurance business model will focus on a strategic view and implementation. It is not only restricted to implementing trend technologies. It should take into consideration the value propositions, financial propositions, and the partner chains. Low-power wide-area technologies (LPWA) could be regarded as the result of endeavors either to raise the range of WLANs and low-power wireless personal area networks (LoWPANs) or to minimize the cost and energy consumption of cellular networks. As the preferred infrastructure for Internet of Medical Things (IoMT) applications, LPWA technologies are highly suggested. The major goal of the LPWA technology is IoT applications that run on affordable low-battery devices and necessarily involve over a large geographic and reasonable data price. This paper reviews the most recent technological developments and the issues they provide. This article explores the significance of interoperability among various LPWA technologies and provides recommendations for selecting the most appropriate LPWA solutions for a variety of IoMT. Finally, problems facing LPWA in IoMT are discussed, and research directions are proposed.

Keywords: LPWA · IoMT · Low power wide area network · Internet of Medical Things · Short Range Wireless Technologies · Long Range Wireless Technologies

1 Introduction

At the beginning of 2020, the novel Corona Virus (COVID-19) pandemic spreads rapidly into various countries around the world. The emergence of Internet of Medical Things (IoMT) plays a core role in the development of health and clinical facts systems will restructure the current business models of healthcare insurance indicator of several nations. The future IoT healthcare insurance business model will focus on a strategic view and implementation. It is not only restricted to implementing trend technologies. It should take into consideration the value propositions, financial propositions, and the partner chains. The new market strategy should have special features to adapt to the acceleration of changes. These features include running to customer-centric and support the relationship with them. Empowering long-term premiums to support and protect

K. Rabie et al. (Eds.): IoTaaS 2022, LNICST 506, pp. 23–37, 2023.
https://doi.org/10.1007/978-3-031-37139-4_3

people healthy and leveraging a new trend in technologies to provide a suitable lifestyle, which ensures well-being and health reversal.

Traditionally, IoT applications could be worked over short-range wireless networks, e.g., Bluetooth; wireless local area networks (WLANs), e.g., IEEE 802.11 (Wi-Fi); wireless home automation, e.g., ZigBee and Z-Wave, and cellular networks, e.g., the global system for mobile communications (GSM) and long-term evolution (LTE). According to the remote monitoring systems, wearable biosensors are utilized either invasive or non-invasive for gathering all necessary biomedical signals and forwarding real-time processed data to the doctors and the patients' dedicated interface. Low-power wide area technologies (LPWA) could be regarded as the result of endeavors either to raise the range of WLANs and low-power wireless personal area networks (LoWPANs) or to minimize the cost and energy consumption of cellular networks [1].

The IoMT has been served all the medical fields, including define recognition, essential signs monitoring, remote monitoring, medical drugs, waste, and equipment monitoring.

Devices through IoMT based wireless could be systematically gathered data and shared with other platforms to manage the environment around us without the need for human intervention. Low-power wireless, in particular IEEE 802.15.4, will therefore continue to play an important role in the future of IoMT as mentioned in Fig. 1.

This review offers researchers with a comprehensive overview of the challenges highlighted in a single article. Thus, it is an interesting and current review for anyone engaged in LPWA networks.

After this section, the paper is structured as follows: Enabling technologies of short-range and long-range wireless in IoMT in Sects. 2 and 3 respectively. In Sect. 4, the development LPWA in IoMT. Section 5 challenges with LPWAs are listed, along with suggestions for future research. The paper is concluded in Sect. 6.

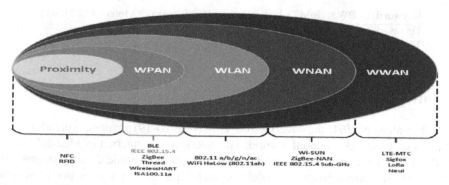

Fig. 1. Wireless communication technologies in IoT applications [1]

2 Short Range Wireless Technologies in IoMT

The short-range communication technologies are utilized for exchange data up to 100 m. There are a number of short-range wireless technologies in IoMT with various features and performances such as Bluetooth, Bluetooth low power (BLE), ZigBee, WiFi, and Light Fidelity (Li-Fi). The BLE and Bluetooth are utilized to transfer the information among peripherals [2]. The short-range communication technologies are specifically useful in the body area networks (BANs) [3]. The technical features and applications of these systems in the domain of IoMT are investigated in the sections below:

2.1 Zigbee

ZigBee is a specification designed wireless technology for offering as long as battery lifetime, a low data rate, and a secure networking [4]. It is a simple network for installing and configuring, which is supported various network topologies (mesh network protocol) and a huge number of nodes. In addition to the capacity, its equipment could be operated for a few years before the battery requires to be changed, which makes it one of the technologies utilized in different medical applications in wireless body area network (WBAN). ZigBee is a secure networking that providing three levels of security mode to avoid the information from being replaced or accessed through attackers [5]. With a range of 100 m, ZigBee can operate at 2.4 GHz, 915 MHz, and 868 MHz frequency bands with a data rate of 250 Kbps, 40 Kbps, and 20 Kbps for each of the operating frequencies respectively. With the utilization of WBAN, ZigBee is targeted healthcare applications that need frequent measurements and text-based transmission of data with low power. It could be utilized for the body temperature monitoring, the pulse monitoring, and others [5]. The limitations of ZigBee are low data rate, capacity, and interference. ZigBee is insignificant for some WBAN healthcare applications which are required high data rate and it is difficult to connect up to 255 devices within a maximum of 100m it in hospitals [4]. Furthermore, interference in 2.4 GHz band is another downside for many wireless systems where can operate.

2.2 Bluetooth

Portable devices can be communicated through using wireless technologies standard called Bluetooth. Bluetooth is a specification designed for short-range wireless technologies standard, where several Bluetooth devices form a short-range personal network known as a piconet [6]. A piconet can contain a device that can work as a master and can establish up to 7 devices known as slaves. The slave device can be only connected with a master device, but cannot establish with other slave devices directly. It can transmit small data packages over multiple 1 MHz channels of bandwidth and utilized short-range radio frequency (RF) from 2.402 to 2.480 GHz ISM bands. Bluetooth is primarily utilized for communication wireless devices distributed in a small area (a maximum of 100 m coverage range). The maximum possible data rate of Bluetooth is 3 Mbps and the time required for communication setup and data transmit is about 100 ms. Multiple radios are allowed a various number of applications such as streaming of audio between a smart phone (Android, iPhone) and speaker, managing healthcare devices from a tablet, or swapping messages among nodes [4].

2.3 BLE

BLE is played a critical role in wireless communication in wearable healthcare ecosystem. it is designed for ultra-low energy, high data transmission rate, strong signal strength, miniaturized size, reliable and secure operations of continuous data streaming applications. It supports over 40 channels using a robust frequency hopping spread spectrum (FHSS) to deliver ranges of data rate between 125 kbps and 2 Mbps, power levels from 1 mW to 100 mW, and security options [4]. The best option for short-range communications in healthcare was found to be Bluetooth Low Energy [7].

2.4 WiFi

WiFi (also called IEEE 802.11) is another short-range technology that allows interconnection among wireless devices within distance limitations. WiFi is utilized radio waves to send data within 100m range, and its utilized for closed environments such as houses and small companies. Smart devices have been communicated and exchanged data through WiFi without a router. It can support 5 GHz and 2.4 GHz in the ISM band. Moreover, there are another type of IEEE 802.11 like 802.11a/b/e/g/h/i/k/n/p/r/ac/ad/ax standards. The main features that have been observed to 802.11ac are to enhance the performance and speed and preferable control the interference. It can achieve these advantages through applying more channel bounding and MIMO and denser modulation [4]. WiFi has benefits over ZigBee and Bluetooth in terms of the data rate and coverage area. The new generations of WiFi are authorizing nodes to interconnect at too high data rates as mentioned in [4].

2.5 Li-Fi

The enormous utilization of the wireless spectrum has many downsides such as the interference and the reduction of radio frequency radiations. One of the revolutionary solutions to dominate these problems is Li-Fi for indoor utilization and for high-speed data network. Li-Fi is short-range technology that utilizes visible light for communication instead of existing Radio Frequency (RF) technology. Li-Fi is supported transmission of data through the illumination of Light Emitting Diodes (LEDs) and a photodetector to examine the signals. Li-Fi is the resolution as it is cheap, much more impressive and it is considered a healthy environment compare to Wi-Fi. Li-Fi has used a light spectrum with wavelengths from infrared (IR) to ultraviolet (UV) containing the visible light (VL) spectrum alternatively of radio waves for relocating of data. From the medical point of view, LED might be made available in homes and hospitals, which can bring the LiFi applicable for WBAN healthcare applications. Moreover, Li-Fi is provided high secure and private connection, low interference, and high bandwidth [69]. These advantages can assist to protect the privacy of the patient while ensuring reliable communication. By contrast, the downside of the utilize of LiFi is due to the requirements for a light source. This limitation is prevented cross-wall communications and imposed the communication to be short-range.

2.6 NFC

Near Field Communication (NFC) is another short-range half duplex wireless technology mode that can allow two-way interaction between two NFC-enabled devices, which can assist contactless transactions and provide an easy way to communicate devices with a single touch. NFC technology is allowed exchange of data among devices within the10 cm range [8]. The advantages of the NFC-based healthcare devices are its small size and nonvolatile memory. It can operate on radio frequency for data access is 13.56 MHz and data which can be transmit at 106.212 or 424 Kbps.

Nowadays different wearable health-related devices are available, such as heart monitors, biosensors, body temperature, etc., which can be helped to send this critical data in real-time. The doctor is tapping his/her reading device at the tag and obtaining the data. Thus, through utilizing NFC, Electronic Health Records (EHR) could be applied, which helps at simplifying the process of including healthcare records and prescriptions. With the assist of NFC tags, the patient's EHR can synchronize and save the real-time data sent by the sensors. Similarly, each patient's record and doctor's prescriptions for the day can be updated.

The NFC devices can afford ways to accelerate the processes in hospitals: the doctors equipped with NFC-enabled smartphones, computers can check all the information about a patient in a moment, without any problems of data being conflicting. NFC-based healthcare is provided not only automation, precision and efficiency in healthcare as well as it is economically feasible in developing countries. There are three types of NFC devices includes Type A, Type B, and FeliCa. These types operated in two modes, namely an initiator (or active mode) and a target (or passive mode). The NFC tag device is a passive device that can include data that is stored some information in it with a unique identification number, but cannot fetch the data included in the other devices [8]. Despite this issue, the active devices can transmit and receive data from other devices. The main benefit of NFC over Bluetooth is that the time required to set up communication among two NFC-cnablcd dcviccs at oncc is one-tenth of a second. NFC-based healthcare is slower in speed than Bluetooth and consumes lesser power [8].

2.7 WirelessHART

WirelessHART (Highway Addressable Remote Transducer) is another open-standard wireless sensor networking technology for process automation, which is developed by ISA, the ISA100.11a. It has been operated in the 2.4 GHz ISM radio band with a 128-bit AES encrypted secure networking technology through leveraging IEEE 802.15.4 compatible Direct-sequence spread spectrum (DSSS) radios with channel hopping on a packet-by-packet basis [9]. The protocol of WirelessHART is deployed Time Division Multiple Access (TDMA) as MAC protocol integrated through precise time synchronization between devices. The network of WirelessHART is organized as a multi-hop mesh network, which means each device could be relayed packets from neighbors in order to achieve multi-hop communication, which can be ensured reliable message delivery leveraging the variant paths available in terms of failures. Both unicast and multicast traffic are supported. WirelessHART was designed with a particular focus on field devices communications to support closed-loop supervisory and regulatory applications because of its high sufficient communication among multiple field devices and efficient routing capabilities in order to guarantee multi-channel frequency hopping [10]. Despite this, external applications could be also utilized as the gateway in order to schedule traffic for field devices. WirelessHART in IoT healthcare sensor networks (IoT-HSNs) control application could be utilized for Parkinson's disease (PD) patients that involve a bio-actuator injection system for this medicine as suggested by measurement and supervisory system [10].

2.8 Infrared

The infrared technology is presented by the Infrared Data Association (IrDA) that utilizes infrared light for short-range wireless technology and mobile object technologies [11]. IrDA is consisted instruction for wireless infrared communication protocols with specifications detailed providing a half-duplex, asynchronous system, and serial communication link up to a few meters, with transmission rates between 2400 bits/s to 115,200 kbits/s. The IrDA protocol stack is divided into three layers: the physical layer, the link access (IrLAP) layer, and the link management layer (IrLMP) layer. The IrLAP protocol is described a basic link-level connection between a pair of devices and is specified the High-level Data Link Control (HDLC) standard for managing access to infrared medium [11]. Thermometers and medical cameras can make use of IrDA's temperature sensing capabilities. High-speed imaging of a body and local temperature measurement with increased precision are both possible with the infrared-based thermal imaging application [12, 13].

3 Long Range Wireless Technologies in IoMT

With long-range communication technologies, the main needs of IoT applications are long range coverage, high capacity, low data rates, low energy consumption, low-cost end devices [1]. It is utilized for transmission of the health-related data up to kilometers relying on the range of the implemented technology such as WiMAX 50 km, LoRa 25 km, LoRaWAN 15–45 km, SigFox [14] 50 km, EC-GSM 100 km. The LPWAN technologies can be divided into two classes: licensed radio spectrum, unlicensed radio spectrum. The licensed radio spectrum includes NB-IoT, LTE-M, EC-GSM-IoT, and Thingstream. The unlicensed radio spectrum can be included SigFox, RPMA, NWAVE, Telensa, Weightless, LoRa, NB-fi, helium, MIOTY, hiber, sata4M2M, CTP. There are other technologies are not classified in LPWAN technologies but has similar features such as WiFi-SUN, WiFi-Halow, Jupiler Mesh, and DASH7.

3.1 LoRa

LoRa is one of the most promising widely adopted LPWAN technologies that originated by Semtech [14]. LoRa is a physical-layer technology for long-range, low-power wireless communication systems. It had become more robust wireless solutions for data collection to interference and long-range coverage (more than 10 km) can offer the possibility by utilizing Mary frequency-shift keying (FSK) modulation (symmetric for uplink (UL) and downlink (DL)) and chirp spread spectrum (CSS) modulation, a technique when the signal is modulated through chirp pulses [15]. It has four vigorous parameters that usually control the performance of LoRa including the transmit power, Spreading Factor (SF), Code Rate (CR), and the Bandwidth (BW).

Using the 868 MHz ISM band within a maximum SF as well as transmit power of 14 dBm, the authors of [16] show that LoRa can travel more than 15 km on land and over 30 km on water.

LoRaWAN protocol provides an architecture for medium access control that developing for battery-based end devices. The end devices allow connecting to the concentrator in a basic star topology. The connection in end devices allows one or more gateways through utilizing single-hop LoRa or FSK communication, whilst the gateways and network servers are connected through standard IP connections [4].

LoRa runs on the sub-1 GHz spectrum, the frequencies of LoRa utilized in European Union in the range of 868 MHz, while in Asia in the range of 433 MHz and in the Americas in the range of 915 MHz [17]. These frequency bands are unlicensed, which can offer the LoRa adoption very straightforward for IoMT applications.

3.2 Sigfox

Sigfox is one of the LPWAN technology originated by Ludovic Le Moan and Christophe Fourtet in 2010 and it set rolling the first global 0G network that used to connect billions of things that broadcasting data without launching or preserving the network. It's a substitutional network operator that offers end to end solutions technology for different IoT application connectivity. It's used the Ultra-Narrow-Band (UNB) carrier and operates in the 200 kHz band of the ISM band. The UNB band gives ultra-communication range for 1–50 km and decreases the noise level as it used a Binary Phase Shift Keying modulation (BPSK) and because of its managed by one operator no roaming needs to be involved for operating that technology in different countries [18]. Sigfox technology offers a low data bit rate to transfer 100 kHz with a data rate of 100 bps. Because its work on the ISM band it's restricted with the limitation of the band and must respect the duty cycle regulation. Sigfox security features including messages singed with a private key, encryption and scrambling methods, limits to transmit 140 transmissions of 12 bytes payload UL and 8 bytes payload for and DL per day per device. Due to the restricted number and the small size of messages that can be sent per day utilizing the low power consumption. Sigfox technology is pushing the heavy processing to the base station which gives in result affordable devices and drastically extends the battery life of the devices [4].

3.3 Wi-Fi HaLow

IEEE 802.11a is the Wi-Fi Alliance technology that has especially IEEE launched for IoT in 2010, also referred to as Wi-Fi HaLow, which was officially released in 2017. There are no commercially available chips yet. The core members of Wi-Fi Alliance consist of some of the world's largest chip manufacturers, including Broadcom, Qualcomm, Mediatek, and Intel. There should be no issues for future IoT chips to be accommodated in Wi-Fi HaLow technology. It is very important for Wi-Fi Alliance to complete promotion before the IoT market boosting [19].

Wi-Fi HaLow is employed multiple-input multiple-output orthogonal frequency-division multiplexing (MIMO-OFDM), which can support ultra-high data rates, multiple bandwidths, and streams in terms to increase the data rate up to 347 Mbps based on the application [20]. The frequency band of the Wi-Fi HaLow application is adapted to be available sub 1 GHz, with more than 6,000 users access, ultra-low power consumption, strong penetration through obstacles, long-range connectivity, and reliable data throughput.

3.4 NB-IoT

3GPP developed and standardized a new LPWA solution named NB-IoT. While NB-IoT does have a definition in LTE Release 13 [21], it is generally viewed as a separate technology. To alleviate the pressure on devices' resources, NB-IoT uses a lower data rate (maximum of 158.5 kbps on the UL and 106 kbps on the DL [22]). Due of this, it cannot support LTE capabilities like carrier aggregation, dual connectivity, or channel quality measures. Healthcare applications can benefit from NB-IoT because of its low cost, low power consumption, and extensive indoor coverage [23].

3.5 DASH7

Another well-defined LPWAN standard is the DASH7 Alliance Protocol (D7AP). D7AP is an open-source international standard, which is provided technical specifications on RFID tags and sensor nodes for Wireless Sensor and Actuator Network protocol (WSAN). It can operate in the Sub-1 GHz bands according to the ISO/IEC 18000-7 standard and identify by DASH7 Alliance. The ISO/IEC 18000-7 is an open standard which is defined the parameters of the ISM band air interface for wireless communications at 433 MHz. The 433 MHz frequency generates D7A with long propagation coverage and better deployment. A full OSI stack (7 OSI layers) known as D7A protocol (D7AP) is specified [29]. This stack supports a high level of functionality applied for active RFID and WSAN. It provides a quite long-range (up to 2 km), tag-to-tag communication, less delay especially for moving nodes, extended battery lifetime for connecting the objects, and a fairly high data rate (up to 167 kbps). The less frequency of DASH7 can bring a high propagation with penetration capability on multi-floored buildings, thus can operate with less power consumption.

D7A builds around the concept of BLAST network technology, and the features of D7A are:

- Bursty: refers to sending short transfer of data in response to an event or operation and sporadic sequences of data.
- Light: Specifies small packet size limited to 256 bytes per transaction.
- Asynchronous: Communication is a transfer of command and response approach between gateways (GWs) and End-devices (EDs) without periodic synchronization.
- Stealth: EDs communicate towards pre-paired the GWs and hence the devices no need any periodic discovery beacons for the ability to respond in communication.

- Transitive: D7A Supports mobility which allows ED to move freely within various GWs coverages and, at the same time, does not lose connectivity.

In this section, the DASH7 Alliance protocol communication is illustrated along with the various layers belonging to mobility in terms to explain the role of each one in the communication. In the uplink, EDs make utilize of Carrier Sense Multiple Access with Collision Avoidance (CSMA/CA) protocol to access the channel and transmit data in the PHY layer. In the downlink, EDs utilize the transmission, reception, scan automation, and multiple access processes in the data link layer (DLL). DASH7 provides Gaussian Frequency Shift Keying (GFSK) modulation scheme and adapts for either a star, tree, or node-to-node network topology. The gateways have the functionality of receiving data and processing it, whereas the endpoints are simpler devices, containing sensors that monitor the needed data and information. The endpoint is designed to be in a sleep mode, which enables low energy consumption and allows for periodically receiving and sending data to the gateways.

The architecture of D7AP is similar to LoRa, which is supported three classes of devices: EDs, gateways, and sub-controllers as shown in Fig. 2. An ED is the least power-demanding platform consisting of sensors and actuators with a transceiver. It can be collected data and transmitted to a gateway when required in asynchrony mode. This platform is redesigned in terms to operate less power consumption and sleeping most of the time. It does not contain all D7AP features, and it utilizes a periodic wake-up mechanism to listen to the possible incoming packets. The sub-controller device is similar to an ED and can use as a relay for packets between an ED and a gateway. However, all D7AP functionalities can be deployed on the sub-controller device. The gateway can be also deployed to all D7AP functionalities and can be always in receiving mode until sending. It received information from an ED, processed them, and transmitted them to the IP-Network or forwarded them to another DASH7 network. The network service can be shared the same functionalities as the network service in LoRaWAN, it can be aggregated the received data, delete duplicates when is required, and select

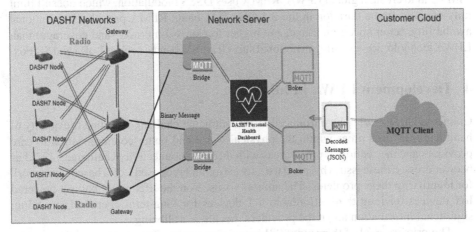

Fig. 2. DASH7 architecture in IoMT.

the nearest gateway for an ED in the downlink. Finally, the customer cloud such as a temperature sensor can be programmed or coded executing at the edge of the network. It receives the information and updates or configures the ED. DASH7 has high reliability in the domain of the healthcare environment compared to Wi-Fi, Bluetooth, and ZigBee as it is not suffering from interference issues whilst acquiring the advantages of less power with high connectivity coverage at low cost [24].

3.6 eMTC

The enhanced machine-type communication (eMTC) technology is typed of the long-term evolution technology. The goal of eMTC technology is to enhance the reliability of packets, low-cost design, less complexity, and security [25]. The eMTC is redesigned based on the 3rd Generation Partnership Project (3GPP) standards in terms to recognize a low power and expand the existing service coverage. The eMTC network is considered a multi-carrier network that can spread radio resources in the frequency domain and in the time domain through implementing respectively a frequency-division duplex (FDD) mechanism, a single carrier (SC-FDMA) mechanism, a TDD mechanism and an orthogonal frequency-division multiple access (OFDMA) mechanism for uplink and downlink health packet transmissions. In the eMTC, the radio access network protocol is utilized universal terrestrial radio access network (E-UTRAN). Moreover, the eMTC MAC protocol is implemented scheduling methods to schedule health packet transmissions in order to guarantee the transmission of the health packet successfully in the context of the WBAN-enabled IoT to achieve a better performance in terms of throughput and a spectrum efficient health packet transmission.

3.7 RPMA Technology

Ingenu proposed the Random Phase Multiple Access (RPMA) [26] LPWA technology (formerly On-Ramp). Unlike LoRa and SigFox, RPMA leverages the global 2.4 GHz ISM band to create a global LPWA. RPMA uses DSSS modulation, which doesn't limit duty cycle or frame duration in the 2.4 GHz ISM band. RPMA provides international availability, better spectrum usage, and higher transmission power (and coverage) than LPWA technologies operating in regional sub-GHz ISM bands, such as LoRa and SigFox.

4 Development LPWA in IoMT

Connected health could be introduced more significant challenges among the quality of healthcare for rural areas within the physical world and better communication to care providers and the section of urban areas with different connectivity challenges. [27] has been addressed these issues by using user scenarios and proposed LoRa based framework for identifying these problems. The authors focused on the lifetime of battery-powered IoT devices for long-term, affordable IoT devices for long-term operation, providing significant information about the providers' health or wellbeing.

The primary goal of this study [28] is to focus on the implementation of the synergies between state-of-the-art communication and AI techniques under smart wearable devices; thus, preparing the development of rightful innovative services and wearable ecosystems. The experimental study is proposed in which the performance of long-range connectivity provided wearable devices helping LPWAN communications and TinyML-based computation is analyzed. Furthermore, the limitation of resource-constrained units such as wearable devices for operating intelligent mechanisms is analyzed. A new architecture [29] proposed a health IoT architecture using LoRa technology. it represented the improvement and progress of current medical infrastructure of IoT. The authors in [30] presented technology and system that utilizes viable, low cost, and low power consumption with data processing, which can assist through LoRa communication technologies and ESP32-based MCU. The aim of the proposed system is to control sensors that discover and predict dangers that will happen for elderly people. This article concluded that the prototype can be enhanced the user's life quality, specifically for those who lived in remote rural areas.

The work in [31] demonstrates the advantages and disadvantages of current communication systems and technologies, suggesting new IoT platforms in the medical area, devoted to home and hospital care services, which is built on LoRa technology.

In [32] has been proposed a proof of concept for monitoring and supporting elderly people using the LoRaWAN communication technologies, the Things Network, and ESP32-based MCU. It has been focused on providing real-time data. The LoRa gateway is configured and connected to The Things Network, receiving the periodically transmitted data from the LoRa nodes. The LoRa nodes are segmented into two distinct types personal LoRa nodes and residential LoRa nodes. This article showed that it is possible to deploy sensor networks to control the elderly using the LoRa gateway and other low-cost technologies. [33] has been proposed an advanced framework with integrated AI that combines Edge computing and Fog computing, LoRa, and IoT-based technologies to build a five-layer system, namely, sensor layer, edge layer, fog layer, cloud layer, and the application layer. The proposed framework could inherit the advantages of these technologies to improve and support health monitoring tasks such as fall detection system or electrocardiogram (ECG) monitoring and satisfy both requirements of high data rate-applications and Lora duty cycle regulation.

5 Challenges and Future Research Directions

In this section, we'll talk about the problems and restrictions of the currently available LPWA for IoMT, as well as the ways in which future research might attempt to address those problems.

5.1 Real Time Communication

Real-time measurements of patients should have been collected by health care systems using the appropriate sensors, then transmitted to medical centers where they should be analyzed and classified according to the complexity of situations require urgent medical assistance. There are a variety of licensed and unlicensed choices accessible for this application. LoRaWAN, RPMA, or NB-IoT can all be utilized for two-way real-time medical control, which requires a minimum of 28.8 kbps. However, there are times when even doctors who can see their patients remotely need to meet with them via video chat. Thus, RPMA and NB-IoT can provide real-time video-based monitoring of health issues, much to how smart home applications can monitor a home's security and temperature. Finally, with the exception of SigFox, all other technologies under consideration are appropriate for use in medical periodic reports and event-driven alerts. Implemented systems for telemedicine should naturally be energy efficient and support numerous devices across a wide range. With 53,547+ versus 40,000 nodes and a 15 km against 5 km coverage, respectively, LoRaWAN and NB-IoT are the right solution in terms of network throughput and range. When looking at available long-range communications solutions, NB-IoT was proven to be the dominant solution for healthcare [7]. For healthcare, it is suggested to use both short-range and long-range M2M communications. The central node of the WBAN and sensors would be connected with technologies such as Bluetooth and ZigBee, while the WBAN would be connected to the provider's base station with a suitable LPWA technology [7]. Even though a system like this is good since it can use short-range M2M architectures, it is highly improbable to have low power use, be scalable, or be less complex and difficult.

5.2 Radiation Absorption in Human Bodies

Exposure to radiofrequency radiation may be harmful to humans, especially to more delicate bodily systems. For example, 15 min of exposure to infrared radiation at an absorption rate of 8 W/Kg in the head or chest might trigger serious damage to the eyes [34]. Even though the highest exposure rate accepted in Europe is 2 W/kg and the highest exposure rate permitted in the US is 1.6 W/kg. Therefore, lowering the rate of radiation exposure is one of the primary problems in WBAN [35]. As a result, sensors must keep their power efficiency high and their power absorption low [36] to reduce the amount of energy collected by the human body to minimize the number of energy received by the human body. Because of this, WBAN devices should require less maintenance and have a lower minimum transmit power requirement. With their low transmission power and short duty cycles, LPWAN technologies offer a potential answer in this context.

5.3 LPWAN Protocols

The LPWAN is a promising technology with a long range and low power consumption, but more work needs to be done on the LPWAN protocols before they can be used to serve e-health applications. Many medical applications necessitate the immediate or on-demand transmission of data. These types of data transfers are not permitted by LPWAN protocols such as LoRaWAN, which are designed primarily for uplink data transfers. However, because many of these protocols do not allow mobile devices can communicate with each other [37], these protocols must also deal with problems that emerge when patients move.

6 Conclusion

The best LPWA technology in IoT-based healthcare depends on the application. Each application's needs determine its technology. Various connectivity solutions must be implemented in order to interface and interconnect IoT devices within a major healthcare application. The administrator must develop an architecture for an overlay that may include edge computing at the hospital facility; cloud computing resources for connectivity to remote devices, and local connectivity through Bluetooth from an IoT technology device to a smartphone that acts as a relay. The level of heterogeneity of the wireless technologies that are integrated into such an architecture will influence the ultimate complexity of the architecture to its maximum capacity. DASH7 has high reliability in the domain of the healthcare environment compared to Wi-Fi, Bluetooth, and ZigBee. Healthcare applications can benefit from NB-IoT because of its low cost, low power consumption, and extensive indoor coverage. The eMTC technology can achieve a better performance in terms of throughput and a spectrum-efficient health packet transmission in the context of the WBAN-enabled IoT.

References

1. Baddeley, M.: Software Defined Networking for the Industrial Internet of Things (2020)
2. Vidakis, K., Mavrogiorgou, A., Kiourtis, A., Kyriazis, D.: A comparative study of shortrange wireless communication technologies for health information exchange. In: 2020 International conference on electrical, communication, and computer engineering (ICECCE), Istanbul, Turkey (2020)
3. Ahad, A., Tahir, M., Yau, K.L.A.: 5G-based smart healthcare network: architecture, taxonomy, challenges and future research directions. IEEE Access **7**, 100747–100762 (2019)
4. Qadir, Q.M., Rashid, T.A., Al-Salihi, N.K., Ismael, B., Kist, A.A., Zhang, Z.: Low power wide area networks: a survey of enabling technologies, applications and interoperability needs. IEEE Access **6**, 77454–77473 (2018)
5. Chung, Y.-F., Liu, C.-H.: Design of a wireless sensor network platform for tele-homecare. Sensors **13**(12), 17156–17175 (2013)
6. Negra, R., Jemili, I., Belghith, A.: Wireless body area networks: applications and technologies. Procedia Comput. Sci. **83**, 1274–1281 (2016)
7. Baker, S.B., Xiang, W., Atkinson, I.: Internet of things for smart healthcare: technologies, challenges, and opportunities. IEEE Access **5**, 26521–26544 (2017)
8. Patil, V., Varma, N., Vinchurkar, S., Patil, B.: NFC based health monitoring and controlling system. In: 2014 IEEE Global Conference on Wireless Computing & Networking (GCWCN) (2014)
9. Maass, A.I., Neši´c, D., Postoyan, R., Dower, P.M., Varma, V.S.: Emulation-based stabilisation of networked control systems over WirelessHART. In: Proceedings of the 2017 IEEE 56th Annual Conference on Decision and Control (CDC), Melbourne, Australia (2017)
10. Devan, P.A.M., Hussin, F.A., Ibrahim, R., Bingi, K., Khanday, F.A.: A survey on the application of wirelessHART for industrial process monitoring and control. Sensors **21**(15), 4951 (2021)
11. Williams, S.: IrDA: past, present and future. IEEE Pers. Commun. **7**(1), 11–19 (2000)
12. Rozlosnik, A.: Potential contribution of the Infrared Industry in the future of IoT/IIoT. In: Proceedings of the 14th Quantitative InfraRed Thermography Conference, Berlin, Germany (2018)

13. Baker, B.C.: Wireless Communication Using the IrDA Standard Protocol. Microchip Technology (2008)
14. Semtech. http://www.semtech.com/
15. Liao, C.-H., Zhu, G., Kuwabara, D., Suzuki, M., Morikawa, H.: Multi-hop LoRa networks enabled by concurrent transmission. IEEE Access 5, 21430–22144 (2017)
16. Petajajarvi, J., Mikhaylov, K., Roivainen, A., Hanninen, T., Pettissalo, M.: On the coverage of LPWANs: Range evaluation and channel attenuation model for LoRa technology. In: Proc. 14th Int. Conf. ITS Telecommun. (ITST) (2015)
17. Zorbas, D., Papadopoulos, G.Z., Maille, P., Montavont, N., Douligeris, C.: Improving LoRa network capacity using multiple spreading factor configurations. In: 2018 25th International Conference on Telecommunications, ICT (2018)
18. Foubert, B., Mitton, N.: Long-range wireless radio technologies: a survey. Future Internet 12(1), 13 (2020)
19. Qiao, L., Zheng, Z., Cui, W., Wang, L.: A survey on Wi-Fi HaLow technology for internet of things. In: 2018 2nd IEEE Conference on Energy Internet and Energy System Integration (EI2) (2018)
20. Shin, J.O., Chan, A., Kung, H., Tarokh, V.: Design of an OFDM cooperative space-time diversity system. IEEE Trans. Vehicular Technol. 56(4) (2007)
21. Meredith, J.M.: Evolved Universal Terrestrial Radio Access (E-UTRA); NB-IOT; Technical Report for BS and UE radio transmission and reception (2017)
22. Hoglund, et al.: Overview of 3GPP release 14 enhanced NB-IoT. IEEE Network 31(6), 16–22 (2017)
23. Tengshe, R.R., Sahoo, A.: NB-IoT for healthcare. In: Principles and Applications of Narrowband Internet of Things (NBIoT), pp. 127–152. IGI Global (2021)
24. Yearp, A., Newell, D., Davies, P.,Wade, R., Sahandi, R.: Wireless remote patient monitoring system: effects of interference. In: 2016 10th International Conference on Innovative Mobile and Internet Services in Ubiquitous Computing (IMIS) (2016)
25. Ali, W.H., Uysal, M.: Next generation M2M cellular networks: challenges and practical considerations. IEEE Commun. Mag. 53(9), 18–24 (2015)
26. rpma (2022). https://www.ingenu.com/technology/rpma/
27. Dimitrievski, A., et al.: Rural Healthcare IoT Architecture Based on Low-Energy LoRa. Int. J. Environ. Res. Public Health (2021)
28. Sanchez-Iborra, R.: LPWAN and embedded machine learning as enablers for the next generation of wearable devices. Sensors 21(15) (2021)
29. Subramanian, P.M., Rajeswari, A.: LoRa-based infrastructure for medical IoT system. In: Rao, Y.V.D., Amarnath, C., Regalla, S.P., Javed, A., Singh, K.K. (eds.) Advances in Industrial Machines and Mechanisms. LNME, pp. 331–337. Springer, Singapore (2021). https://doi.org/10.1007/978-981-16-1769-0_30
30. Lousado, J.P., Pires, I.M., Zdravevski, E., Antunes, S,.: Monitoring the health and residence conditions of elderly people, using LoRa and the things network. Electronics 10(14) (2021)
31. Drăgulinescu, A.M.C., Manea, A.F., Fratu, O., et al.: LoRa-based medical IoT system architecture and testbed. Wireless Pers. Commun. (2020) (2020)
32. Lousado, J.P., Antunes, S.: Monitoring and support for elderly people using LoRa communication technologies: IoT concepts and applications. Future Internet 12(11) (2020)
33. Queralta, J.P., Gia, T.N., Tenhunen, H., Westerlund, T.: Edge-AI in LoRa-based health monitoring: fall detection system with fog computing and LSTM recurrent neural networks. In: 42nd International Conference on Telecommunications and Signal Processing (TSP) (2019)
34. Ahmed, G., et al.: Rigorous analysis and evaluation of Specific Absorption Rate (SAR) for mobile multimedia healthcare. IEEE Access 6, 29602–29610 (2018)
35. Foster, K.R.: Thermal and nonthermal mechanisms of interaction of radio-frequency energy with biological systems. IEEE Trans. Plasma Sci. 28(1), 15–23 (2000)

36. Fernandez, M., Espinosa, H.G., Guerra, D., Peña, I., Thiel, D.V., Arrinda, A.: RF energy absorption in human bodies due to wearable antennas in the 2.4 GHz frequency band. Bioelectromagnetics **41**(1), 73–79 (2020)
37. Ayoub, W., Samhat, A.E., Nouvel, F., Mroue, M., Pre´votet, J.-C.: Internet of mobile things: overview of lorawan,dash7, and nb-iot in lpwans standards and supported mobility. IEEE Commun. Surv. Tutorials **21**(2), 1561–1581 (2018)

Design of Performance Enhanced Metamaterial-Enabled Absorber for Low-Power IoT Networks

Kozhakhmet Abdugapbar, Kassen Dautov, Mohammad Hashmi,
and Galymzhan Nauryzbayev[✉]

School of Engineering and Digital Sciences, Nazarbayev University,
Astana 010000, Kazakhstan
{kozhakhmet.abdugapbar,kassen.dautov,mohammad.hashmi,
galymzhan.nauryzbayev}@nu.edu.kz

Abstract. A single-band metamaterial absorber (MTMA) for Internet-of-Things (IoT) networks, working at 5.8 GHz, is presented. The proposed unit cell with a size of 16×16 mm^2 has circular and square rings designed on a Rogers RO4350B substrate with a thickness of 1.54 mm. The material properties of the absorber are extracted and used to show the double negative metamaterial behavior. The real and imaginary values of impedance demonstrate the matching of MTMA with the free space. Furthermore, MTMAs with various configurations are designed to validate the impact on the absorption level and operating frequency. All array configurations exhibit nearly perfect, 99.9% absorbance. The physical mechanism of MTMA is discussed using an electric field and surface current distributions. The obtained results of the study reveal that the proposed MTMA can be used to charge low-power IoT devices.

Keywords: Array · Electromagnetic waves · Internet-of-Things (IoT) · Metamaterial absorber · Unit cell

1 Introduction

Recently, the Internet-of-Things (IoT) is a rapidly evolving technology that is present in every part of industry and daily life. In general, these devices are powered by batteries, which cause high maintenance costs due to the regular replacement [1]. Since difficulties with a big size and weight are also present, an alternative sustainable powering becomes a challenge [2,3]. Radio frequency (RF) energy harvesting (EH) is one of the viable solutions because of its availability [4]. Numerous wireless technologies operate using electromagnetic (EM) waves that can be transformed into useful energy. However, the RF power density is low, between $0.2 \, \text{nW/cm}^2$–$1 \, \mu\text{W/cm}^2$, therefore, an efficient absorber is needed for the EH purposes [5].

This research was funded by Nazarbayev University under Collaborative Research Program Grants #11022021CRP1513 (G. Nauryzbayev) and #021220CRP0222 (M. Hashmi).

K. Rabie et al. (Eds.): IoTaaS 2022, LNICST 506, pp. 38–47, 2023.
https://doi.org/10.1007/978-3-031-37139-4_4

Absorbers are introduced as a key enabling component of the EH-based system that scavenges energy from the radio waves. There are several energy harvester types: the high-gain antenna, the dipole antenna, the graphene-based and the metamaterial absorber (MTMA). Nowadays, MTMAs are considered an effective absorber type and attract many researchers. MTMA has extraordinary properties such as the beating diffraction limit, negative permeability (μ) and permittivity (ε) [6]. MTMA is a composite structure that has the potential to reduce the incoming EM wave reflections and, therefore, provides a variety of benefits over traditional absorbers in terms of effective size reduction, vast flexibility, and low profile.

Recently, the work on MTMAs that have high absorption levels and different operating frequencies has been reported. The design of absorbers is important due to the impact on an absorption rate, and researchers presented various unit cells (UCs) with patterns such as square, double, split rings, *etc.* For example, single-band MTMA working at 2.4 GHz had a pattern with two circular rings, the parameters of which were optimized to define the frequency and absorption level [7]. Furthermore, UCs were combined into an array that led to an increased absorption efficiency of 84.7%. Another single-band absorber was designed to have 93% absorption at 2.45 GHz [8]. Alternatively, multi-band absorbers have several resonance frequencies, which increase the amount of harvested energy. One of the examples was dual-band MTMA working at 6.46 GHz and 7.68 GHz, which showed 95% absorbance at both frequencies [9]. The design of UC was done step-by-step, first obtaining two resonance frequencies and then increasing the absorption rate by implementing another resonator. Furthermore, a triple-band split ring resonator-based absorber operating at 4.19 GHz, 6.64 GHz and 9.95 GHz had an efficiency of 97.5%, 96.5% and 98.85% [10].

This paper proposes high-absorbance MTMA working at practical ISM (industrial, scientific and medical) frequency bands used in WiFi and radio local area networks. It should be noted that effective MTMA may result in efficient RF EH and replace batteries of IoT devices. To achieve a high absorbance rate, the proposed UC geometry was thoroughly analyzed. MTMA was investigated for the presence of any metamaterial behavior and showed a double-negative nature. Then, designed UC was used to construct MTMA with various array configurations. The final absorbance rate of optimal array-type MTMA was 99.9%.

The remaining sections of this paper are organized as follows. Section. 2 discusses the step-by-step design of UC and its associated challenges. The metamaterial properties of proposed UC are extracted and discussed in Sect. 3. Furthermore, developed MTMA using UCs is presented in Sect. 4. The design of MTMA and corresponding results are concluded in Sect. 5.

2 Unit Cell Design

The effectiveness of the absorber depends on the level of absorption, which is calculated using reflected (S_{11}) and forward transmission (S_{21}) waves as

$$A(\omega) = 1 - |S_{21}| - |S_{11}|. \tag{1}$$

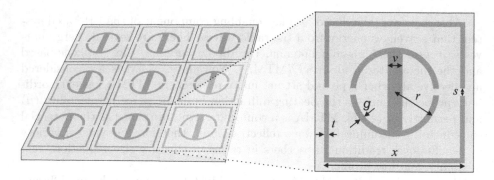

Fig. 1. The proposed UC design.

The proposed design of UC has a copper layer at the bottom of a structure, which reflects all coming waves to the incident port. As a sequence, this leads to the zero transmittance and (1) becomes as follows

$$A(\omega) = 1 - |S_{11}|.\tag{2}$$

The considered UC geometry was analyzed to identify the optimal parameters that result in superior performance. Designed UC consists of square and circular rings with a line, as presented in Fig. 1. The structure of UC consists of the dielectric material and the copper layers at the bottom and top. The thickness of the copper layers are 0.035 mm, while the Rogers RO4350B with dielectric constant 3.66 and loss tangent 0.0037, substrate's height is 1.54 mm. The parameters, which affect the performance, are the radius of the inner circular ring (r) with width (g) and the length of outer square ring (x) with width (t). Both the rectangular and circular rings have two slits with width (s) while the line in the circular ring has width (v). All the discussed parameters are analyzed to increase absorption at the intended working frequency of 5.8 GHz.

2.1   Performed Analysis

As previously discussed the parameters of UC play a major role in MTMA's performance. Changing the parameters of the proposed design affects the absorption and resonance frequencies, simultaneously, and certain parameters with a higher absorption may have different frequency than needed. The pattern of UC defines the absorption rate and bandwidth. The design is developed step-by-step, adding more complex elements. The initial design of UC consists of a square ring with gaps, as presented in Fig. 2. This design results in a single resonance frequency at a higher frequency with a low absorption rate. The second step is to add another resonator, a circular ring inside of the square one, and this modification shifted the operating frequency to 5.8 GHz. The reason of adding another resonator is that the first square is not enough to shift down the frequency further. Additionally, the last design includes a line connecting two semicircles, which

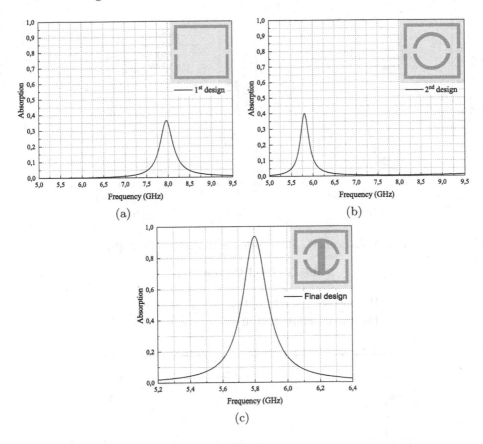

Fig. 2. The UC design steps.

significantly raises the absorption level. The performed analysis aims to find the optimal values for the highest possible absorption rate while keeping the resonance at 5.8 GHz.

The optimal UC design is obtained from completing the parametric analysis, which is done by alternating g and t. Figure 3a presents the absorbance with changing t. When the width is 0.2 mm, it reaches the high absorption rate and satisfies the needed frequency, while for higher values of t, there is a shift of the resonance frequency. Furthermore, Fig. 3b shows the absorption ratio at different values of g. It is observed that 0.4 mm width is perfect in terms of both absorbance level and frequency. On the other hand, if the width grows, the operating frequency will get higher than 5.8 GHz. From the performed analysis, the most absorbance was obtained, when $g = 0.3$ mm and $t = 0.2$ mm. The UC, with optimal parameters presented in Table 1, shows 94% absorbance as depicted in Fig. 4.

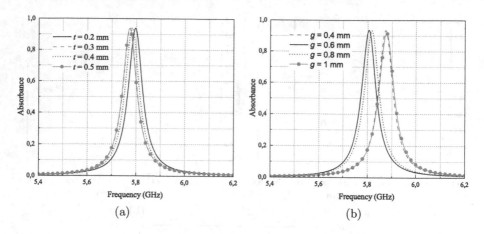

Fig. 3. Frequency vs absorption with varying: (a) t; (b) g.

Table 1. The UC parameters.

Parameter	t_{sub}	t_{cop}	r	g	t	s	x
Dimension (mm)	1.54	0.035	8	0.7	0.2	0.5	2

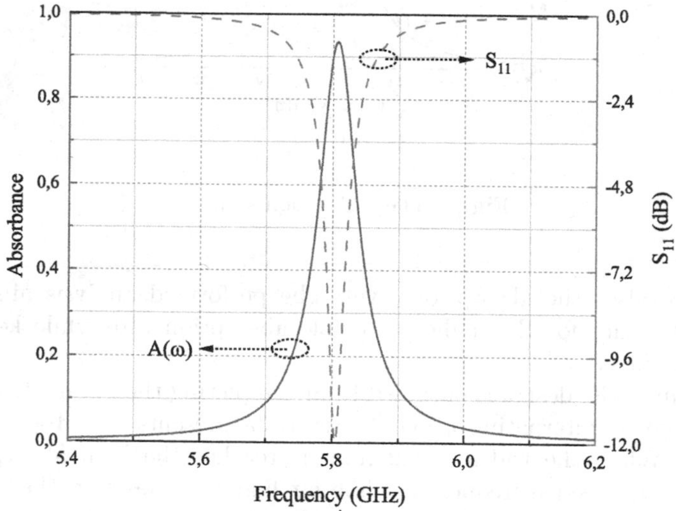

Fig. 4. The results for optimized UC.

3   Material Parameter Retrieval

For the further analysis of the MTMA behavior, the material properties (*i.e.*, ε, μ, impedance (z), refractive index (n)) of UC are extracted by using the retrieval method [12]. The S_{11} and S_{21} values are needed for obtaining the MTMA proper-

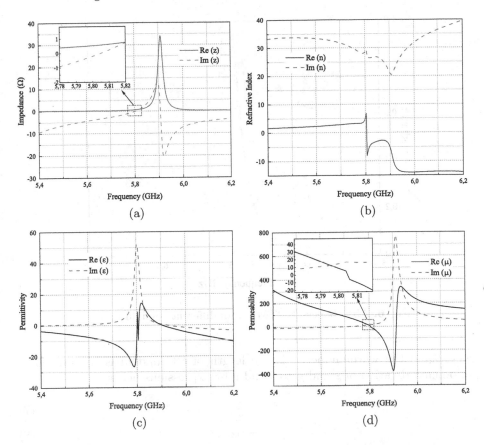

Fig. 5. Metamaterial properties: (a) z; (b) n; (c) ε; (d) μ.

ties. At the bottom layer, three holes were etched to allow waves to pass through and obtain the S_{21} values for the ε and μ calculations. These holes are small and have no impact on the absorption or resonance frequency. The scattering parameters can be described by the equations below

$$S_{11} = \frac{R_{01}\left(1 - e^{i2nk_0l}\right)}{1 - R_{01}^2 e^{i2nk_0l}},$$ (3)

$$S_{21} = \frac{\left(1 - R_{01}^2\right) e^{i2nk_0l}}{1 - R_{01}^2 e^{i2nk_0l}}.$$ (4)

The method of the extracting metamaterial properties with S_{11} and S_{21} values comes from inverting (3) and (4) and obtaining z and n.

$$z = \sqrt{\frac{\left(1 + S_{11}\right)^2 - S_{21}^2}{\left(1 - S_{11}\right)^2 - S_{21}^2}},$$ (5)

$$n = \frac{1}{k_0l}\left[\left(\left[ln\left(e^{ink_0l}\right)\right]'' + 2m\pi\right) - i\left[\left[ln\left(e^{ink_0l}\right)\right]'\right]\right],$$ (6)

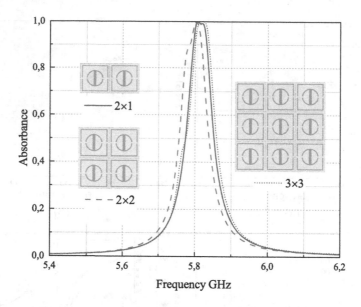

Fig. 6. Absorbance of MTMA with different configurations.

where k_0 is the wavenumber, l is the length of UC and m is the branch of periodicity. Relation of ε and μ to z and n by expressions below

$$\varepsilon = \frac{\text{n}}{\text{z}}, \tag{7}$$

$$\mu = \text{nz}. \tag{8}$$

The functions of ε and μ are complex and need analysis to identify the metamaterial nature of UC.

Figure 5 depicts the material properties calculated using (5)–(8) with the S_{11} and S_{21} values. The value of real impedance reaches 1 Ω and the imaginary part is close to 0 Ω at the resonance frequency, as shown in Fig. 5a, which indicates the impedance matching between the absorber and free space [13]. Figure 5b shows that the real part of the refractive index is negative at 5.8 GHz. The positive impedance and the negative refractive index at the resonance frequency represent the metamaterial behavior of UC.

The metamaterials are divided into four types depending on the values of μ and ε which determine the metamaterial behavior [14]. There are three types of medium: *double − positive medium*, when both μ and ε are positive; *epsilon − negative medium*, where only ε is negative, *mu − negative medium*, where μ is lower than zero; and *double − negative medium*, where both parameters are below zero. Figures 5c and 5d show that the real parts of μ and ε at 5.8 GHz are −10 and −8, respectively. The negative values of μ and ε define the double-negative metamaterial property. Furthermore, the plots of refractive index, permeability, and permittivity demonstrate an incline from positive to

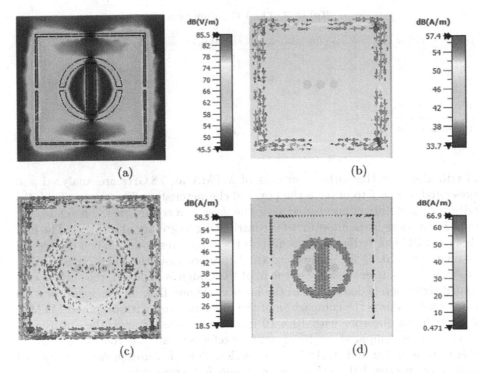

Fig. 7. (a) The electric field distribution; (b) The surface current of 1st design; (c) The surface current of 2nd design; (d) The surface current of final design;

negative values at 5.8 GHz. It is worth noting that this phenomenon appears with only artificial metamaterial devices. All these prove that proposed UC has metamaterial properties.

4   Metamaterial-Based Absorber Development

The size of IoT devices is different, which varies from small-sized to huge sensors. It is important to examine the impact of an array size on the frequency and absorption, since the possibility to change the array size without a major shift in the frequency and absorption loss, gives wider coverage area and, therefore, more harvested energy. Designed UC is used to construct the arrays of 2×1, 2×2, and 3×3, as shown in the inset of Fig. 6.

It is imperative to note that all three array-based MTMAs demonstrated 99.9% absorption. The array size has a negligible impact on the frequency shift and increases the absorption rate, making it nearly perfect. The slight changes in the frequency may be caused by the mutual coupling between adjacent UCs. The presented MTMA's efficiency is capable of powering small devices and sensors. It is compact and can be attached to most small sensors and can be used to cover large areas without a shift in the resonance frequency. The electric field

Table 2. The UC parameters.

Ref	UC size, mm^2	Frequency, GHz	Absorbance, %	UC thickness, mm	Application
[7]	50 × 50	2.4	88.5	1	Radio wave absorber
[9]	35 × 35	6.46 / 7.68	95	1.6	Multi-functional sensors
[10]	14 × 14	4.19 / 6.64 9.95	97.5 / 96.5 98.85	1.6	Stealth technology, radar applications
[15]	20 × 20	2.25	99	0.5	EH
[16]	10 × 10	3.5	98.5	1.6	Radar cross section, antenna reduction
This work	16 × 16	5.8	99.9	1.61	EH for IoT devices

distribution and the surface currents of MTMA at 5.8 GHz are analyzed and presented in Fig. 7 to observe the physical characteristics. The electric field distribution is mainly concentrated near the gaps of a square ring. Therefore, the gaps in UC design are important for contributing to greater absorption. The first design of UC has surface current around the square resonator. When the second resonator is added, the surface current is present near the inner circle. In Fig 7d, where the current density of the final UC design is depicted, the surface current distribution is dense around the inner circle and line, increasing absorption rate. Table 2 shows the comparison of the previous work with proposed MTMA. Although the absorber with 10 × 10 mm^2 has a smaller area, the absorbance level is lower compared to [16]. It can be referred that the absorbance rate of this work is higher and the UC size is smaller. These features make the proposed design an effective EH method for low-power IoT networks.

5   Conclusion

Single-band MTMA for RF EH has been designed and analyzed in this paper. MTMAs with different configurations, constructed from proposed UCs, show a high absorption of 99.9% at 5.8 GHz. From the analysis of metamaterial behavior, MTMA has double-negative medium characteristics. The metamaterial properties and insensitivity of frequency to the array configurations make proposed MTMA suitable for EH to power IoT devices. The number of UCs may be set to any necessary value and used to cover different surface areas.

References

1. Dautov, K., et al.: Quantifying the impact of slow wave factor on closed-loop defect-based WPT systems. IEEE Trans. Instrum. Meas. **71**, 1–10 (2022)
2. Quy, V.K., et al.: IoT-enabled smart agriculture: architecture, applications, and challenges. Appl. Sci. (2076-3417), **12**(7), 3396 (2022)
3. Nauryzbayev, G., et al.: On the performance analysis of WPT-based dual-hop AF relaying networks in α - μ fading. IEEE Access **6**, 37138–37149 (2018)
4. Altinel, D., Kurt, G.K.: Modeling of multiple energy sources for hybrid energy harvesting IoT systems. IEEE Internet Things J. **6**, 10846–10854 (2019)
5. Arzykulov, S., et al.: On the capacity of wireless powered cognitive relay network with interference alignment. IEEE Glob. Commun. Conf. 1–6 (2018)

6. Dautov, K., et al.: Assessment of compact digital metasurface with beam control for WBAN applications. In: EuMC. pp. 151–154 (2022)
7. Manohar, R., Joseph, S., Ratheesh, R.: An efficient metamaterial radio wave absorber for 2.4GHz ISM band. In: 2018 3rd IEEE International Conference on Intelligent Computer Communication and Processing, pp. 648–651 (2018)
8. Xu, P., et al.: Design of an effective energy receiving adapter for microwave wireless power transmission application. In: AIP Advances. p. 6 (2016). https://doi.org/10.1063/1.4966050
9. Bakir, M., et al.: Microwave metamaterial absorber for sensing applications. Opto-Electron. Rev. **25**(4), 318–325 (2017)
10. Singh, A.K., et al.: Dual- and triple-band polarization insensitive ultrathin conformal metamaterial absorbers with wide angular stability. IEEE Trans. Electromagn. Compat. **61**(3), 878–886 (2019)
11. Wei, Y., et al.: A multiband, polarization-controlled metasurface absorber for electromagnetic energy harvesting and wireless power transfer. IEEE Trans. Microw. Theory. Tech. **70**(5), 2861–2871 (2022)
12. Chen, X., et al.: Robust method to retrieve the constitutive effective parameters of metamaterials. Phys. Rev. E - Stat. Nonlinear Soft Matter Phys. **70**(1 2), 016608-1–016608-7 (2004)
13. Paul, J.J., et al.: Compact triple-band metamaterial absorber for RF energy harvesting. In: 2020 IEEE 4th Conference on Information and Communication Technology, pp. 1–6 (2020)
14. Ma, Y., et al.: Miniaturized and dual-band metamaterial absorber with fractal Sierpinski structure. J. Opt. Soc. Am. B **31**, 325–331 (2014)
15. Amin, M., et al.: An interference-based quadruple-L cross metasurface absorber for RF energy harvesting. IEEE Antennas Wirel. Propag. Lett. **20**(10), 2043–2047 (2021)
16. Garg, P., Jain, P.: Analysis of a novel metamaterial absorber using equivalent circuit model operating at 3.5 GHz. In: 2020 IEEE International Conference on the Computation of Electromagnetic, pp. 246–247 (2020)

Effective Exploitation of Ambient EM Energy for Driving Emerging IoT Devices: Case Study

Kamila Shalpeneyeva, Kassen Dautov, Mohammad Hashmi,
and Galymzhan Nauryzbayev[✉]

School of Engineering and Digital Sciences, Nazarbayev University, Astana 010000,
Kazakhstan
{kamila.shalpeneyeva,kassen.dautov,mohammad.hashmi,
galymzhan.nauryzbayev}@nu.edu.kz

Abstract. Radio-frequency (RF) energy harvesting-enabled sensor
nodes can alleviate the charging challenges by exploitation of electromagnetic waves in the ambient proximity and contribute to more
efficient use of energy resources that is essential to deploy numerous
Internet-of-Things (IoT) nodes. An RF spectrum survey was conducted
at Nazarbayev University campus to discover potential RF energy sources
and their available power levels which revealed four prospective frequency
bands. Consequently, two frequencies that demonstrated sufficient power
levels and stability for an efficient RF energy harvesting were selected
from the analysis of a full week data measurements. Then, the rectangular patch microstrip-fed dual-band antenna operating on those frequencies was designed and fabricated. The proposed meander-line antenna
design allowed miniaturization of the effective surface area that is useful for IoT sensor applications. The fabricated prototype and simulation
measurements were in good agreement.

Keywords: Energy harvesting (EH) · Internet-of-Things (IoT) ·
multi-band antenna · radio-frequency (RF) spectral survey

1 Introduction

The rapid growth and development of an Internet-of-Things (IoT) infrastructure
are leading to the increase in a number of sensor nodes in wireless networks [1].
The extensive deployment of IoT networks has led to exploring complications
of battery charging and high maintenance cost of numerous devices [2]. Therefore, wireless charging approaches, that enable maintenance-free sensor nodes,
became more attractive in comparison to the conventional battery charging techniques [1,3,4]. The advancement and extensive use of wireless communication

This research was funded by Nazarbayev University under Collaborative Research
Program Grants #11022021CRP1513 (G. Nauryzbayev) and #021220CRP0222 (M.
Hashmi).

K. Rabie et al. (Eds.): IoTaaS 2022, LNICST 506, pp. 48–57, 2023.
https://doi.org/10.1007/978-3-031-37139-4_5

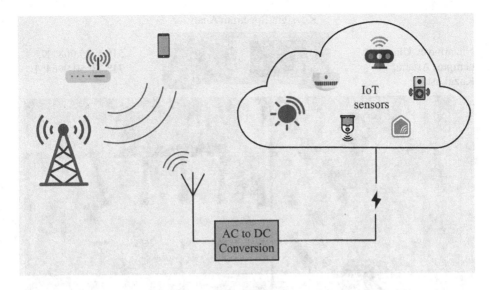

Fig. 1. Exploitation of EM pollution for wireless charging.

have made urban areas crowded with a myriad of user devices, Wi-Fi routers, cell phones, and sensors emitting electromagnetic (EM) waves that saturate the environment with radio-frequency (RF) energy [5]. The wireless devices emit the EM waves to communicate with each other, however, indeed only a fragment of that energy is processed for information decoding while the remaining part freely flows polluting the environment [6]. Considering the inevitability of this, the unused energy in an ambient environment could be utilized to satisfy the charging requirements of ultra low-power devices [3,7]. This could enable the deployment of autonomous IoT sensor networks. Recycling the unused EM waves contributes toward achieving the green communication paradigm through RF energy harvesting (EH) [8–10].

Available RF signal power needs to be determined and quantified to design and implement an effective EH system. This has been reportedly achieved by conducting spectrum surveys, one of which emphasized that maximum signals' power levels are more informative measurement rather than their density [11]. The measurements reported in [12,13] considered the conditions of a location, time and possible effects they had on the acquired results recognizing varying RF energy presence with respect to those conditions. An initial step of RF EH is antenna design that is tuned to operate within certain bands. Owing to the low-power levels of available RF signals, it would be beneficial to have a few sources to harvest from. Previous works have reported dual-band [14–16] and multi-band [9,17] antenna for RF EH applications.

In an aim to address the above-mentioned need, this paper proposes to realize simultaneous RF energy harvesting from multiple energy carriers. Keeping this in a perspective, an RF spectrum survey was performed on the campus of Nazarbayev University (NU, Astana, Kazakhstan) to determine the frequency

Keysight Spectrum Analyzer

Nazarbayev University
campus, Astana,
Kazakhstan

51° 5' 25.908" N,
71° 23' 50.9964" E

Fig. 2. Location of spectrum analyzer for RF survey (from the Google Maps).

bands eligible for efficient RF EH. The location of the RF spectrum survey represented a customary public place where an IoT network would likely be installed. This allowed estimating the potential for EH of the site from the taken data measurements. As a result, two frequencies of 1.74 GHz and 2.4 GHz were selected as prominent sources demonstrating the power levels above −30 dBm throughout the data measurement period. A dual-band antenna of a miniaturized size operating at those frequencies was designed and experimentally validated.

This paper is organized as follows. Section 2 introduces the proposed model of exploitation of EM pollution for IoT sensors powering. In addition, it provides a basis for conducting an RF spectral survey with observed measurements. Section 3 describes the design approach, simulation and experimental validation results of the dual-band antenna. Sections 4 and 5 cover the discussion of the results and conclusion of this paper, respectively.

2   Ambient RF Measurements

Nowadays, wireless networks are strongly packed with various devices communicating through RF signals. As a consequence, the areas with such networks have a lot of freely roaming EM waves that are not used for data transfer. Figure 1 depicts a scenario of the crowded network with RF signals available for EH. Ambient RF energy can be therefore recycled and used to power IoT sensors

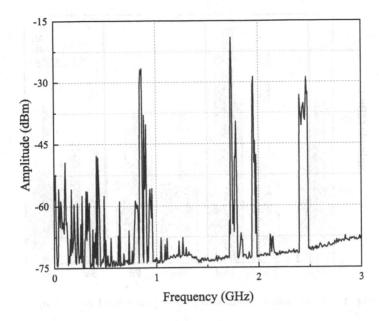

Fig. 3. The measured RF spectrum.

that require small amounts of energy. This option is a promising approach to enable independent IoT devices and contribute toward the green communication. The first step of collecting unused EM waves is capturing the signals with a dedicated antenna optimized to the present frequencies in that proximity. Moreover, the proper design of the EH system requires identifying the feasible spectral bands for RF harvesting. The signal with peak power above −30 dBm is treated as a prominent source for RF EH [11].

2.1 Methodology

To approach realizing efficient RF EH, it was necessary to determine the present frequency bands and their power levels. This was achieved by conducting an RF spectrum survey over a period of time to establish the power availability and consistency. The survey location was the NU campus, as illustrated in Fig. 2. The measurements were conducted during the working hours from 9 a.m. to 6 p.m. in a period of one week assuming that RF signals were more active during the daytime. The equipment used was the Keysight N9320B Spectrum Analyzer operating between 9 kHz−3 GHz. The resolution bandwidth was 100 kHz, the attenuation was set at 5 dB to avoid a compression of small signals [12]. The antenna used for signal capturing had a broad bandwidth of 800 MHz−8 GHz. The measurement setup recorded the maximum available peaks of incoming signals throughout the average day.

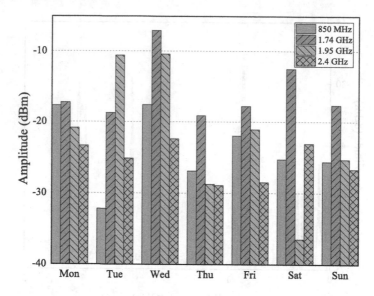

Fig. 4. The measured maximum power: power level vs week days.

2.2 Obtained Results and Analysis

As a result of the spectral survey at NU, multiple active frequency bands were observed to persist consistently in a period of the taken measurements. Figure 3 demonstrates the RF spectrum recorded on an average day. It is apparent that there are four main frequency peaks that are centered at 850 MHz, 1.74 GHz, 1.95 GHz, and 2.4 GHz which stand for the GSM (Global System for Mobile) and Wi-Fi bands. These frequency bands were measured and analyzed during a period of one week. Figure 4 depicts the maximum power levels of four distinguished bands that were recorded on each day of the week. As depicted, 1.74 GHz frequency signal demonstrated the highest activity throughout the week with a power level above −20 dBm at all times peaking at −6 dBm. Similarly, 2.4 GHz signal showed a stable trend with power level fluctuating between −20 dBm and −30 dBm. In general, the other two frequency bands showed potential for EH feasibility by having power levels within −20 dBm and −30 dBm during most days but were below the minimum power threshold of −30 dBm. Therefore, the two most active and stable frequencies of 1.74 GHz and 2.4 GHz were chosen for RF EH at the NU campus. For this purpose, the dual-band antenna was designed which is thoroughly described in Sect. 3.

3 Dual-Band Antenna Design

As stated above, simultaneous RF EH from two frequencies is realized by a means of a dual-band antenna. The rectangular patch antenna was selected due to its easy and low-cost fabrication. Figure 5 shows the antenna of dimensions 50 × 35

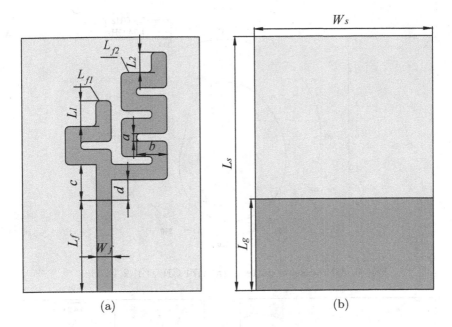

Fig. 5. The dual-band antenna structure: (a) top view (b) bottom view.

Table 1. The final optimized antenna parameters.

Parameter	W_s	L_s	W_f	L_q	a	b	c	d	L_1	L_2
Value (mm)	35	50	3	18	1.5	6	7	4	3.2	7

mm which was designed in CST Studio Suite. The meander-line approach that allows minimizing the surface area was chosen to shape the radiating element. The antenna's radiating patch comprises two meander lines each corresponding to a single resonant frequency. The lengths of line segments were calculated to be $\lambda/4$ of the resonant frequency and tuned to the desired values of 1.74 GHz and 2.4 GHz. Figure 7(a) depicts a single meander line (L_{f_1}) response, while Fig. 7(b) illustrates obtaining dual-band characteristic by adding a second meander line (L_{f_2}) to the radiating element. The microstrip feed line was calculated to have a characteristic impedance of 50-Ω with (1) and (2).

$$L_f = \frac{\lambda_0}{4\sqrt{\epsilon_{eff}}}, \tag{1}$$

$$Z_0 = \begin{cases} \frac{60}{\sqrt{\epsilon_{eff}}} \ln\left[\frac{8h}{W_f} + \frac{W_f}{4h}\right], & \frac{W_f}{h} \leq 1, \\ \frac{120\pi}{\sqrt{\epsilon_{eff}}\left[\frac{W_f}{h}+1.393+0.667\right]\ln\left[\frac{W_f}{h}+1.444\right]}, & \frac{W_f}{h} > 1. \end{cases} \tag{2}$$

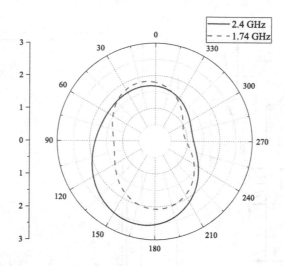

Fig. 6. 3D radiation pattern: (a) 1.74 GHz; (b) 2.4 GHz.

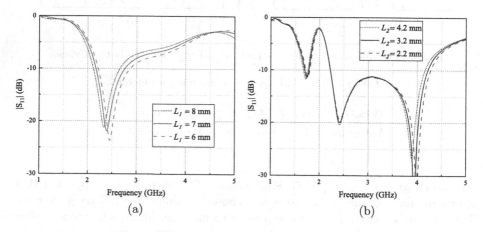

Fig. 7. The parameter variation: (a) L_1; (b) L_2.

3.1   The Effects of Antenna Configuration

The dual-band antenna design was realized by combining two meander-line segments of corresponding lengths each responsible for a respective frequency. L_{f_1} and L_{f_2} were varied to observe the effect on antenna performance at resonant frequencies of $f_1 = 2.4$ GHz and $f_2 = 1.74$ GHz, respectively, as it was dependent on the meander-line length. Figure 7(a) depicts the length variation of the first line path (L_{f_1}) and its effect on the resonant frequency that should correspond to f_1. L_{f_1} was varied by incrementing the stub (L_1) from 3.2 mm to 4.2 mm to monitor the change in the desired first resonance. It can be seen that increasing the line segment's length results in the lower resonant f_1. Similarly, Fig. 7(b) demonstrates the L_{f_2} line segment length variation and its effect on

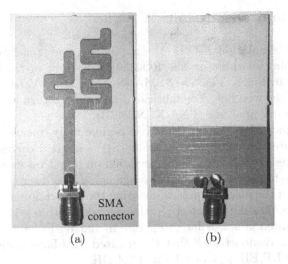

Fig. 8. The fabricated antenna: (a) top view (b) bottom view.

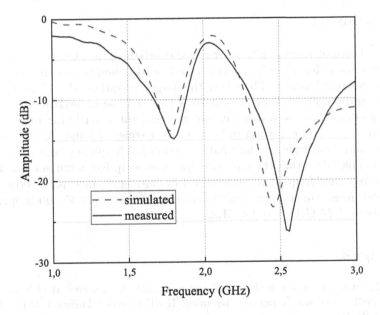

Fig. 9. The obtained results: S_{11} vs frequency.

second resonant frequency. The stub L_2 length was modified from 6 mm to 8 mm to increase the total line segment L_{f_2}, and it is observed that the second resonant frequency f_2 shifts toward the lower value. Finally, the lengths of the line segments were optimized to obtain resonances at f_1 and f_2. The radiation pattern is depicted in Fig. 6. The antenna gain reached 2.1 dBi and 2.6 dBi for 1.74 GHz and 2.4 GHz, accordingly, which are the characteristic gains of meander-line structured antennas.

4   Results and Discussion

To validate the simulation results, the antenna design was fabricated by the LPKF prototyping machine on the RO4350B substrate of thickness 1.54 mm which is shown in Fig. 8. The 50-Ω SMA (SubMiniature Version A) connector was soldered to the feed line. The fabricated antenna's return loss was measured by a vector network analyzer (PNA-X, N5247B).

Figure 9 shows the simulated and experimentally measured S_{11} of the meander-line patch antenna. The measured S_{11} is in good correspondence with the simulation results having a slight deviation on a first resonance. This difference in f_1 is due to the losses at higher frequencies. The discrepancy is accountable as a result of the machine precision during the fabrication and SMA connector soldering. Despite the deviation f_1, that remains within -10 dB bandwidth, the fabricated antenna is feasible to operate in the Wi-Fi band. The validation of the design has demonstrated that the realized dual-band antenna prototype is applicable for RF EH at 1.74 GHz and 2.4 GHz.

5   Conclusion

The abundance of unused EM waves in the urban environment can be conveniently exploited for charging multiple IoT sensor nodes and to enable their independent functionality. Therefore, this paper investigated and analyzed the spectrum and power levels of present RF energy on the university campus. The campus grounds was a suitable location as a general scenario for a public place with many users and expected to have active frequency bands to choose from. The spectrum measurements inferred two potential frequency bands eligible for RF EH and based on that the meander-line microstrip-fed patch antenna is realized. The resonant frequencies were tuned by finding optimal parametric values of meander lines. The antenna has dimensions (in mm) 50×35 and is optimized to operate on 1.74 GHz and 2.4 GHz.

References

1. Gu, X., et al.: Dynamic ambient RF energy density measurements of Montreal for battery-free IoT sensor network planning. IEEE Internet Things J. 8(17), 13209–13221 (2021)
2. Dautov, K. et al.: Quantifying the impact of slow wave factor on closed-loop defect-based WPT systems. In: IEEE Transactions on Instrumentation and Measurement, vol. 71, pp. 1–10 (2022)
3. Dhungana. A., Bulut, E.: Opportunistic wireless crowd charging of IoT devices from smartphones. In: 16th International Conference on Distributed Computing in Sensor Systems (DCOSS), pp. 376–380 (2020)
4. Toro, U.S., Wu, K., Leung V.C M.: Backscatter Wireless Communications and Sensing in Green Internet of Things. In: IEEE Transactions on Green Communications and Networking, vol. 6, no. 1, pp. 37–55 (2022)

5. Nauryzbayev, G., Abdallah, M., Rabie, K. M.: Outage Probability of the EH-Based Full-Duplex AF and DF Relaying Systems in $\alpha - \mu$ Environment. In: 2018 IEEE 88th Vehicular Technology Conference (VTC-Fall), pp. 1–6 (2018)
6. Raghavandaar, M. et al.: Energy harvesting using 2.45 GHz rectenna for powering sensors in IoT devices. In: International Conference on Electronics, Information, and Communication, pp. 1–3 (2020)
7. Dautov, K. et al.: Analysis and experimental validation of circularly slotted near-field WPT systems. In: 2021 IEEE International Midwest Symposium on Circuits and Systems (MWSCAS), pp. 263–266 (2021)
8. Nauryzbayev, G. et al.: Ergodic capacity analysis of wireless powered AF relaying systems over alpha-μ Fading Channels. In: GLOBECOM 2017–2017 IEEE Global Communications Conference, pp. 1–6 (2017)
9. Vu, H.S. et al.: Multiband ambient RF energy harvesting for autonomous IoT devices. In: IEEE Microwave and Wireless Components Letters, vol. 30, no. 12, pp. 1189–1192 (2020)
10. Ruchi et al.: A rectenna for RF energy harvesting for application in powering IoT device. In: IEEE Wireless Antenna and Microwave Symposium (WAMS), pp. 1–4 (2022)
11. Kwan, J.C., Fapojuwo, A.O.: Measurement and analysis of available ambient radio frequency energy for wireless energy harvesting. In: 2016 IEEE 84th Vehicular Technology Conference, pp. 1–6 (2016)
12. Pinuela, M., Mitcheson, P.D., Lucyszyn, S.: Ambient RF energy harvesting in urban and semi-urban environments. IEEE Trans. Microw. Theory Techn. **61**(7), 2715–2726 (2013)
13. Andrenko, A.S., Lin, X., Zeng, M.: Outdoor RF spectral survey: a roadmap for ambient RF energy harvesting. In: TENCON 2015–2015 IEEE Region 10 Conference, pp. 1–4 (2015)
14. Bhatt, K. et al.: Highly efficient 2.4 and 5.8 GHz dual-band rectenna for energy harvesting applications. In: IEEE Antennas and Wireless Propagation Letters, vol. 18, no. 12, pp. 2637–2641 (2019)
15. Wong, K. et al.: Very-low-profile grounded coplanar waveguide-fed dual-band WLAN slot antenna for on-body antenna application. In: IEEE Antennas and Wireless Propagation Letters, vol. 19, no. 1, pp. 213–217 (2020)
16. Yadav, M. et al.: Gain enhanced dual band antenna backed by dual band AMC surface for wireless body area network applications. In: 2021 IEEE Indian Conference on Antennas and Propagation, pp. 494–497 (2021)
17. Boursianis, A.D., et al.: Multiband patch antenna design using nature-inspired optimization method. IEEE Open J. Antenn. Propag. **2**, 151–162 (2021)

Evaluating Direct Link IoT-LoRa Communication via LEO Nanosatellite: DEWASAT-1

Reem Al-Ali[1]([✉]) [ID], Sidi Ahmed. Bendoukha[1] [ID], Zineddine N. Haitaamar[1,1] [ID], Mireya Arora[1,2] [ID], Jayakumar V. Karunamurthy[1], and Tareg Ghaoud[1]

[1] Research and Development Department, Dubai Electricity and Water Authority (DEWA), Dubai, UAE
`reem.saleh@dewa.gov.ae`
[2] College of Engineering, University of Michigan, Ann Arbor, MI 48109, USA

Abstract. The rapid growth of the Internet of Things (IoT) opens the possibility for multiple applications catering to a variety of needs. Combined with Long Range (LoRa) technology, it can provide a global coverage network that connects devices and communicates valuable information. This manuscript evaluates the direct link of IoT-LoRa to the satellite by presenting various ground trials and uplink/downlink tests. The IoT substation communication to the tracked satellites based on predicted passes over the target is tested for coverage and environment losses. Using orbital data analyses and simulation plots, we estimate and validate the Radio Frequency (RF) output data of the received power, signal strength, and Bit Error Rate (BER) of the ground receiver through the telemetry phase. The paper validates the novel concept of using LoRa - Chirp Spread Spectrum (CSS) modulation by varying the spreading factor, elevation, and antenna gain for direct communication from the IoT terminal to Low Earth Orbit (LEO) CubeSat. This is done by excluding the master gateway and establishing a standard for future validations with untried and onboard data by attaining a positive link margin.

Keywords: BER · DEWASAT-1 · Direct Communication · IoT · LoRa-CSS · Spreading Factor · Signal to Noise Ratio

1 Introduction

The Internet of Things (IoT) is a network connecting several devices as sensors, software, machines – things – to improve real-time decisions and operational awareness. The technology can apply to a small household, a larger industrial workspace, and even a global framework. IoT nodes are connected via the network and process data from the sensors before sending it to the cloud. There has been a growing interest in IoT technology, with forecasts predicting that 75 billion devices will be connected by 2025 [1].

© ICST Institute for Computer Sciences, Social Informatics and Telecommunications Engineering 2023
Published by Springer Nature Switzerland AG 2023. All Rights Reserved
K. Rabie et al. (Eds.): IoTaaS 2022, LNICST 506, pp. 58–70, 2023.
https://doi.org/10.1007/978-3-031-37139-4_6

Different protocols have been developed for different use cases. For instance, for devices that have a short communication range and require low power, the IEEE, Bluetooth Low Energy, and ZigBee standards are used as communication protocols [2]. Long Range (LoRa) is based on Chirp Spread Spectrum (CSS) technology and serves as a method of spread spectrum modulation. It is a more resilient modulation scheme and particularly useful when handling IoT technology because its relatively low power consumption can perform long-range communication. LoRa is popular for use cases that involve monitoring large geographical areas with many nodes and less data per node [3].

A common infrastructure setup for an IoT network involves three key components: the IoT devices, a gateway, and the network. The devices perform their respective functions and transfer information to the gateway. The gateway sends data from and to the network, serving as a central node when communicating in a large or rural area. The gateway then sends information back to the devices. Using a gateway reduces the investment required for infrastructure; however, it is not effective in remote areas [4]. According to reference [5], the author recommends a constellation of satellites to solve the remote connectivity problem. This would cover a significantly larger geographical area and opens the possibility of achieving global coverage. This can be done by connecting a series of CubeSats, which have increased in popularity due to recent technological advancements and lower costs associated with the launch [6]. Here a Low Power Wide-Area Network (LPWAN) is used called LoRaWAN to form the connection. Each device can transmit signals directly and independently in this network using bidirectional communication. In 2021, there were about 178 million devices connected to LoRa networks [7].

For optimum transmission of LoRa messages in the network, certain parameters need to be configured. The Spreading Factor (SF) refers to the ratio of chips per symbol and has typical values from 7 to 11 [8]. As SF values get larger, the Signal-to-Noise Ratio (SNR) increases because there are more chips in each transmission. This means longer data packets are required, and the receiver sensitivity is less. The second parameter works to ensure that messages are transmitted without errors. To do this, data packets often have redundant bits added to them. The number of these bits is determined by the Code Rate (CR), which works by collecting and correcting information received [9]. The frequency Bandwidth (BW) used affects the airtime required for a signal to reach the satellite. Since LoRa generally works between 125–500 kHz [10], a bandwidth of 500 kHz would have the lowest airtime but will reduce sensitivity at the receiver. The bandwidth of LoRa modulation defines the maximum shift of central frequency, which is approximately 25% of the BW.

New research recommended using IoT for space-based systems. The suggestion enables a wide communication coverage. Despite the benefits of using a satellite, communicating with devices in space comes with a set of challenges. One of these is the Doppler frequency shift which becomes higher when in space. There are also more channel losses, likely because of atmospheric interference [11]. Some of these effects are combatted using an LPWAN and a constellation of CubeSats, they still need to be accounted for in calculations, simulations, and results. This paper presents the analysis and results done for one of Space-D projects. Space-D is a project initiated by the Dubai Electricity and Water Authority (DEWA) Research and Development (R&D) Center. The project aims to build a constellation of CubeSats equipped with advanced space technology and Commercial off-the-shelf (COTS). DEWASAT-1 is part of this program and was launched on January 13th, 2022. The mission objective is to establish a direct communication link using satellited based IoT communication without utilizing gateways. Figure 1(a) illustrates the IoT terminal used on the ground to communicate with the DEWASAT-1, and the CubeSat structure is presented in Fig. 1(b). The focus of this paper is on DEWASAT-1's primary mission which is the evaluation of the link margin of LoRa CSS communication.

The paper is organized as follows; Sect. 1 includes the literature review LoRa IoT network; Sect. 2 is methodology and simulation, including IoT system architecture, link budget study of DEWASAT-1, and simulations; Sect. 3 presents the results and analysis; and Sect. 4 the conclusions.

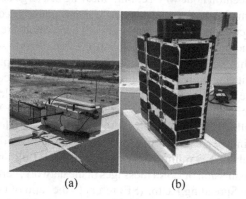

(a)   (b)

Fig. 1. (a) IoT Terminal-left (b) DEWASAT-1 flight model-right

2   Methodology and Simulation

2.1   IoT-LoRa System

The utilization of a CubeSat constellation as a LoRa gateway enables reasonable coverage for IoT devices in remote areas. DEWASAT-1 is a 3U nanosatellite that is part of the Space-D project and includes the LoRa receiver as a payload. The IoT terminal is developed by the R&D center at DEWA to communicate with the satellite through LoRa CSS modulation. As shown in Fig. 2, the IoT terminal transmits using LoRaWAN Protocol and a CSS modulation. The transmission signal parameters can vary within guidelines set by authorities such as the Telecommunications and Digital Government Regulatory Authority (TDRA) in UAE or limitations created by interference with other transmissions. Figure 2 displays the IoT space architecture where two nanosatellites are used to assess the uplink communication under varying conditions.

During the downlink of telemetry data, the nanosatellite receives housekeeping information and sends it to the ground station via an onboard S-band transceiver. The antenna on the satellite can be a Left-Hand Circular Polarization (LHCP) or a Right-Hand Circular Polarization (RHCP). The downloaded data is received at a specified bit rate through

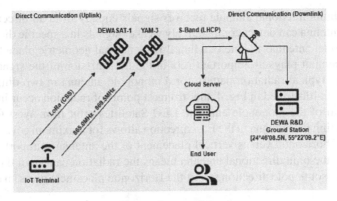

Fig. 2. IoT Space architecture

S-X bands at the ground station. Alternatively, the data received by the ground station can be uploaded to the cloud, where it may be used for various IoT Platforms by different end-users.

An IoT Terminal model is designed to meet the requirements and perform the tests defined in the simulations discussed in Sect. 2.2. The IoT Terminal consists of 2 main subsystems, as shown in Fig. 3. The lower part of the system architecture consists of a host processor that controls the main system and scripts. A script is configured with the transmission parameters: frequency, SF, and CR. The upper section comprises the ARM node processor, which hosts the SX1262 based radio for transmission. This radio is capable of transmitting with up to +22 dBm at a low power rating according to the datasheet [12].

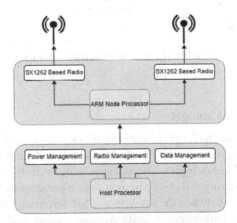

Fig. 3. Hardware architecture of the IoT terminal

The transmitted power is configured to 22 dBm at the 865.07 MHz channel. The gain of the antenna can vary based on which antenna is used. In the scope of this paper, two possibilities are evaluated, a 2 dBi and 10 dBi gain antenna with monopole propagation.

Monopole Omnidirectional antenna receives signals equally from all directions whilst directional antenna can detect comparatively weaker signals in a specific direction [13]. Omnidirectional antennas radiate in a flat, 2-Dimensional geometric plane [14]. Hence antenna placement plays an important role in the transmission of the signal. Figure 4 illustrates the typical radiation pattern for a monopole antenna in two dimensions (X and Y) [15]. As illustrated in Fig. 4, the strongest points of radiation occur in the above-ground region of the monopole antenna. LEO Satellites orbit from West to East [16] therefore placing the antenna in the East direction allows for maximum coverage. Lastly, the choice of horizontal versus vertical placement of the antenna is important. Vertical placement of the omnidirectional antenna means the radiation pattern of the antenna is in the north to south pole direction whilst the Horizontal placement gives an east to west radiation.

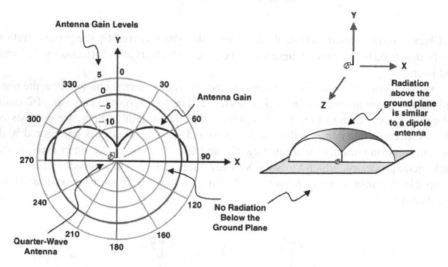

Fig. 4. Typical omnidirectional monopole antenna radiation pattern [15]

2.2   DEWASAT-1: Link Budget

Space communication is challenging, and a high link margin is difficult to achieve due to channel losses. Thus, it is necessary to study, evaluate and determine the feasibility of using IoT space-based technologies. The assessment of the link budget of DEWASAT-1 is conducted by considering different communication parameters for uplink to validate the communication link between the satellite and IoT terminal. This section focuses on evaluating the essential parameters in LoRa communication, such as BW, SF, and CR.

The study includes the effect of elevation angle on the SNR for different SF. Two studies are conducted, varying the gain value to evaluate and determine the link margin based on these conditions. A positive link margin defines a good communication link where it is calculated based on

$$Link\ Margin = E_s/N_0 - E_s/N_{0,\ required} \tag{1}$$

where E_s/N_0 is the signal-to-noise ratio, the estimated value in dB, and $E_s/N_{0, required}$ is measured in dB and it is the required value to establish a communication link. The link margin is influenced by serval factors, so different parameters are varied to verify to evaluate its effect on the communication link.

The data rate is an important parameter in terms of data downloading. It is dependent on the factors that impact LoRa communication. In the second simulation, these parameters were varied to observe their impact on the data rate. To consider different scenarios, the study includes considering two bandwidths that are 125 kHz and 250 kHz. The data rate is calculated by

$$Data\ Rate = \left[BW/2^{SF} \right][4/(4 + CR)]SF \tag{2}$$

where the *Data Rate* is in bps, *BW* is the bandwidth in bps, *SF* is the spreading factor, *CR* is the code rate.

Another study involves varying SF to understand its influence on the probability of bit error rate (BER). As the modulation scheme used has a critical effect on the signal BER. Investigating the BER provides sufficient information to evaluate the quality of the communication link. The probability of BER for CSS is calculated using

$$P_e = 0.5\ Q\left(1.28(E_s/N_0)^{0.5} - 1.28\ SF^{0.5} + 0.4 \right) \tag{3}$$

Doppler shifts affect the signal, particularly for space communication, as it is dependent on satellite motion. The dynamics associated with the satellite speed influence the Doppler shift. Thus, it is essential to demonstrate that the maximum Doppler shift is within the signal's BW to ensure communication. This value depends on the satellite speed which is 7.6 km/s. Doppler shift is calculated using the equation

$$\Delta f = (\Delta v/c)f_o \tag{4}$$

Where Δf is the doppler shift in Hz, Δv is the satellite velocity in km/s, c is the speed of light in km/s, and f_o is the central frequency in Hz. The maximum experienced doppler shift is 21.9 kHz, where the central frequency is 865.07 MHz.

2.3 Orbital Simulations

Developing a test with the IoT terminal allows for the evaluation of simulated data against real orbital data. Eutelsat [YAM-3] and DEWASAT-1 were tested to assess the direct uplink test for the LoRaWAN Protocol. The first test setup done was with Eutelsat's 3U CubeSat (YAM-3), where a pass was predicted with the parameters outlined in Table 1. It should be noted that the test is conducted for YAM-3 and DEWASAT-1 for the testing purposes of the IoT terminal, and to ensure a successful LoRa link is established in the two scenarios regardless of the satellite orbit.

Table 1. YAM-3 predicted pass time

Time	Azimuth (°)	Elevation (°)	Range (km)
04-06-2022 01:58:00	160.7	3.0	2361
04-06-2022 02:03:11	77.8	62.9	590
04-06-2022 02:08:22	354.1	3.1	2357

As seen in Table 1, the satellite's entry time, known as the Acquisition of Signal (AOS), to the Ground Station's (GS) transmitter is at 01:58:00 local time (UTC + 4:00). The mid-pass is when the satellite is directly above the GS transmitter and offers the best elevation, also known as the Time of Closest Approach (TCS). Finally, Loss of Signal (LOS) is when the satellite is below the ground station's horizon. The higher the elevation, the better the link margin meaning greater success in transmission. Figure 5 shows the satellite's position at the entry pass and the path to be taken. Also, it shows the orbital parameters of the satellite on the right side in real-time such as Coordinates, Altitude, Velocity, and Range (km).

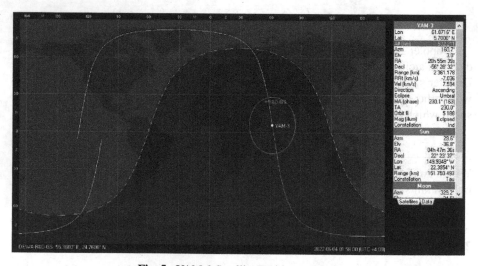

Fig. 5. YAM-3 Satellite Position and Path

A second test is done on DEWASAT-1 to evaluate and compare the results obtained. In Fig. 7, the path of the DEWASAT-1 satellite is predicted using Orbitron, and the pass details obtained are shown in Table 2. Furthermore, using the Orbitron Software [17], the satellites can be tracked to indicate key orbital parameters of the satellite in real-time such as coordinates, altitude, velocity, and range (km). A Two-Line-Element (TLE) set can be obtained from sites like NORAD [18], which provide the Azimuth and Elevation angle, as well as the Uplink/Downlink frequency used by the satellite. A sample TLE is shown in Fig. 6 for DEWASAT-1, which defines the orbital parameters of the satellite in its orbit.

```
DEWASAT-1
1 51067U 22002CM  22165.79182470  .00007128  00000+0  40346-3 0  9996
2 51067  97.4839 232.6714 0010066  94.0309 266.2073 15.13303242 23009
```

Fig. 6. TLE for DEWASAT-1

Table 2. DEWASAT-1 predicted pass time

Time	Azimuth (°)	Elevation (°)	Range (km)
04-06-2022 17:48:20	160.8	3.0	2361
04-06-2022 17:53:31	77.9	63.1	589
04-06-2022 17:58:43	354.1	3.0	2364
06-06-2022 10:52:34	357.0	3.0	2346
06-06-2022 10:57:30	284.6	34.2	866
06-06-2022 11:02:26	211.7	3.1	2340

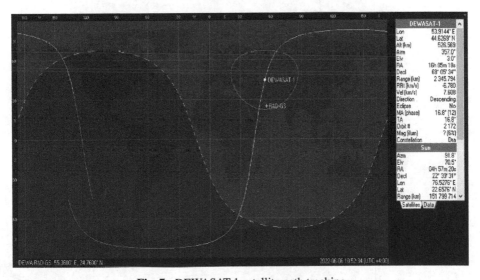

Fig. 7. DEWASAT-1 satellite path tracking

3 Results and Analysis

The assessment and results of the link budget of DEWASAT-1 are represented in this section. Figure 8 demonstrates the effect of elevation angle on the signal-to-noise ratio for different SF values. Several conclusions can be drawn from this plot. First, the figure displays calculations performed at two values of antenna gain, 2 and 10. For each SF and elevation angle value, a higher gain causes a higher E_s/N_0. This is because a larger antenna gain provides a higher signal-to-noise ratio, therefore a more reliable communication link. The second result seen in Fig. 8 is that, for any SF or gain value, as the elevation angle increases, the E_s/N_0 continues to rise until it reaches 90°, where the best communication link occurs. Third, for every gain and elevation value, increasing SF from 7 to 11 causes E_s/N_0 to grow by about 10 dB. Based on these results, the simulation using an antenna gain margin of 2 requires a minimum elevation angle of 20-degrees to establish a communication link. However, using a gain margin of 10 presents positive link margins at lower angles.

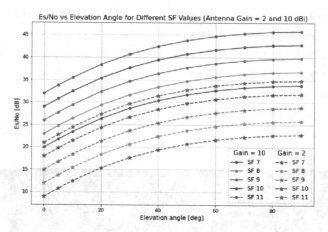

Fig. 8. Signal-to-noise ratio for different elevation angle and antenna gain

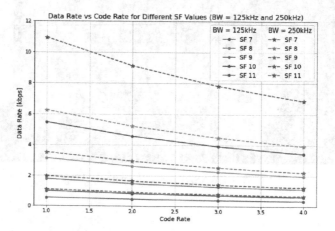

Fig. 9. Data rate for different SF and BW

Figure 9 showcases the relationship between data rate and code rate for different values of SF at two possible bandwidths based on LoRa's capabilities. CR shows an almost insignificant effect on the data rate when SF is high. However, smaller values of SF experience a visible reduction in data rate as CR increases. The study performs the calculation at two BW and demonstrates the effect of BW on the data rate and CR. The results show that, at any given code rate and SF, a higher data rate is associated with higher BW.

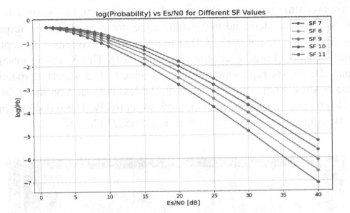

Fig. 10. Probability of BER for various SF

Another study done involved varying SF to observe its influence on the probability of BER, as shown in Fig. 10. This investigation is done as lower BER is desirable for the communication. As illustrated from the results, a high signal-to-noise ratio has a lower probability of BER, where the SF of LoRa has a small influence on the P_b.

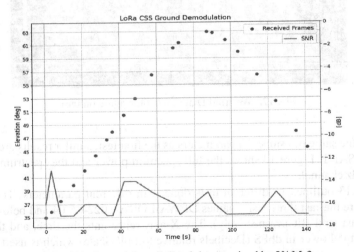

Fig. 11. Ground demodulated data received by YAM-3

Using the parameters above, the transmitting IoT Terminal can be set up. The parameters for the above test case: a transmission frequency of 865.070 MHz, a spreading factor of 9, a payload of 15 bytes, and the transmission cycle period was 5 s. In Fig. 11, the demodulated LoRa received frames from the satellite are plotted against the time (X-Axis) and SNR (Y-Axis). The figure shows the corresponding SNR at each LoRa demodulated frame with the respective elevation. As the elevation is higher, the SNR is also high signifying a better-received frame.

A spectrogram is also used, as a method of analyzing the level of intensity (Transmitted Power) on a time-frequency domain. The spectrogram, also known as a Waterfall diagram, allows us to understand and evaluate the power at different frequencies and evaluate the SNR on a visual basis. Often in a waterfall diagram, blue represents low pressure, and red is the highest recorded intensity [19]. The X-axis represents the frequencies, and the Y-axis represents the time spanned. The waterfall spectrum of the received data is shown below in Fig. 12 with the levels legend on the right indicating the low and high-power points in blue and red respectively. The red signal in the figure below is at the center frequency of transmission (865.070 MHz).

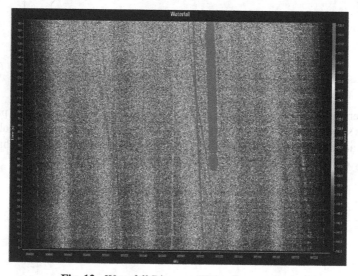

Fig. 12. Waterfall Diagram (Color figure online)

Using the same transmission parameters as the first test, similar results are obtained on DEWASAT-1. Figure 13 shows the full spectrum power and the spectrum power at the 125 kHz channel.

Figure 13 outlines 11 different tests done with different parameters. The ones to highlight are the last three tests' names DEWA-LORA-2022-06-04 and below colored (Lime, Aqua, and Blue respectively). The X-axis represents the time, and the Y-axis represents the Power in dbFS (Decibels relative to Full Scale) which is used in digital signals. Focusing on the lower part of the figure, it can be seen that all 3 tests have similar power values, distinctly different from the unsuccessful tests. This means they have a lower dbFS signifying a stronger signal. The lime and aqua signals have a shorter time scale as opposed to the blue signal due to the different pass time of the satellite.

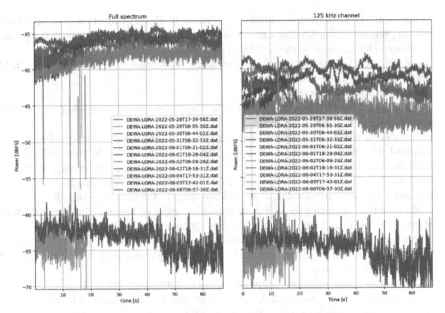

Fig. 13. Full and 125kHz spectrum power comparison for DEWASAT-1

4   Conclusion

This paper proposes a novel method to evaluate and assess the direct link between IoT-LoRa enabled devices and LEO nanosatellite DEWASAT-1. The results of the direct communication link between the satellite and IoT terminal using LoRa-CSS technology shows a successful link margin establishment signifying positive communication from the IoT terminal to LEO satellite. Despite atmospheric losses and power limitations of the IoT Terminal, a successful uplink was achieved. Orbital data results show a step in the correct direction with multiple LoRa frames demodulated at the ground using CSS.

For future work, the collection of orbital data will continue from DEWASAT-1 and other satellites in the constellation to further analyze the data and enhance the design of the IoT Terminal for improved reliability. Furthermore, the use of multiple IoT Terminals simultaneously will be implemented to evaluate the satellite receiver with multiple joint transmissions.

References

1. Vailshery, L.S.: IOT devices installed Base Worldwide 2015–2025. https://www.statista.com/statistics/471264/iotnumber-of-connected-devices-worldwide/
2. Lavric, A.: Lora (long-range) high-density sensors for internet of things. J. Sens. **2019**, 1–9 (2019). https://doi.org/10.1155/2019/3502987
3. Wu, T., Qu, D., Zhang, G.: Research on Lora adaptability in the Leo satellites internet of things. In: 2019 15th International Wireless Communications and Mobile Computing Conference (IWCMC) (2019)

4. Colombo, R.M., Mahmood, A., Sisinni, E., Ferrari, P., Gidlund, M.: Low-cost SDR-based tool for evaluating Lora Satellite Communications. In: 2022 IEEE International Symposium on Measurements and Networking (M&N) (2022)
5. Qu, Z., Zhang, G., Cao, H., Xie, J.: Leo satellite constellation for internet of things. IEEE Access. **5**, 18391–18401 (2017)
6. CubeSat. http://www.cubesat.org/
7. Everything you need to know about Lora. https://hyphabit.io/everything-you-need-to-know-about-lora/
8. Edward, P., El-Aasser, M., Ashour, M., Elshabrawy, T.: Interleaved chirp spreading Lora as a parallel network to enhance Lora Capacity. IEEE Internet Things J. **8**, 3864–3874 (2021)
9. Marcelis, P.J., Kouvelas, N., Rao, V.S., Prasad, R.V.: DaRe: data recovery through application layer coding for LoRaWAN. IEEE Trans. Mob. Comput. **21**, 895–910 (2022)
10. Karunamurthy, J.V., Bendoukha, S.A., Nikolakakos, I., Ghaoud, T., Ebisi, F., Alkharrat, M.R.: Adaptive Technique for lora communication with Leo Nanosatellite. In: 2021 IEEE Microwave Theory and Techniques in Wireless Communications (MTTW) (2021)
11. Fernandez, L., Ruiz-De-Azua, J.A., Calveras, A., Camps, A.: Assessing Lora for satellite-to-earth communications considering the impact of ionospheric scintillation. IEEE Access **8**, 165570–165582 (2020)
12. SX1261. https://www.semtech.com/products/wireless-rf/lora-core/sx1261
13. Neely, M., Hamerstone, A., Sanyk, C.: Basic radio theory and introduction to radio systems. Wirel. Reconnaissance Penetration Test. 7–43 (2013)
14. Contributor, T.T.: What is omnidirectional antenna? - definition from whatis.com. https://www.techtarget.com/whatis/definition/omnidirectional-antenna
15. Farahani, S.: RF propagation, antennas, and regulatory requirements. ZigBee Wirel. Netw. Transceivers, 171–206 (2008)
16. Types of orbits. https://www.esa.int/Enabling_Support/Space_Transportation/Types_of_orbits
17. Stoff, S.: Orbitron - satellite tracking system. http://www.stoff.pl/
18. NORAD GP Element Setscurrent Data. http://www.celestrak.com/NORAD/elements/
19. Sorama: Spectrogram Analysis Waterfall Diagram. https://www.sorama.eu/blog/spectogram-analysis-waterfall-diagram

Wireless Communications, Vehicular Networks, Resource Optimization, Satellite communications and Machine Learning

Bit Error Rate Performance of Wireless Communication Systems with Passive Intermodulation Interference

Lu Tian, Zhan Xu[✉], Chenrui Shi, Lele Guan, and Yuming Shi

Key Laboratory of Modern Measurement and Control Technology, Ministry of Education, Beijing Information Science and Technology University, Beijing 100101, China
{tianlu,xuzhan}@bistu.edu.cn

Abstract. The development of wireless communication systems tends to be high-power, multi-carrier and broadband, which makes the problem of passive intermodulation (PIM) interference in the communication systems more and more serious. When PIM interference falls into the receiving passband of communication systems, the receiving sensitivity of receivers will be reduced and the performance of the receiver will be affected. In this paper, a model is established to analyze the influence of PIM interference on the demodulation link in two cases. One is the constant signal-to-interference ratio (SIR), and the center frequency of PIM interference is the same as the carrier frequency of the uplink received signal, the other is time-varying SIR. Due to numerical simulations, the analysis curve and simulation curve of the bit error rate is basically consistent with each other, indicating that the analysis model is reasonable.

Keywords: passive intermodulation interference · bit error rate · demodulation link · signal-to-interference ratio

1 Introduction

PIM is the phenomenon of interference caused by intermodulation signals generated when two or more transmit carriers are input to fall into the receive passband in a high-power multichannel communication system [1]. Various passive components in the transmitting system have a certain degree of nonlinear characteristics, and in high-power, multi-channel systems, the nonlinearity of these passive components will generate harmonics of a higher order than the operating frequency, and the mixing of harmonics with the operating frequency will generate a new set of frequencies, which will eventually generate a set of interference spectrum in the air and affect normal communication.

In the transceiver communication system, the transmitted signal and the received signal pass through the transceiver duplexer, high-power cable, antenna feed source at the same time. If the PIM products generated between different carriers of the transmitted signal fall into the receive band, the PIM products will enter the receiver together with the received signals at the same time, forming an interference signal. This problem cannot

K. Rabie et al. (Eds.): IoTaaS 2022, LNICST 506, pp. 73–81, 2023.
https://doi.org/10.1007/978-3-031-37139-4_7

be solved by using traditional filter and isolation methods. When the PIM level is low, the bottom noise of the received signal will be raised, so that the receiver signal-to-noise ratio (SNR) decreases and the bit error rate increases; when the PIM level increases further, it will affect the normal operation of the entire communication system, and in serious cases, the PIM will flood the received signal, resulting in channel blockage and communication interruption, which will paralyze the entire communication system.

The impact of passive intermodulation interference on the communication system is mainly reflected in the following two links, namely the demodulation link and the synchronization capture link. Among them, PIM interference affects the demodulation link of the communication system means that when PIM interference is superimposed on the uplink received signal, it will deteriorate the Error Vector Magnitude (EVM) of the uplink received signal so that the verdict of the uplink received signal will be affected and the error code elements will appear in the uplink signal transmission, and then affect the demodulation performance of the uplink communication link. For the impact of PIM interference on the demodulation link of the communication system, the BER of the uplink transmission is used to measure.

The intermodulation phenomenon generated by nonlinear devices in the process of signal transmission has been an important research problem, especially with the development of communication systems towards high-power and multi-carrier, scholars all over the world pay more attention to the research of intermodulation. However, among the many studies of PIM, most of them focus on the analysis of the mechanism of PIM and microwave devices. There are fewer studies on the impact of PIM on the communication system, and the analysis of the influence of more general multi-carrier PIM on system performance needs to be improved. There is little analysis has been done on the statistical properties of PIM and its effects on the system such as bit error rate (BER) performance [2–5]. However, the existing results have focused on analyzing the impact of dual-carrier PIM on the bit error rate of the communication system, and have not analyzed the impact of multi-carrier PIM, which is more common in the actual situation. At the same time, in the existing analysis, the assumption of PIM interference signal is too ideal to achieve an accurate prediction of the influence of PIM on the performance of the communication system.

In this paper, the impact of PIM interference on the demodulation performance of the communication system will be analyzed according to the statistical signal processing theory in combination with the characteristics of PIM interference. In the following analysis model of the effect of PIM interference on the demodulation performance of communication system, the analysis of the effect of PIM interference on the demodulation link under constant SIR, and the analysis of the effect of PIM interference on the demodulation link under time-varying SIR are separately described according to whether the SIR is constant or not.

The rest of this paper is organized as follows. In Sect. 2, the influence of PIM interference on the demodulation link is analyzed when the SIR is constant and the center frequency of PIM interference happens to fall on the carrier frequency of the uplink received signal. In Sect. 3, the influence of PIM interference on the demodulation process is analyzed in the case of time-varying SIR, followed by a brief conclusion in Sect. 4.

2 Bit Error Rate Performance of PIM Interference with Constant SIR

Since any memoryless nonlinear behavior can be described by the power series model, the power series model is used to analyze the influence of PIM interference on demodulation.

$$Y(t) = a_1 X(t) + a_2 X^2(t) + a_3 X^3(t) + \cdots + a_n X^n(t)+ \tag{1}$$

where $Y(t)$ is the PIM interference signal; $X(t)$ is the downlink m-way carrier signal, which can be expressed as

$$X(t) = \sum_{i=1}^{m} R_i(t) \cos(2\pi f_i t) \tag{2}$$

where f_i is the frequency of the downlink carrier signal; $R_i(t)$ is the baseband shaping signal with downlink frequency f_i.

Due to the design characteristics of the upstream and downstream signal bands, only the PIM products in the region I (i.e., PIM products with PIM frequencies lower than the second harmonic frequency) are usually considered, so only the PIM interference generated by odd powers of $X(t)$ is considered.

Since the PIM product grows nonlinearly with the number of downlink carriers, only the PIM product of the downlink with dual-carrier and BPSK modulation is considered next. The PIM products of the downlink signal with multi-carrier and other modulation modes can also be analyzed using this method, but it is more complicated.

The downlink $X(t)$ can be expressed as

$$X(t) = \sum_{i=1}^{2} R_i(t) \cos(2\pi f_i t) \tag{3}$$

Then the n ($n = 2p + 1$, p is a positive integer) order PIM product that falls into the receive band can be expressed as

$$Y_n(t) = R_1^{p+1} R_2^p \cos(2\pi((p+1)f_1 - pf_2)) \tag{4}$$

When the baseband signal is modulated using rectangular pulse BPSK (binary phase shift keying), $R_1 = \pm 1$ and $R_2 = \pm 1$, so $R_1^{p+1} R_2^p \cos(2\pi((p+1)f_1 - pf_2))$. If R_1 and R_2 take the value of ± 1 with equal probability, then the values of $R_1^{p+1} R_2^p$ are also taken with equal probability.

When the uplink signal frequency $f_{up} = (p+1)f_1 - pf_2$, then the PIM interference has the greatest impact on the reception of the uplink signal. The PIM interference signal after down-conversion to get the baseband signal can be expressed as

$$Y_b(t) = R_1^{p+1} R_2^p = \pm 1 \tag{5}$$

At the uplink signal receiving end, the signal entering the adjudicator can be expressed as

$$z = \sqrt{P_s} X + \sqrt{P_I} Y_b + n \tag{6}$$

where X is the uplink signal per unit energy; Y_b is the interference signal per unit energy; n is the additive Gaussian white noise; P_S is the signal power; P_I is the interference power.

The BER is calculated for $Y_b = +1$ and $Y_b = -1$, respectively. The BER can be expressed as

$$
\begin{aligned}
P_e &= P(Y_b = +1)PX = +1P(z\langle 0|Y_b = +1, X = +1) \\
&+ P(Y_b = -1)PX = +1P(z\langle 0|Y_b = -1, X = +1) \\
&+ P(Y_b = +1)PX = -1P(z > 0|Y_b = +1, X = -1) \\
&+ P(Y_b = -1)PX = -1P(z > 0|Y_b = -1, X = -1)
\end{aligned}
\tag{7}
$$

When $X = \pm 1$ with equal probability and $Y_b = \pm 1$ with equal probability (In the BPSK system), Eq. (7) can be expressed as

$$
\begin{aligned}
P_e &= \frac{1}{4}P(z\langle 0|Y_b = +1, X = +1) + \frac{1}{4}P(z\langle 0|Y_b = -1, X = +1) \\
&+ \frac{1}{4}P(z > 0|Y_b = +1, X = -1) + \frac{1}{4}P(z > 0|Y_b = -1, X = -1)
\end{aligned}
\tag{8}
$$

The statistical distribution of the signals entering the adjudicator is considered below. Four probability density functions for the conditions $X = \pm 1$ and $Y_b = \pm 1$ can be written as

$$
f_{X=+1, Y_b=+1}(z) = \frac{1}{\sqrt{2\pi}\sigma} exp\left(-\frac{(z - (\sqrt{P_S} + \sqrt{P_I}))^2}{2\sigma^2}\right)
\tag{9}
$$

$$
f_{X=+1, Y_b=-1}(z) = \frac{1}{\sqrt{2\pi}\sigma} exp\left(-\frac{(z - (\sqrt{P_S} - \sqrt{P_I}))^2}{2\sigma^2}\right)
\tag{10}
$$

$$
f_{X=-1, Y_b=-1}(z) = \frac{1}{\sqrt{2\pi}\sigma} exp\left(-\frac{(z - (-\sqrt{P_S} + \sqrt{P_I}))^2}{2\sigma^2}\right)
\tag{11}
$$

$$
f_{X=-1, Y_b=-1}(z) = \frac{1}{\sqrt{2\pi}\sigma} exp\left(-\frac{(z - (-\sqrt{P_S} - \sqrt{P_I}))^2}{2\sigma^2}\right)
\tag{12}
$$

Substituting Eqs. (9) to (12) into Eq. (8), the uplink received BER of the system can be expressed as

$$
\begin{aligned}
P_e &= \frac{1}{4}\int_{-\infty}^{0} f_{X=+1, Y_b=+1}(z)dz + \frac{1}{4}\int_{-\infty}^{0} f_{X=+1, Y_b=-1}(z)dz \\
&+ \frac{1}{4}\int_{-\infty}^{0} f_{X=-1, Y_b=+1}(z)dz + \frac{1}{4}\int_{-\infty}^{0} f_{X=-1, Y_b=-1}(z)dz
\end{aligned}
\tag{13}
$$

By simplifying Eq. (13), it can be expressed as

$$
\begin{aligned}
P_e &= \frac{1}{2}\int_{-\infty}^{0} f_{X=+1, Y_b=+1}(z)dz + \frac{1}{2}\int_{-\infty}^{0} f_{X=+1, Y_b=-1}(z)dz \\
&= \frac{1}{4}erfc\left(\left(1 + \frac{1}{\sqrt{SIR}}\right)\sqrt{SIR}\right) + \frac{1}{4}erfc\left(\left(1 - \frac{1}{\sqrt{SIR}}\right)\sqrt{SIR}\right)
\end{aligned}
\tag{14}
$$

where *SIR* is the signal-to-interference ratio, $SIR = P_S/P_I$, P_S is the signal power; *SNR* is signal to noise ratio, $SNR = P_S/N_0$, N_0 is the noise power, $N_0 = 2\sigma^2$.

The analysis and simulation curves of BER with SIR for uplink communication receivers under SNR = 0 dB and SNR = 5 dB are given in Fig. 1.

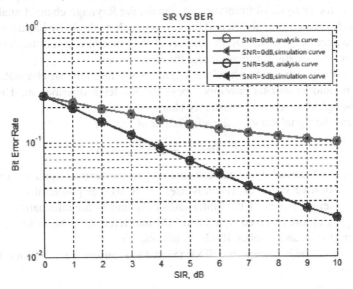

Fig. 1. Analysis and Simulation Curves of BER vs Signal-to-interference Ratio at Constant SNR

From Fig. 1, it can be seen that the analytical curve of the BER variation with the SIR is consistent with the general trend of the simulation curve. The simulation curve basically matches the analysis curve, which indicates that the analysis model is basically reasonable.

The above analysis is based on the assumption that the PIM interference power is constant, the center frequency of the PIM interference is exactly equal to the center frequency of the uplink received signal and the phase of the PIM interference is consistent with the phase of the uplink received signal. The impact of PIM interference on the uplink received signal is the largest, i.e., the above analysis gives the worst performance of the uplink received signal demodulation performance with constant SIR.

3 Bit Error Rate Performance of PIM Interference with Time-Varying SIR

The previous section focused on the effect of PIM interference on the demodulation link at constant SIR, but PIM interference is time-varying and with a constantly changing SIR. This section will focus on the analysis of the impact of PIM interference on the demodulation link at the time-varying SIR. The general idea is to analyze the statistical characteristics of the time-varying SIR, and then find out the variation of the average BER with the average SIR for that period.

The uplink received power of the Rice channel includes the power of the direct signal and the power of the non-direct fading signal, and the uplink received power of the Rayleigh channel has only the power of the non-direct fading signal. Since the power of the direct signal is basically constant, the time-varying part of the received power of both the Rice and Rayleigh channels is the power of the non-direct fading signal. It is easy to see that, in the analysis of time-varying signals, the Rayleigh channel analysis is the basis of the Rice channel analysis, and the two research methods are basically the same, but it is also necessary to analyze the impact of PIM interference on the demodulation link of the communication receiver under the Rice channel.

In the Rayleigh channel, when the signal passes through the channel, its signal amplitude is random and its envelope obeys the Rayleigh distribution. The received power of the uplink receiver is constantly changing.

Represent the signal entering the adjudicator as

$$Z = \sqrt{P_S}h_0x + \sqrt{P_I}h_1y + n \tag{15}$$

where x is uplink received signal per unit energy; y is interference signal per unit energy; n is AWGN(Additive White Gaussian Noise); P_S is average power of uplink received signal; P_I is average power of PIM interference; h_0 and h_1 are attenuation coefficients of the changing uplink received signal and PIM interference. In the following analysis, it is assumed that h_0 and h_1 obey Rayleigh distribution.

After entering the judgment, the SINR (Signal to Interference plus Noise Ratio) can be expressed as

$$SINR = \frac{X}{Y + \sigma^2} \tag{16}$$

where $X = |h_0|^2 P_S$, $Y = |h_1|^2 P_I$, X and Y obey exponential distribution. Their probability density functions are denoted as

$$f_X(X) = \frac{1}{P_S}exp\left(-\frac{X}{P_S}\right) \tag{17}$$

$$f_Y(Y) = \frac{1}{P_I}exp\left(-\frac{Y}{P_I}\right) \tag{18}$$

The statistical properties of the SINR are discussed below. The cumulative distribution function of the SINR can be expressed as

$$F_{SINR}(\gamma) = Pr(SINR \leq \gamma) = \int_0^{+\infty} Pr\left(X \leq \gamma\left(Y + \sigma^2\right)\right)f_Y(Y)dY \tag{19}$$

Substituting Eq. (17) and Eq. (18) into Eq. (19), Eq. (19) can be simplified as

$$F_{SINR}(\gamma) = 1 - \frac{P_S}{P_S + \gamma P_I}exp\left(-\frac{\gamma\sigma^2}{P_S}\right) \tag{20}$$

In the case of time-varying SINR, the effect of PIM interference on the receiver BER can be expressed as

$$SER_L = \int_0^{+\infty} a_{mod}Q\left(\sqrt{2b_{mod}\gamma}\right)f_{SINR}(\gamma)d\gamma \tag{21}$$

where $Q(\cdot)$ is Gaussian Q function; a_{mod} and b_{mod} are parameters related to the modulation mode.

Substituting the Q function into Eq. (21), Eq. (21) can also be expressed as

$$SER_L = \frac{a_{mod}\sqrt{b_{mod}}}{2\sqrt{\pi}} \int_0^{+\infty} \frac{exp(-b_{mod}\gamma)}{\gamma^{1/2}} F_{SINR}(\gamma)d\gamma \qquad (22)$$

Under BPSK modulation, $a_{mod} = 1$ and $b_{mod} = 1$. Substituting Eq. (21) into Eq. (22), the relation between BER, average SIR and average SNR under BPSK modulation can be obtained after calculation as

$$P_e = \frac{1}{2} - \frac{1}{2}\sqrt{SIR}*exp(SIR(1 + 1/(2SNR)))\Gamma\left(\frac{1}{2}, SIR(1 + 1/(2SNR))\right) \qquad (23)$$

where $SIR = P_S/P_I$; $SNR = P_S/N_0$; $N_0 = 2\sigma^2$; and $\Gamma(a, x)$ is defined as follows:

$$\Gamma(a, x) = \int_x^{+\infty} e^{-t}t^{a-1}dt \qquad (24)$$

Figure 2 gives the analytical and simulation curves of the BER variation with the average SIR for the uplink with SNR = 5dB and SNR = 25dB under PIM interference.

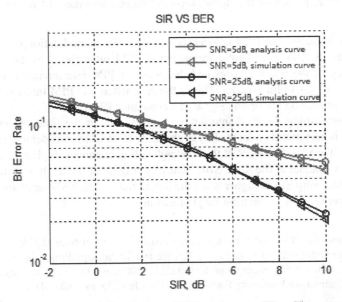

Fig. 2. Analytical and Simulation Curves of BER vs Average SIR at Time-varying SNR

From Fig. 2, it can be seen that the analytical curve of BER variation with SIR is consistent with the general trend of the simulation curve. The error between the simulation curve and the analysis curve is within 2dB, which shows that the analysis of the effect of PIM interference on the demodulation performance of the communication receiver under the time-varying SIR is basically reasonable.

The above analysis is analyzed on basis of that the uplink received power and PIM interference power are subject to an exponential distribution, if the uplink received power and PIM interference power are subject to other statistical characteristics, then the analysis with the above ideas can also get more satisfactory results.

The model of the effect of PIM interference on the demodulation performance of communication receivers under time-varying SIR is more suitable for analyzing the effect of PIM interference on the demodulation performance of communication systems for a long time continuous communication than the model of the effect of PIM interference on the demodulation performance of communication receivers under constant SIR. This is mainly because the communication time of long-time continuous communication is long, and its PIM interference power is constantly changing, and the longer the time, the more its SIR distribution approximately obeys its theoretical SIR statistical characteristics, and the method can be used to analyze the BER of PIM interference on uplink communication link under time-varying SIR.

4   Conclusion

In this paper, the influence of PIM interference on the receiver demodulation performance in the case of constant SIR and the center frequency of PIM interference is the same as the carrier frequency of the uplink received signal, and the SIR is time-varying is analyzed.

(1) The effect analysis of PIM interference on receiver demodulation performance at a constant SIR and the center frequency of PIM interference is the same as the frequency of the uplink carrier and the phase of PIM interference is the same as the phase of the uplink carrier. This is the case where the PIM interference has the greatest impact on the uplink signal at a constant SIR.

(2) When performing the PIM interference analysis under the time-varying SIR, the analysis is performed under the Rayleigh fading channel to consider the time-varying nature of the SIR. The BER of the Rayleigh fading channel is higher than that of the Gaussian channel at the same SIR. That is, the BER of the analytical model under the time-varying SIR is higher when the SIR in the constant SIR analysis is the same as the average SIR in the time-varying SIR analysis.

Acknowledgments. This work was supported in part by National Natural Science Foundation of China under Grant 62201070, in part by Science and Technology Project of Beijing Municipal Education Commission under Grant KM202211232009, and in part by Beijing Information Science and Technology University Foundation (2121YJPY223 and 2021XJJ25).

References

1. Kai, Y.E., Yue, O.C.: High-order intermodulation effects in digital satellite channels. IEEE Trans. Aerosp. Electron. Syst. AES **17**(3), 438–445 (1981)
2. Lojacono, R., et al.: Simulation of the effects of the residual low level PIM to improve payload design of communication satellites. In: IEEE Aerospace Conference. IEEE (2005)

3. Suzuki, Y., Narahashi, S., Nojima, T.: Bit error probability in the presence of third-order intermodulation distortion component from power amplifier of different mobile systems. IEEE Commun. Lett. **15**(10), 1041–1043 (2011)
4. Al-Mudhafar, A., Hartnagel, H.: Bit error probability in the presence of passive intermodulation. IEEE Commun. Lett. **16**(8), 1145–1148 (2012)
5. Tian, L., Wang, Y., Wang, R., Bu, X.: Modified Cauchy distribution model of high-order passive intermodulation. In: International Symposium on Antennas and Propagation (ISAP). IEEE (2016)

User-Oriented Dynamic MEC Application Deployment in Edge Cloud Network

Yinan Guo[1], Yanzhao Hou[2]([✉]), Jiaxiang Geng[1], Hao Chen[3], and Whai-En Chen[4]

[1] Beijing University of Posts and Telecommunications, Beijing, China
[2] Beijing University of Posts and Telecommunications Shenzhen Institute, Shenzhen, China
houyanzhao@bupt.edu.cn
[3] Department of Broadband Communication, Peng Cheng Laboratory, Shenzhen, China
[4] Department of Computer Science and Information Engineering, National Ilan University, Yilan, Taiwan

Abstract. Multi-Access Edge Computing (MEC) have become the core technologies to meet users' needs for 5G and beyond wireless networks. MEC applications can be flexibly created and placed at the network edge through virtual network functions (VNFs) to provide users with specific services with lower latency. In this paper, we consider a multi-user dynamic MEC network, where user trajectories follow Lévy walks, and each user has a set of requested target MEC applications. Our goal is to obtain an online deployment algorithm that is able to serve dynamic user requests within a tolerable latency while balancing the computational load among Mobile Edge Platforms (MEPs) as much as possible. This requires real-time processing of intractable NP-hard optimization problems. To tackle this problem, we propose an online deployment framework for MEC applications based on deep reinforcement learning, whose policy-based features adapt to the characteristics of the large action space in the problem. The framework learns binary deployment decisions from experience without solving NP-hard optimization problems, which greatly reduces computational complexity. Through simulations, we demonstrate the ability of our scheme to balance the computational load among the available MEPs and to satisfy the dynamic service requests of users.

Keywords: MEC application placement · Multi-access Edge Computing (MEC) · Reinforcement learning

1 Introduction

Ultra Reliable Low Latency Communications (URLLC), one of the typical application scenarios of 5G, requires high reliability and ultra-low latency access (about 1ms in the radio access network (RAN)) [1,2]. Traditionally, centralized cloud-based applications cannot meet the low-latency requirements of some

© ICST Institute for Computer Sciences, Social Informatics and Telecommunications Engineering 2023
Published by Springer Nature Switzerland AG 2023. All Rights Reserved
K. Rabie et al. (Eds.): IoTaaS 2022, LNICST 506, pp. 82–93, 2023.
https://doi.org/10.1007/978-3-031-37139-4_8

real-time applications due to their long-distance communication with user equipment. In this case, multi-access edge computing (MEC) can deploy applications or some of their components at the edge in the form of virtual network functions (VNFs) to maintain low latency for key URLLC services [3]. Based on the standard ETSI MEC model [4], MEC applications are deployed on the MEC platform (MEP) in the form of virtual machines or containers. According to the operator's deployment strategy, one MEP can cover a group of gNodeBs. We consider MEC applications as a whole and can only be deployed on a single MEP. When deploying MEC applications at the edge, the MEC orchestrator (MEO) must select the best MEP to meet the application latency and required resource capacity (CPU, storage, etc.). However, in actual deployment, some MEPs may not be able to carry some MEC applications, mainly due to the following three difficulties: (i) Unlike the centralized cloud with super-large capacity located in the data center, the computing power of a single MEP cannot meet the requirements of some MEC applications for computing or storage resources, and the number of MEC applications that it can carry is also limited; (ii)The unpredictable time-varying wireless channel conditions brought about by the randomness of user distribution lead to uncertain transmission delays between users and MEPs, and it is difficult to guarantee the tolerance delay of MEC applications required by users; (iii) Considering the diverse dynamic service requests of different users, it is difficult to quickly meet the needs of all users for the required MEC applications. Therefore, the challenging question raised by the above difficulties is where to deploy MEC applications in order to better meet their application requirements in terms of computing and storage resources and latency, while meeting the user's dynamic specific service needs.

Only a few works address the placement of MEC applications in edge clouds. For example, a tabu search-based deployment algorithm for MEC applications in federated MEPs is proposed in [5], which uses short-term memory to iteratively find optimal solutions from a neighborhood solution space. Both [6, 7] have made meaningful work on the deployment of MEC applications, and [6] proposed a method to schedule the optimal location of MEC applications based on temporal network-wide delay fluctuations using optimal stopping theory, [7] proposed a genetic-based heuristic algorithm to solve the optimal placement problem for MEC applications. However, these works either do not consider the changing network state caused by the user's movement pattern, or require a large number of iterations to reach a satisfactory local optimum, and crucially, do not consider the needs of different users for specific MEC applications

Our work is inspired by the advantages of deep reinforcement learning in dealing with reinforcement learning problems with large state and action spaces. At present, there are some works that use deep reinforcement learning to study the task offloading decision problem in MEC networks. MEC application deployment decision problem is similar to it, both problems are learned from training data samples, and finally generated Integer decisions and assess their quality, so we can learn from and reference. [8,9] studied task offloading strategies in MEC networks based on DQN. [10,11] studied offloading and resource allocation based on dual DQN and duel DQN, respectively. [12] proposed a mapping method to improve the slow convergence of DQN in a large action space, but its algorithm is more likely to fall into local optimum in some scenarios. In general, these value-based reinforcement learning algorithms are not suitable for handling problems with high-dimensional action spaces, and it is difficult to obtain good convergence in our problem.

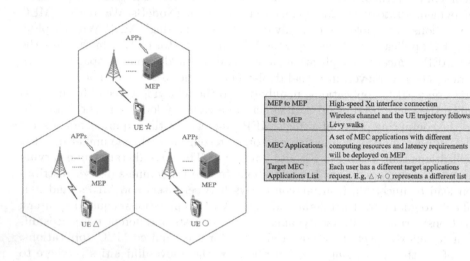

MEP to MEP	High-speed Xn interface connection
UE to MEP	Wireless channel and the UE trajectory follows Lévy walks
MEC Applications	A set of MEC applications with different computing resources and latency requirements will be deployed on MEP
Target MEC Applications List	Each user has a different target applications request. E.g, △ ☆ ○ represents a different list

Fig. 1. An example of the considered MEC network, Where the MEP is attached to the gNodeB, all User Equipments (UEs) are dynamically mobile and have requests for specific MEC applications.

In this paper, we consider a multi-user MEC network, as shown in Fig. 1, each MEP can deploy MEC applications within its available resources, and the MEPs are connected through a high-speed Xn interface. In particular, there are multiple users randomly distributed in each cell, and each user has a specific service request. Our goal is to optimize deployment decisions for MEC applications. To this end, we propose a deep reinforcement learning-based online MEC application deployment framework to balance the computational load among the available MEPs, while ensuring that the user access latency of MEC applications satisfies constraints, as well as satisfying user-specific service requests. Our contributions are summarized as follows:

- A user-oriented MEC application deployment problem was studied that considers user-specific service requests and latency uncertainty caused by user mobility, with the goal of balancing the computational load among MEPs.
- The problem is shown to be NP-hard, and the search space for its solution grows exponentially. The proposed algorithm learns from past deployment experience under user distribution and user service request conditions, and automatically improves its action generation policy, so the computational complexity does not explode with network size.

- Different from many existing value-based reinforcement learning algorithms, our proposed algorithm is policy-based, and it also has a good convergence effect when the number of applications to be deployed is large and the action space is large, avoiding the curse of dimensionality.
- The performance of the proposed algorithm is demonstrated by simulations, showing that our scheme can balance the load among MEPs under various user distributions and different service requests, while ensuring that the requirements of MEC applications are met.

The rest of this article is organized as follows. Section 2 introduces the system model and formulates the optimization problem. Section 3 introduces the detailed design of the proposed algorithm. The obtained experimental results are discussed in Sect. 4. Finally, the paper is concluded in Sect. 5.

2 System Model

As shown in Fig 1, there is one MEP attached to the gNodeB in each cell, and there are E MEPs in total, denoted as $\mathcal{E} = \{1, 2, ..., E\}$, the available computing resources of the ith MEP is denoted as R_i, and their values vary in order to simulate real scenarios. There are M MEC applications to be deployed, denoted as $\mathcal{M} = \{1, 2, ..., M\}$, the maximum tolerable delay of the jth MEC application is denoted as l_j, and the required computing resources are denoted as r_j. There are N user equipments (UEs) in the network, denoted as $\mathcal{N} = \{1, 2, ..., N\}$. Each UE has a set of target MEC applications, and the target MEC application list of the kth UE is denoted as v_k. There is wireless channel transmission between UE and MEP, and high-speed Xn interface connection between MEPs, which can transmit service data of MEC applications. In this paper, we will make MEC application deployment decisions based on the user's dynamic channel conditions, as well as their list of different target MEC applications.

2.1 User Mobility

Due to the mobility of users, the deployment of MEC applications faces challenges. On the one hand, it is necessary to ensure that the target applications requested by users can arrive within the maximum tolerable delay. On the other hand, the capability difference between MEPs should also be considered, so as to avoid a system crash caused by the overload of a certain MEP as much as possible. Lévy walks [13] are a widely used way of simulating human flow trajectories. In this paper, the action trajectories of N users in the MEC network conform to Lévy walks. The user's initial position is randomly distributed in each cell, and to constrain the step size to the simulation region, we use a Lévy stable distribution to generate user trajectories. The coordinate set of the user at time t in the network area is recorded as $\mathbf{c}_t$.

2.2   Delay Model

In this paper, we consider a typical Orthogonal Frequency Division Multiplexing(OFDM) network with a frequency reuse factor of 1. There are K subchannels in each cell, the subchannel bandwidth is denoted as B, and the subchannels used by users are randomly allocated. The transmit power allocated by the base station to a single user is P, the white Gaussian noise power is denoted as σ^2, and the path loss model refers to the typical empirical formula of the UMi scene in 3GPP TR 38.901 [14], denoted as h_k, which can be expressed as

$$h_k = 32.4 + 21 \log_{10}(d_k) + 20 \log_{10}(f_c) \tag{1}$$

where d_k is the distance from the gNodeB to the user k, and f_c is the center carrier frequency.

The scenario considered in this paper is that the MEC application provides services for users, so the interference mainly comes from the downlink transmission power of the base station in the cell where the user sharing the subchannel resides. The distance between the base station generating interference and the user k can be denoted as d_{ik}, so the interference power can be expressed as

$$N_k = \sum_i h_{ik} P \tag{2}$$

Based on the above definition, the downlink transmission rate of the $k-th$ user can be expressed as

$$R_k = B \log_2 \left(1 + \frac{h_k P}{N_k + \sigma^2}\right) \tag{3}$$

Denote the size of the data packet delivered when the MEC application provides services as D_j, assuming that service data can be transmitted between MEPs through the fixed-rate Xn interface, the transmission rate is denoted as R^*, and the processing delay of one forwarding is denoted as t^*, then the delay of user k when it obtains its target MEC application j deployed in MEPi can be expressed as

$$T_{ik} = \begin{cases} D/R_k & \text{if application } j \text{ in } k\text{'s cell} \\ D/R_k + D/R^* + \alpha t^* & \text{otherwise} \end{cases} \tag{4}$$

where α is the forwarding times.

2.3   Problem Formulation

The goal of this paper is to balance the computing load among MEPs as much as possible, and the balance degree index can be formulated as follows:

$$Q(\mathbf{c}, \mathbf{x}, \mathbf{v}) \triangleq \sum_{i=1}^{i=E-1} \sum_{i'=i+1}^{i'=E} \left(\left| \frac{\sum_{j=1}^{j=M} x(i,j) r_j}{R_i} - \frac{\sum_{j=1}^{j=M} x(i',j) r_j}{R_{i'}} \right|\right) \tag{5}$$

where $\mathbf{c} = \{c_k \mid k \in \mathcal{N}\}$, $\mathbf{v} = \{v_k \mid k \in \mathcal{N}\}$, and $\mathbf{x}$ represents the binary deployment decision.

In order to find optimal or satisfactory sub-optimal application deployment decisions, satisfy the requests of different users for MEC applications, and ensure the delay and resource constraints required by these MEC applications, based on the previous definition, the optimization problem can be formulated as follows :

$$\min Q(\mathbf{c}, \mathbf{x}, \mathbf{v}) \tag{6}$$

s.t.

$$C1 : \sum_{i=1}^{i=E} X(i,j) = 1, \forall j \in \mathcal{M}$$

$$C2 : \sum_{i=1}^{i=E} \sum_{j=1}^{j=M} X(i,j)r_j \leq R_i \tag{7}$$

$$C3 : X(i,j)T_{ik} \leq l_j, \quad \forall j \in v_k, k \in N, i \in E$$

The problem (6) is to minimize the sum of load percentage differences between MEPs. $X(i,j)$ is the deployment decision matrix of MEC applications, where $x(i,j) = 1$ if application j is deployed on the MEP i. $C1$ guarantees that a MEC application can only be deployed on one MEP. $C2$ guarantees that the resources occupied by MEC applications on each MEP do not exceed the available resources. $C3$ guarantees that the user's delay in using the service of the target MEC application is less than the maximum tolerable delay of the application. It can be seen that problem (6) is an NP-hard problem.

The main difficulty in solving problem (6) lies in the deployment decision. Traditional optimization algorithms need to iteratively adjust deployment decisions to achieve optimality, which is infeasible when the number of users and MEC applications is large. In order to solve the complexity problem, we propose a novel online deployment algorithm based on deep reinforcement learning, whose policy-based characteristics can be well applied to large action spaces and meet the needs of users.

3   The Proposed Algorithm

Our goal is to design a deployment strategy function π, which can quickly generate optimal deployment actions. For example, when there are 4 MEPs, the deployment decision of each MEC application can be represented by 2 bits, so the deployment decision matrix X can be Reshape into a decision vector $\mathbf{x} \in \{0,1\}^{2M}$ of length $2M$. As users move within the network area, we take user coordinates $\mathbf{c}$ every time period T as input to the function, which then gives deployment decisions. This strategy can be expressed as

$$\pi : \mathbf{c} \rightarrow \mathbf{x} \tag{8}$$

The proposed algorithm gradually learns such a policy function π from experience.

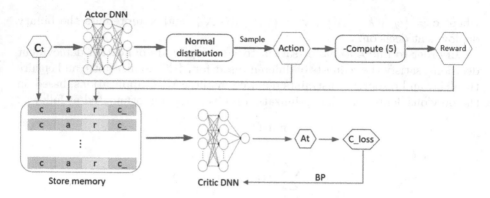

Fig. 2. Partial schematic diagram of the proposed algorithm without policy updates.

3.1 Deployment Action Generation

Part of the structure of the proposed algorithm is shown in Fig. 2. It consists of two alternating phases: deployment action generation and policy update. First, the deployment action generation is introduced. The user coordinate c_t at t time is input into the actor network, the network will construct a normal distribution, perform multiple sampling and output an action, and quantify it to get the deployment vector x. Taking the existence of 4 MEPs as an example, the original sampling output of the network is the continuous value of **action** $\in (0,1)^{2M}$, we quantify it to get the required deployment decision $x \in \{0,1\}^{2M}$, the quantization rule is shown in Eq. (9)

$$x_{t,j} = \begin{cases} 1 & \text{action }_{t,j} > 0.5 \\ 0 & \text{action }_{t,j} \le 0.5 \end{cases} \tag{9}$$

for $j = 1, ..., 2M$

Then use c, x, v as a parameter to calculate formula (5), and since reinforcement learning uses gradient ascent to maximize rewards and, we take its negative value as the reward for the current action. When the constraints in (7) are not met, we will punish the action and reduce the reward value. Store this set of $[c_t, a_t, r, c_{t+1}]$ in store memory, and then loop this process multiple times until the number is at least reach a batch.

3.2 Policy Update

Our scheme is a deep reinforcement learning algorithm based on PPO (Proximal Policy Optimization) [15], and the data stored in store memory will be used to update the parameters of Deep Neural Network (DNN). Overall, our goal is to make the deployment actions output by the network have an advantage, for which the proposed algorithm uses an actor-critic architecture. The At calculated by the critic network output is called the advantage function, which can be

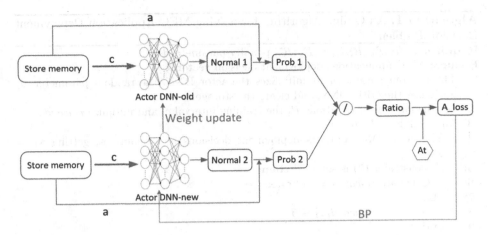

Fig. 3. Schematic diagram of policy update of proposed algorithm.

used to evaluate the advantage of the actor network output action. It should be pointed out that the At here is the cumulative conversion advantage of the entire experience pool. As shown in Fig. 2, the critical network output state value is used to estimate the advantage function value At, which uses MSE loss as the loss function, and updates the network parameters through backpropagation to achieve a more accurate estimate.

Then, as shown in Fig. 3, the actor network starts to update. Through the $[\mathbf{c}, \mathbf{a}]$ stored in memory and the At obtained by using the critic network, use the following loss function to update the parameters:

$$L^{CLIP}(\theta) = \hat{\mathbb{E}}_t \left[\min \left(r_t(\theta)\hat{A}_t, \text{clip} \left(r_t(\theta), 1 - \epsilon, 1 + \epsilon \right) \hat{A}_t \right) \right] \tag{10}$$

where $r_t(\theta)$ represents the state-action probability ratio between the new policy and the old policy, and ϵ is a hyperparameter that controls the distance between the old and new policies. The actor DNN uses this backpropagation to update its own network parameters, thereby maximizing the advantage, that is, getting the maximum reward. We provide pseudocode for our scheme in Algorithm 1.

4   Simulation Results

4.1   Simulation Setup

In this section, we use simulations to evaluate the performance of the proposed algorithm. We simulated a scenario with 4 MEPs, the Gaussian white noise power is -114 dBm, and the downlink transmit power is 29 dBm. Each user occupies 5 Resource Blocks (RBs), plus the protection bandwidth, a total of 1 MHz. Then, the occupied resources r_j and the maximum tolerable delay l_j of each MEC application are randomly generated. We use Pytorch [16] to implement the proposed algorithm in Python, and set the policy update interval delta $= 256$, the

---

Algorithm 1. An Online Algorithm for Solving MEC Application Deployment Decision Problem

---

Require: $c_t, h_k, \mathcal{L}_k, R_i, l_j, r_j, D_j, R^*$, penalty parameter$\beta$
Ensure: MEC applications deployment decision vector **x**
1: The random parameter θ_1 initializes the actor DNN, the random parameter ω_1 initializes the critic DNN, and clears the storage.
2: Set the number of iterations P, the training interval δ, and initialize $reward_0$.
3: **for** $t = 1, 2, ..., P$ **do**
4:    The actor DNN outputs deployment decisions and quantifies, getting $\mathbf{x}_t = f_{\theta_t}(\mathbf{x}_t)$
5:    **if** Constraint (7) is satisfied **then**
6:       Calculate $reward_t = -Q(\mathbf{c}_t, \mathbf{x}_t)$
7:    **else**
8:       $reward_t = reward_{t-1} - \beta$
9:    **end if**
10:   Save $[\mathbf{c}_t, \mathbf{x}_t, reward_t, \mathbf{c}_{t+1}]$ to memory
11:   **if** $t \% \delta = 0$ **then**
12:      Input memory into critic DNN
13:      Calculate A_t and use MSE loss to update parameter ω_t
14:      Input memory into actor DNN-old and actor DNN-new
15:      Use function (10) as the loss function to update the parameter θ_t
16:      Clear memory
17:   **end if**
18: **end for**

---

policy evaluation interval 5000, the learning rate of both actor and critic are 0.0003, and the penalty parameter $\beta = 0.05$.

To verify the performance of our scheme, we compare it with the DROO algorithm and the unbalanced load algorithm, where the unbalanced load algorithm only ensures that the delay and resource constraints of MEC applications are met, and does not pursue load balance.

4.2   Simulation Results

In Fig. 4(a), we plot the load balancing value of our scheme when $M = 20, N = 100$, which is not the reward value of each training, but the average value of an episode. We can see that when the number of training steps exceeds 15,000,000, its average converges around -0.2. This means that after the model is trained, the sum of the load percentage differences between MEPs can be stably reduced to about 20% under the MEC application conditions given by us.

In Fig. 4(b), we compare the average delay of each MEC application providing services to users and the constrained delay when $M = 20$ and $N = 100$. We can see that the MEC application deployment decision output by the proposed algorithm can fully meet the delay requirements for users to obtain services. It should be pointed out that our randomly generated maximum tolerable delay l_j for each MEC application is relatively strict, so the algorithm decision cannot

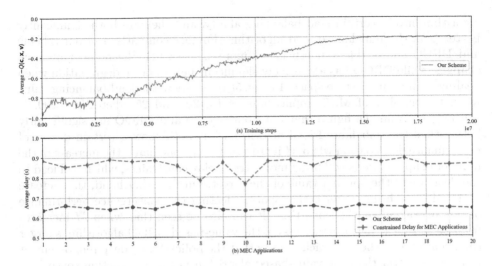

Fig. 4. Evaluated the convergence performance and service delay of our scheme when $M = 20$ and $N = 100$. (a) The load balancing value of our scheme. (b) Average delay for each MEC application to serve users, compared with constrained delay.

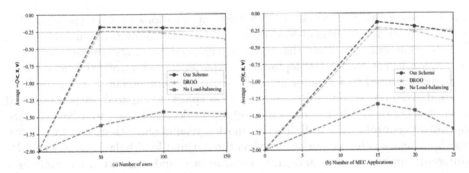

Fig. 5. (a) The load balancing effect of our scheme with different numbers of users when $M = 20$, and its comparison with the baseline. (b) The load balancing effect of our scheme with different numbers of MEC applications when $N = 100$, and its comparison with the baseline

be completely inclined to balance the load and ignore the delay constraint. At the same time, the computing resources required by each MEC application are also designed to be indivisible and of different sizes. Therefore, the load balance value in Fig. 4(a) can only be reduced to 20%, and then it cannot be further reduced due to the constraints of delay and computing resources.

In Fig. 5, we compare the load balancing capabilities of our scheme and the baseline under different numbers of users and MEC applications. In Fig. 5(a), we show the load balancing value when the number of users is 50, 100, and 150 when $M = 20$. As can be seen from the figure, both our scheme and the DROO algorithm have a certain load balancing ability, and they are both significantly better than the unbalanced load algorithm. Further comparison of our scheme and DROO shows that our scheme is more stable when the number of users changes, while DROO has a relatively significant performance degradation when dealing with a larger state space. In Fig. 5(b), we show the load balancing value when the number of MEC applications is 15, 20, and 25 when $N = 100$. It can be seen from the figure that both our scheme and DROO are significantly better than the unbalanced load algorithm, but both show a certain degree of performance degradation when M increases. On the one hand, the increase of the number of applications will bring more strict delay constraints, which will lead to the decrease of the optimal value of the target. On the other hand, the increase of M will also bring larger action space, affecting the convergence performance of the algorithm. At the same time, it can also be seen that when M increases from 20 to 25, the performance loss of the value-based DROO algorithm is larger than that of our scheme, which reflects that the policy-based deep reinforcement learning is better than the value-based algorithm in the large action space.

5   Conclusion

In this paper, we propose an online MEC applications deployment algorithm based on deep reinforcement learning to balance the computational load among MEPs while ensuring that the services requested by users are satisfied. The algorithm learns from past deployment experience to improve the deployment actions generated by the actor network through reinforcement learning, and has a good convergence effect in a large action space. Compared with traditional optimization methods, the proposed algorithm does not need to solve NP-hard optimization problems at all. The simulation results show that, compared with the benchmark scheme, our scheme has the optimal load balancing effect under different number of users and MEC applications, and can satisfy dynamic user service requests at the same time. As future work, we will continue to study the performance of our scheme under burst application requests.

Acknowledgement. This work was supported in part by the National Key R&D Program of China under Grant 2019YFE0114000, in part by the Shenzhen science and technology innovation commission free exploring basic research project (No. 2021Szvup012), in part by the 111 Project of China (No B16006), and the research foundation of Ministry of Education China Mobile under Grant MCM20180101

References

1. Gupta, A., Jha, R.K.: A survey of 5G network: architecture and emerging technologies. IEEE Access **3**, 1206–1232 (2015)
2. Ksentini, A., Frangoudis, P.A., PC, A., Nikaein, N.: Providing low latency guarantees for slicing-ready 5G systems via two-level MAC scheduling. IEEE Netw. **32**(6), 116–123 (2018)

3. Taleb, T., Samdanis, K., Mada, B., Flinck, H., Dutta, S., Sabella, D.: On multi-access edge computing: a survey of the emerging 5G network edge cloud architecture and orchestration. IEEE Commun. Surv. Tutor. **19**(3), 1657–1681, thirdquarter (2017)

4. Mobile Edge Computing (MEC); Framework and Reference Architecture, ETSI Group Specification MEC 003 (2016)

5. Brik, B., Frangoudis, P.A., Ksentini, A.: Service-oriented MEC applications placement in a federated edge cloud architecture. In: ICC 2020–2020 IEEE International Conference on Communications (ICC), pp. 1–6 (2020)

6. Cziva, R., Anagnostopoulos, C., Pezaros, D.P.: Dynamic, latency-optimal VNF placement at the network edge. In: IEEE INFOCOM 2018 - IEEE Conference on Computer Communications, pp. 693–701 (2018)

7. Kiran, N., Liu, X., Wang, S., Yin, C.: Optimising resource allocation for virtual network functions in SDN/NFV-enabled MEC networks. IET Commun. **15**, 1710–1722 (2021)

8. Min, M., Xiao, L., Chen, Y., Cheng, P., Wu, D., Zhuang, W.: Learning-based computation offloading for IoT devices with energy harvesting. IEEE Trans. Veh. Technol. **68**(2), 1930–1941 (2019)

9. Chen, X., Zhang, H., Wu, C., Mao, S., Ji, Y., Bennis, M.: Optimized computation offloading performance in virtual edge computing systems via deep reinforcement learning. IEEE Internet Things J. **6**(3), 4005–4018 (2019)

10. Li, J., Gao, H., Lv, T., Lu, Y.: Deep reinforcement learning based computation offloading and resource allocation for MEC. IEEE Wirel. Commun. Network. Conf. (WCNC) **2018**, 1–6 (2018)

11. Tang, M., Wong, V.W.S.: Deep reinforcement learning for task offloading in mobile edge computing systems. IEEE Trans. Mob. Comput. **21**(6), 1985–1997 (2022)

12. Huang, L., Bi, S., Zhang, Y.-J.A.: Deep reinforcement learning for online computation offloading in wireless powered mobile-edge computing networks. IEEE Trans. Mob. Comput. **19**(11), 2581–2593 (2020)

13. Rhee, I., Shin, M., Hong, S., Lee, K., Kim, S.J., Chong, S.: On the levy-walk nature of human mobility. IEEE/ACM Trans. Network. **19**(3), 630–643 (2011)

14. 5G; Study on channel model for frequencies from 0.5 to 100 GHz, 3GPP TR 38.901 (2018)

15. Xu, C., Zhu, R., Yang, D.: Karting racing: a revisit to PPO and SAC algorithm. In: International Conference on Computer Information Science and Artificial Intelligence (CISAI) 2021, pp. 310–316 (2021)

16. Kim, S., Wimmer, H., Kim, J.: Analysis of deep learning libraries: Keras, PyTorch, and MXnet. In: 2022 IEEE/ACIS 20th International Conference on Software Engineering Research, Management and Applications (SERA), pp. 54–62 (2022)

Joint Design of Caching and Offloading for Mobile Edge Computing in 5G Heterogenous Networks

Jianxiong Xiao[1,2,3], Jing Liu[1], Xiang Chen[2,3(✉)], Yuhan Dong[4],
and Terng-Yin Hsu[5]

[1] College of Electronics and Information Engineering, Shenzhen University,
Shenzhen 518060, China
[2] School of Electronics and Information Technology, Sun Yat-sen University,
Guangzhou 510006, China
chenxiang@mail.sysu.edu.cn
[3] Research Institute of Tsinghua University in Shenzhen (RITS),
Shenzhen 518057, China
[4] Shenzhen International Graduate School, Tsinghua University, Shenzhen, China
[5] Department of Computer Science, National Chiao Tung University,
Hsinchu, Taiwan

Abstract. With the rapid development of the information and communication technology, more and more computation-intensive and also latency-sensitive applications have been emerging. Mobile edge computing (MEC) has been regarded as one of the most significant technologies to satisfy the rigorous requirements of these applications. However, the efficient allocation of MEC resources in multiple dimensions remains an obstacle to further develop MEC in 5G and beyond 5G heterogeneous networks. In this paper, we formulate a joint optimization problem of caching and offloading for MEC systems to minimize the total latency of computation tasks. Following a divide and conquer idea, we first propose a caching scheme oriented to computation tasks with a comprehensive consideration in popularity, data size and computation complexity. Then, we design a caching-aware offloading strategy to make more efficient allocation of communication and computation resources based on the caching situation at the MEC server. Simulation results verify that the proposed joint design can achieve lower total latency comparing to the basic or separate schemes.

Keywords: edge computing · active caching · task offloading

1 Introduction

The recent years have witnessed the explosive growth of the emerging mobile applications like interactive games, virtual reality and natural language process-

The work is supported partly by the State's Key Project of Research and Development Plan under Grants 2019YFE0196400, and partly by the Shenzhen Natural Science Foundation under Grant JCYJ20200109143016563.

ing. Mobile cloud computing (MCC) has played a significant role to facilitate the development of these applications, as it allows the users to upload some computation-intensive tasks to it. As such, even a mobile device with limited capabilities can offer fascinating and high-quality services to its user. Nevertheless, the long physical distance between the users and the MCC server can produce a noticeable transmission delay and greatly infect the experience of some time-sensitive services. Moreover, the transmissions might require multiple forwards or relays, which further brings uncertain delay fluctuation [1]. Mobile edge computing (MEC) is novel paradigm proposed to tackle this problem. The MEC server is usually equipped to a cellular base station that is much closer to the clients. A shorter distance brings a smaller latency and hence, the MEC sever is capable to provide nearly real-time response to the mobile users.

However, comparing with the MCC server, the MEC server only possesses limited storage and computation resources in most cases. Therefore, the management of these resources is crucial to take advantage of the MEC. Task offloading has been an issue of great concern since the MEC is proposed. It is mostly about how to allocate computation resources to a great number of clients, with the objective to satisfy the different requirements on latency from various users. On the other hand, active caching has also been a trending topic all the time. It involves how to selectively store some popular contents like audios, videos or movies, so that the clients no longer need to download them from the remote cloud. Recently, some researchers have argued that the active caching can also be a vital approach to help further reducing the total delay of some computation-intensive tasks [2]. This is because, users within a certain range might share the same computing tasks. Caching the results of these tasks enables the MEC server to respond without any computing latency, and meanwhile prevents from wasting computation resources to duplicated calculation. In fact, offloading and caching can be further associated together to acquire more latency reduction.

MEC is a key component of 5G and beyond 5G (B5G) networks. In 5G and B5G cellular systems, there will be various kinds of base stations (BS) and they can be roughly categorized as micro base station (MBS) and small base station (SBS). This multi-station circumstance actually forms a heterogenous network. As such, a client might be served by several BSs simultaneously. This makes the MEC offloading further couple with the radio resource allocation between different BSs. Therefore, the offloading-caching problem mentioned above will further extend to the joint optimization on the utilization of communication, computation and cache resources in 5G/B5G heterogenous networks. Although there has been a great body of research on offloading and caching separately, this kind of collaborative problem still need further investigation.

In this paper, we focus on the joint design of caching and offloading for MEC in 5G heterogenous networks. Unlike caching content-data like videos, we notice that the caching of computation results should no only take the popularity and data size but also the computational complexity into consideration. Therefore, we design a comprehensive caching strategy based on all these factors. In addition, the caching policy will infect the latency gain of task offloading. Therefore, we further design a offloading method with awareness of the caching situation at the MEC server. Our contributions can be summarized as:

- We formulate a latency optimization problem that involves caching, offloading and base station cooperation. Following a divide and conquer idea, we propose a jointly designed solution to achieve better latency performance.
- We propose a novel caching policy oriented to computation tasks, which simulta-neously considers the popularity, result size and computation complexity of tasks to save more time.
- We design an offloading scheme that takes into account both the caching decisions of the MEC server and the channel conditions between the users and the BSs when allocating computational and bandwidth resources. Through properly prioritizing the clients tasks, the scheme can provide more latency gain.

The rest of this paper is organized as follows: We provide a brief review of the related works in Sect. 2 and present the system model and problem formulation in Sect. 3. The proposed methods are elaborated in Sect. 4 and the numerical results are reported in Sect. 5. Section 6 concludes this work.

2   Related Works

MEC is a promising technology to improve the capabilities of the mobile cellular systems. Recently, some studies have tried to apply MEC to 5G heterogeneous networks. For instance, an energy-efficient computational offloading algorithm via allocating channel resources between the MBS and SBS are proposed in [3]. Besides, some works focus on combing the caching and offloading functions of the MEC. The authors in [4] construct a large dataset to train neural networks that can predict the future popularity of tasks and make better caching decisions. In [5], the authors investigate a computational offloading and data-content caching problem in NOMA-MEC systems and reduce the total completion latency by jointly optimizing the task offloading decision and data-content caching strategy.

In [6], the authors propose an active caching method for computational results but still lack comprehensive consideration on allocating the MEC resources in multiple dimensions. In [7], the authors consider the joint optimization of caching and computation, but the MEC is not deployed in heterogeneous networks and thus the allocation of communication resources between multiple BSs is not involved. In [8], the authors consider the collaborative offloading between the MEC and MCC servers and propose a cloud-edge-end algorithm to optimize the allocation of communicating, computing and caching resources and achieve lower latency. Nonetheless, this work still lacks considerations on the result size and computing complexity of tasks.

In summary, the existing works have investigated the joint design problem in different perspective, yet the optimization of MEC resource allocation based on comprehensive concerns of the popularity, result size and computation complexity of user tasks is still underexplored.

3 Problem Formulation

3.1 System Model

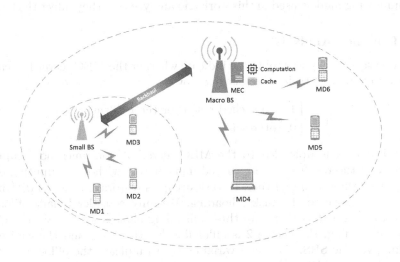

Fig. 1. The scenario of joint offloading and caching in heterogeneous networks.

As shown in Fig. 1, we consider a 5G heterogeneous network that consists of an MBS, an SBS and N mobile devices (MD) denoted as $\mathcal{N} = \{1, 2, \ldots, N\}$ in this paper. The MBS can cover all the users while the SBS only serves those who are within a smaller range around it. The MEC server is only equipped at the MBS, and all the tasks offloaded to the SBS will then be transferred to the MBS through a backhaul link. Suppose that for a period of time, each user only generate a computation-intensive task. The one generated by the i-th user is referred as the i-th task, which is described by a triple

$$T_i = \{d_i^{in}, c_i, d_i^{out}\},$$

where d_i^{in}, d_i^{out} respectively denote the size of the input data and output result, and c_i represents the number of CPU cycles needed to calculate this task.

The MEC server has a certain amount of cache and computation resources. Based on these resources, on the one hand, the MEC server can accelerate the computation of the tasks that are uploaded to it. On the other hand, the MEC server can actively cache the results of some popular tasks to further reduce the latency of task offloading. According to the offloading approach and whether the results have been cached, there are five schemes available to obtain the result of a computation task, which are: (a) Local computing; (b) MBS offloading and MEC computing; (c) MBS offloading and MEC caching; (c) SBS offloading and MEC computing; (e) SBS offloading and MEC caching. Obviously, the latency of processing a task depends on which scheme is used. However, as the resources at the MEC server are limited, it is impossible to cache or offload all the tasks. Therefore, finding a efficient way to allocate these resources and finally reduce the overall latency of the users is important. Yet before diving into the optimization of resource utilization, we first introduce the caching, computing and communicating models used in this work and analyze how they infect the latency.

3.2 Lantency Analysis

First, we use a binary variable y_i to indicate whether the MEC server has cached the result of the i-th task, which is given by

$$y_i = \begin{cases} 1 & \text{no cached result for the } i\text{-th task} \\ 0 & \text{otherwise.} \end{cases}$$

If a cached task is uploaded to the MEC server, it consumes no computing resource and the result can be returned immediately without computing delay. In exchange, the caching of the i-th task occupies a storage space of d_i^{out} bits.

Next, we move to the task offloading. We only consider binary offloading in this work, and thus there are three offloading choices for a task: the choice 1 is not offloading, the choice 2 is offloading via the MBS and the choice 3 is offloading via the SBS. We use a variable $\alpha_{i,j}$ to indicate the offloading choice of the i-th task, which is defined as

$$\alpha_{i,j} = \begin{cases} 1 & \text{the } i\text{-th task adopts choice } j \\ 0 & \text{otherwise.} \end{cases}$$

Notice that $\alpha_{i,3}$ can only be 0 for those that can not access the SBS.

For the users that choose the scheme (a) i.e., local computing, the total delay is only the computation delay. Suppose the CPU frequency of the i-th mobile device is f_i^l, then the latency of using scheme (a) to calculate the i-th task is

$$t_i^l = \frac{c_i}{f_i^l}. \tag{1}$$

If a task is offloaded to the MEC server via the MBS or SBS, it costs time to upload the inputs of this task at first. In this work, we suppose the orthogonal frequency-division multiple access (OFDMA) is adopted by both the MBS and SBS for uplink transmission. The whole frequency band is divided into K orthogonal sub-channels, and each with a bandwidth of W. The MBS and SBS share these sub-channels without overlapping to avoid interference. Assume that k_i sub-channels are allocated to the i-th user. For those that offload tasks via the MSB, the transmission delay of uploading the task is

$$t_i^{m,t} = \frac{d_i^{in}}{r_i^m}.$$

Here, r_i^m is the uplink data rate from the i-th user to the MBS, given by

$$r_i^m = k_i W \log_2(1 + \frac{p_i g_i^m}{\sigma^2}),$$

where p_i is the transmission power of the i-th mobile device, g_i^m is the channel gain between the user and the MBS, and σ^2 is the noise power. Similarly, if the user selects to offload its task via the SBS, the transmission delay is

$$t_i^{s,t} = \frac{d_i^{in}}{r_i^s}, \quad r_i^s = k_i W \log_2(1 + \frac{p_i g_i^s}{\sigma^2}).$$

where g_i^s is the channel gain between the user and the SBS.

Subsequently, the MEC server will compute the result of the task if there is no cached result for it, i.e., $y_i = 1$. In this work, we assume that the MEC server can calculate multiple tasks simultaneously by distributing its computing capabilities. The total CPU frequency of the MEC server is referred to as F while the fraction allocated to the i-th task, if necessary, is denoted as v_i. As such, the computation delay of the task is

$$t_i^c = \frac{c_i}{v_i F}.$$

As the transmission power of the BS is usually much more adequate, and the size of the result is also much smaller than that of the input, the communication delay of returning the result is neglected in this work. Overall, for the users that choose scheme (b) and (c), the total latency is

$$t_i^m = t_i^{m,t} + y_i \cdot t_i^c. \tag{2}$$

For SBS offloading, there is a extra delay to transfer the computation tasks from the SBS to the MBS via the backhaul link. We suppose that the transfer delay is proportional to the data size with a coefficient φ, i.e.,

$$t_i^b = \varphi d_i^{in}.$$

Therefore, for the users that use scheme (d) and (e), the total latency is

$$t_i^s = t_i^{s,t} + t_i^b + y_i \cdot t_i^c. \tag{3}$$

3.3 Optimization Objective

Based on the analysis above, we can establish the optimization objective of this work as

$$
\begin{aligned}
\underset{\{y_i, \alpha_{i,j}, k_i, v_i\}}{\text{minimize}} \quad & \sum_{i \in \mathcal{N}} \left(\alpha_{i,1} \cdot t_i^l + \alpha_{i,2} \cdot t_i^m + \alpha_{i,3} \cdot t_i^s \right) \\
\text{subject to} \quad & C1 : y_i, \alpha_{i,j} \in \{0, 1\}, \quad \forall i \in \mathcal{N}, j \in \{1, 2, 3\}, \\
& C2 : \sum_{i \in \mathcal{N}} (1 - y_i) \cdot d_i^{out} \leq M, \\
& C3 : \sum_{i \in \mathcal{N}} k_i \leq K, \\
& C4 : \sum_{i \in \mathcal{N}} v_i \leq 1, \\
& C5 : \sum_{j=1}^{3} \alpha_{i,j} = 1, \quad \forall i \in \mathcal{N}
\end{aligned}
\tag{4}
$$

which is to minimize the total latency of the system. Thereinto, C2 to C4 are constraints with respect to the resources of the MEC server or BSs. C2 restrains the space to cache the selected tasks is smaller than a given maximum M. C3 limits the number of sub-channels used by the MBS and SBS not to exceed the given amount. C4 states that the summation of the computation capabilities arranged to different tasks should be under the total capability of the MEC server. C5 ensures that each user chooses and only chooses one offloading scheme.

In the problem (4), there are binary variables $\alpha_{i,j}, y_j, k_i$, continous variables $v_i \in [0, 1]$ and the objective is comprised of non-linear terms derived from multiplying these undetermined variables. Actually, this optimization problem is a mixed integer nonlinear programming (MINLP) problem [9], which is non-convex and difficult to be solved directly. Therefore, we adopt a divide and conquer strategy to cope with it, which will be detailed in the next section.

4   Proposed Method

4.1   Caching Scheme Oriented to Computation Tasks

Since the storage resources are limited at the MEC server, it is impossible to cache all the task results. We assume that all the users generate tasks in an identical pattern and the generating probability of each task is different. It is intuitive that the MEC server should preferentially cache those tasks with higher generating probability. This is greatly reasonable for data-content caching. However, the caching of computation results has another significant factor that should be taken into consideration, which is the computation complexity. A task with relatively high generating probability and small space cost is not necessarily a good choice to be cached. If the computation complexity is quite low, the user are likely not to upload this task and the caching space is wasted. Therefore, we design a new policy that is more dedicated to caching computation tasks.

We suppose that there are totally L possible tasks, and the generating probabilities of these tasks follow the Zipf's distribution, which is commonly used in the literature [10]. The generating probability of the l-th task is given by

$$P_l = \frac{1/l^z}{\sum_{l=1}^{L} 1/l^z},$$

where z is the Zipf exponent. We suppose that the system has worked for a long time. Hence, the MEC is capable to build a Zipf's distribution accurate enough, according to the historical data. Then, we propose a novel metric for the MEC server to determine the caching strategy, which is defined as

$$T_l = \frac{P_l \cdot c_l}{d_l^{out}}. \tag{5}$$

It measures how much computation cost is expected to reduce per cache bit. Larger T_l means higher efficiency. Therefore, using (5) as a criterion, the MEC server can first sort the L tasks into an ordered list $\{T_{x_1}, T_{x_2}, \ldots, T_{x_L}\}$, where $T_{x_1} \geq T_{x_2}$, and then cache the first X tasks. Here, X is the largest value that satisfies

$$\sum_{l=1}^{X} d_{x_l}^{out} \leq M.$$

4.2   Caching-Aware Offloading Algorithm

Once the MEC server has determined the caching scheme, we can remove the constraint C2 from the problem (4). And the next questions are which users should offload their tasks and how should they offload. To answer these two questions, we propose a two-step solution, which takes the caching decision into consideration to achieve better performance.

For the i-th task, we can first calculate the local-computing delay t_i^l with (1). However, the MBS-offloading and SBS-offloading delays are not available at this time, as the allocation of communication and computation resources is undecided yet. Hence, we alternatively define a concept of "full-resource delay" t_i^f to determine which tasks are more deserved to be offloaded. We suppose that all the bandwidth and computation resources are allocated to the i-th task, that is, $k_i = K$ and $v_i = 1$. Based on this, we can get the "full-resource" versions of the MBS-offloading and SBS-offloading delays according to (2) and (3), which are referred to as $t_i^{m,f}$ and $t_i^{s,f}$, respectively. For those users that are within both the coverage of the SBS and MBS, we define the latency gain as

$$\Delta D_i = t_i^l - \min(t_i^{m,f}, t_i^{s,f}),$$

while for those that are only covered by the MBS, the latency gain is given by

$$\Delta D_i = t_i^l - t_i^{m,f}.$$

Next, we sort the tasks into $\mathcal{N}_{sort} = \{n_1, n_2, \ldots, n_N\}$ in a descending order, where $D_{n_i} \geq D_{n_j}, \forall N > i > j > 0$. Then, we sequently determine the offloading and resource allocating for each task with a greedy strategy.

We denote the set of users choosing local computing as $\mathcal{N}_l$ while the sets of those offloading tasks via the MBS and the SBS are denoted as $\mathcal{N}_m$ and $\mathcal{N}_s$, respectively. Then the optimization objective in problem (4) can be equivalently transformed to

$$\underset{\{k_i, v_i\}}{\text{minimize}} \, L(\mathcal{N}_l, \mathcal{N}_m, \mathcal{N}_s) = \sum_{i \in \mathcal{N}_l} t_i^l + \sum_{i \in \mathcal{N}_m} t_i^m + \sum_{i \in \mathcal{N}_s} t_i^s. \qquad (6)$$

The sets $\mathcal{N}_m, \mathcal{N}_s$ are initialized as empty sets while $\mathcal{N}_l$ is set to be $\mathcal{N}_{sort}$. Here, we take the first user in $\mathcal{N}_{sort}$ to illustrate how to update the user sets: If the n_1-th user can only access the MBS, then it is directly moved to $\mathcal{N}_m$. That is, we update

$$\mathcal{N}_m \leftarrow \mathcal{N}_m \cup \{n_1\}.$$

If the user are in the coverage of both the MBS and SBS, then we update

$$\begin{cases} \mathcal{N}_m \leftarrow \mathcal{N}_m \cup \{n_1\} & \text{if } t_i^{m,f} < t_i^{s,f} \\ \mathcal{N}_s \leftarrow \mathcal{N}_s \cup \{n_1\} & \text{otherwise.} \end{cases}$$

In both cases, we then exclude n_1 from $\mathcal{N}_l$ as

$$\mathcal{N}_l \leftarrow \mathcal{N}_l \backslash \{n_1\}.$$

Given the sets $\mathcal{N}_l, \mathcal{N}_m, \mathcal{N}_s$, the constraints and objective functions are convex functions, and the feasible domains of k_i and v_i are convex sets. The problem (6) becomes a convex optimization problem [11]. Therefore, we can obatin the current minimal total delay

$$T_1 = \underset{\{k_i, v_i\}}{\text{minimize}}\ L(\mathcal{N}_l, \mathcal{N}_m, \mathcal{N}_s)$$

by using the CVX toolkit to determine $\{k_i, v_i\}$. After that, we can move $n_2, n_3, \ldots$ to $\mathcal{N}_m$ or $\mathcal{N}_l$ until $T_i < T_j$, which mean no more latency gain can be obtain through task offloading.

So far, we have set up a complete procedure to cope with the collaborative optimization of caching and offloading in a heterogeneous network. And we will verify the benefits of this algorithm in the next section.

5   Numerical Result

5.1   Simulation Setup

In the simulation environment, the MBS covers a radius of 500 m, and the SBS is located 150 m away from the MBS with a covering radius of 150 m. The latency coefficient φ of transmission via backhaul link between the MBS and SBS is set to 0.0001 s/KB. The total bandwidth is 20 MHz and evenly divided into $K = 20$ sub-channels. The MEC server has a CPU frequency F of 40 GHz and it can only cache the results of half of the possible tasks. The number of users is 30, and 60% of these users are randomly located at the whole area while the rest 40% are set to be randomly located within the coverage of the SBS. The input size d_i^{in} (KB) for Sect. 5.2 and 5.3 is set to follow uniform distributions $U[1000, 5000]$ and $U[500, 1000]$, respectively. For each task, the CPU cycle c_i (GHz) follows a uniform distribution $U[1, 2]$ and the result size d_i^{out} (KB) follows a normal distribution $\mathcal{N}(50, 80)$ for all simulations.

5.2   Benefits of the Proposed Caching Scheme

We have proposed a caching scheme oriented to computation tasks in Sect. 4.1, which particularly takes the output size and computation complexity of tasks into consideration. In this section, we evaluate the benefits of this comprehensive consideration by comparing it with two basic schemes: Basic Scheme 1 randomly

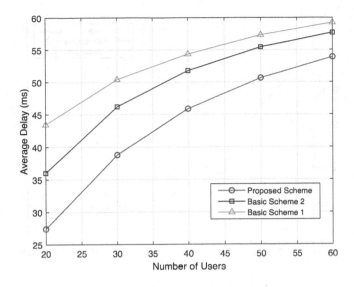

Fig. 2. Comparing the delay of the proposed caching scheme versus two basic schemes

caches a proportion of the tasks under the limitation of caching space. Basic Scheme 2 only considers the popularity of the tasks, and thus caches a certain number of tasks with the highest generating probability [12]. All of them use the offloading strategy proposed in Sect. 4.2. We use the average latency of all the users as metric and the results are presented in Fig. 2. It can be seen that for all the three schemes, the latency increases when more users are served. However, no matter how many users are given, the proposed method provides a lower latency than the other two basic schemes.

5.3   Benefits of the Proposed Offloading Scheme

We have proposed a caching-aware offloading scheme in Sect. 4.2, which takes the caching results into consideration to determine which tasks should be uploaded and how many communication and computation resources should be allocated to them. To show the advantages of the proposed strategy, we compares it with two basic schemes: Basic Scheme 1 has no cache space and thus provides an upper bound, while the Basic Scheme 2 determines the offloading policy regardless of the caching decision at the MEC server. The proposed scheme and the Basic Scheme 2 both use the caching method proposed in Sect. 4.1. The results are reported in Fig. 3, which reveal that the proposed method always outperforms the other two basic schemes under different configurations. Moreover, it brings higher latency gain when F is relatively small, which indicates that the caching-aware offloading method can play a important role when the MEC is not powerful enough.

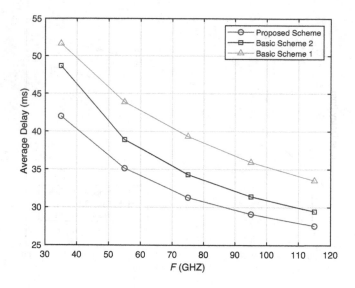

Fig. 3. Comparing the delay of the proposed offloading scheme versus two basic schemes

6   Conclusion

In this paper, aiming at optimizing the resource utilization in 5G heterogeneous networks, we propose a joint design of caching and offloading for MEC systems. We analyze the latency of different caching and offloading schemes and formulate an optimization problem to minimize the total latency of users. With a divide and conquer idea, we first design a caching scheme oriented to computation tasks with comprehensive consideration of popularity, data size and computation complexity. And then, we propose a caching-aware offloading method to make more reasonable and efficient allocations on communication and computation resources. The simulation results verify that the proposed schemes can bring benefits in various situations.

References

1. Meng, S., Wang, Y., Miao, Z., Sun, K.: Joint optimization of wireless bandwidth and computing resource in cloudlet-based mobile cloud computing environment. Peer-to-Peer Networking Appl. **11**(3), 462–472 (2018)
2. Hu, Y.C., Patel, M., Sabella, D., Sprecher, N., Young, V.: Mobile edge computing-a key technology towards 5G. ETSI White Paper **11**(11), 1–16 (2015)
3. Zhang, K., et al.: Energy-efficient offloading for mobile edge computing in 5G heterogeneous networks. IEEE Access **4**, 5896–5907 (2016)
4. Chen, B., Liu, L., Sun, M., Ma, H.: IoTCache: toward data-driven network caching for internet of things. IEEE Internet Things J. **6**(6), 10064–10076 (2019)

5. Huynh, L.N., Pham, Q.V., Nguyen, T.D., Hossain, M.D., Shin, Y.R., Huh, E.N.: Joint computational offloading and data-content caching in NOMA-MEC networks. IEEE Access **9**, 12943–12954 (2021)
6. Elbamby, M.S., Bennis, M., Saad, W.: Proactive edge computing in latency-constrained fog networks. In: 2017 European Conference on Networks and Communications (EuCNC), pp. 1–6. IEEE (2017)
7. Li, S., Li, B., Zhao, W.: Joint optimization of caching and computation in multi-server NOMA-MEC system via reinforcement learning. IEEE Access **8**, 112762–112771 (2020)
8. Zhao, H., Wang, Y., Sun, R.: Task proactive caching based computation offloading and resource allocation in mobile-edge computing systems. In: 2018 14th International Wireless Communications & Mobile Computing Conference (IWCMC), pp. 232–237. IEEE (2018)
9. Chen, X., Jiao, L., Li, W., Fu, X.: Efficient multi-user computation offloading for mobile-edge cloud computing. IEEE/ACM Trans. Network. **24**(5), 2795–2808 (2015)
10. Golrezaei, N., Dimakis, A.G., Molisch, A.F.: Scaling behavior for device-to-device communications with distributed caching. IEEE Trans. Inf. Theory **60**(7), 4286–4298 (2014)
11. Borst, S., Gupta, V., Walid, A.: Distributed caching algorithms for content distribution networks. In: 2010 Proceedings IEEE INFOCOM, pp. 1–9. IEEE (2010)
12. Suyu, Z., Jiang, L.: Cloud edge and collaborative offloading strategy based on active caching. J. Comput. Eng. Des. **42**(8), 2124–2129 (2021)

A Percolation-Based DTNs Routing Using Fountain Coding

Ruxin Zhi[1,2(✉)], Bilei Zhou[3], and Zhigang Tian[4]

[1] Key Laboratory of Information and Communication Systems, Ministry of Information Industry, Beijing Information Science and Technology University, Beijing 100101, China
zhiruxin@bistu.edu.cn

[2] Key Laboratory of Modern Measurement and Control Technology, Ministry of Education, Beijing Information Science and Technology University, Beijing 10010, China

[3] Shanghai Institute of Satellite Engineering, Shanghai 200240, China

[4] Tsinghua University, Beijing 100080, China
zgtian@tsinghua.edu.cn

Abstract. In Delay/Disruption Tolerant Networks (DTNs), an upper bound of the propagation delay and a persistent bi-direction link is not required. Thus, DTNs is considered as an effective extension to the existing network infrastructures and targeted to solve the problems that it is unable to communicate under extreme conditions. However, the long delay and frequent interruption of links in DTNs lead to routing strategy, a hot issue in DTNs research. From the perspective of efficient data transmission and information security, PFC-DRP, a DTNs routing protocol based on percolation and fountain coding is proposed. Since data theft and interception on a single path does not pose a serious threat to the leakage of complete data, the security of data transmission is guaranteed. At the same time, the proposed protocol effectively improves routing robustness. According to the simulation results, compared with other protocols, the proposed protocol achieves higher message delivery performance and reduces the overhead of delivery.

Keywords: Delay/Disruption Tolerant Networks (DTNs) · Routing · Percolation · Fountain Code

1 Introduction

Compared with traditional mobile wireless networks, the routing policy in DTNs faces the challenges of lack of global topology information, limited energy resources of nodes, limited storage space, and prominent security risks [1].

In DTNs, multipath is able to compensate for network performance defects due to long delays and intermittent connections. Multipath routing is dedicated to discovering more than one end-to-end transmission path, which has been studied in the Internet, MANETs, and WSNs [2, 3]. In wireless networks, such as MANETs, the discovery and maintenance of multi-hop paths requires more overhead, but also brings

K. Rabie et al. (Eds.): IoTaaS 2022, LNICST 506, pp. 106–116, 2023.
https://doi.org/10.1007/978-3-031-37139-4_10

many advantages, such as balanced link load, increased fault tolerance, increased bandwidth, and reduced end-to-end delay. In addition, in traditional Internets and MANETs, the transport layer-related security mechanisms are based on end-to-end connection acknowledgments.

In DTNs, the mechanism for discovering multiple routes at the same time in MANETs requires high network overhead, which is difficult to implement efficiently. Therefore, in order to balance network load and improve transmission efficiency and security, a routing protocol combining percolation transmission and coding techniques is presented [4]. Further, for the purpose of reducing the delivery cost, this paper converts the end-to-end mechanism into a single-hop acknowledgment mechanism. The rateless digital fountain code is used, which not only has a small coding overhead, but also effectively increases the channel capacity. According to the simulation comparison results, the proposed protocol is an efficient routing protocol.

The rest of this paper is organized as follows. Section 2 introduces the work related to multipath routing, fountain code and percolation. Section 3 presents a notion of the utility value of PFC-DRP and the routing mechanism. Section 4 constructs and simulates the model of the proposed protocol, and compares and analyzes the simulation results. Section 5 provides a brief summary of the research in this paper.

2   Routing in DTNs

The coding technique in DTNs routing compensates for network performance degradation caused by link failure and reduces the overall transmission overhead of the network [5]. There are two types of conventional codes, erasure code and network coding. The erasure code encodes the message at the source node, and increases the reliability by redundancy. The network coding allows the intermediate node to encode the message and encode different messages together. That improves the robustness of the network transmission and reduces the overhead ratio.

The digital fountain code is a type of erasure code. The source node performs fountain coding on the generated message, and encodes the k original packets into any number of encoded packets. The source node continuously transmits the data packets, and the receiving node successfully decodes through any $k(1 + \varepsilon)$ coded packets (ε is the decoding efficiency), recovering information of all k original packets. The source node continuously generates coded packets, like a fountain erupting water droplets, so it is called "fountain code." The source node stops transmitting the encoded packet after receiving the ACK message from the destination node, and then starts a new encoding and sending process. The digital fountain code not only has a low overhead and low complexity of coding and decoding, but also effectively increases the channel capacity and increases the robustness of the network. Even if several code blocks on a certain path cannot be transmitted because of link interruption, the decoding of the destination node will not be seriously impaired. As long as the destination node receives enough code blocks, it will decode correctly. In addition, the transmission of different coded packets on the multipath also ensures the security of data transmission. The interception and cracking of any single path data cannot reproduce the complete raw data [7].

3   The PFC-DRP Protocol

This paper proposes a DTNs Routing Protocol based on Percolation and Fountain Coding (PFC-DRP). The protocol combines the technology of multi-path routing penetration transmission and fountain coding, and is committed to achieving high security and balanced network load data transmission.

In this section, we first presents the relevant notions of percolation, then introduces the maintenance of local data and the computation of the utility value, and finally educes the routing mechanism and process of the proposed protocol.

3.1   Percolation

According to the small-world network phenomenon, any two people in the world can be connected by a limited number of hops (5 or 6). When there are enough nodes in the network, each node randomly associates with other nodes to form a small-world model. In such a network, data sent by any one node is able to be forwarded to the destination node with a high probability through the transit of several nodes. In order to achieve efficient forwarding, the choice of intermediate nodes is very critical. Certain social relationships between nodes can be used as a basis for selection.

For the PFC-DRP protocol, the following definitions are proposed:

Definition 1: In the network layer of DTNs, after fountain encoding, the source data packets are sent in parallel through different nodes or paths until they reach the destination node. This process is defined as percolation.

Definition 2: The end-to-end path through which the packet passes from the source node to the destination node is defined as the percolation path.

Definition 3: A fountain-encoded packet transmitted on the percolation path is defined as a percolation packet.

This paper proposes a data transmission technology based on percolation. When any node in the network sends data to a node, the data is segmented and handed over to one or more neighbour nodes that are most likely to transfer the data to the destination node. The same principle is applied to the intermediate node. The amount of data transmitted on the selected plurality of paths is different, related to the forwarding capability of the next hop node.

Since the intermittent connection state between nodes in DTNs cannot guarantee the existence of multipath every moment, the percolation transmission is actually a "quasi" concurrent multipath transmission process. Moreover, due to the sparseness of nodes in DTNs, the number of neighbor nodes cannot be ensured. Therefore, there may be multiple links or multiple node data aggregated to the same node and the continuous occurrence of single-path transmission in actual percolation transmission. Unlike traditional MANETs, which goes from the beginning to the end, more in the DTNs is to judge each step. Hence, multipath is selected as much as possible in each step to achieve multipath distributed transmission of the entire path.

In DTNs, the percolation path is connected to the destination node with a specific probability. The percolation packets of the partial percolation path unlikely to reach the destination are discarded in the network. Figure 1 shows a complete transmission process without the loss of percolation packets. The benefit of fountain coding is that no matter

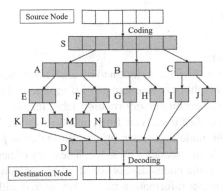

Fig. 1. Percolation Packet Transmission

which path a small number of packets are lost, it does not have a decisive influence on the integrity of the final reception, thus optimizing the efficiency of the transmission. Table 1 summarizes the variables used in our model and their definitions.

Table 1. Variables and Definitions of PFC-DRP

Variable Name	Description
N	set of all the nodes in the network
NB	set of neighbors nodes
NH	set of next hop nodes
U_S^D	unity value of node S for node D
ε	coding rate
k	number of original messages
q	loss rate of packets
M	number of messages generated by source node
K	minimum number of messages that can be decoded correctly in destination node
X	number of messages received by destination node
$encntUtil(v_i, v_j)$	utility value of node v_i and node v_j
$numEncnt(v_i, v_j)$	number of encounter time between node v_i and node v_j
$tsLastEncnt(v_i, v_j)$	last time when node v_i and node v_j meet
$tsNow$	simulation time
γ	decay factor

3.2 The Utility Value

Local Maintenance Data

In the PFC-DRP protocol, the data maintained by each node includes a node encounter information table and a neighbor node encounter information table for route calculation.

The entry of the node encounter information table includes the node address, the number of encounters, the last encounter time, and the most recent update time of the entry. The content of the node encounter information table is periodically sent to the neighbor node along with the broadcast message. The entry of neighbor node encounter information table includes the node address and all of its encounter information entries. The neighbor node encounter information table is not shared with neighbor nodes.

Computation of the Utility Value

In the social network analysis, the attributes that measure the tie strength of the connection between individuals mainly include frequency, intimacy, recency, regularity, and social homogeneity. Applied to DTNs, the frequency of encounters between the pairs of nodes and the number of encounters reflect the closeness of relationship and the possibility of future encounters, so it is suitable as a basis for the forwarding policy. The encounter utility value reflected by the social connection relationship between the two nodes is composed of the number of encounters and the attenuation of the two nodes, expressed as Eq. (1)

$$encntUtil(v_i, v_j) = numEncnt(v_i, v_j) \times \frac{1}{(tsNow - tsLastEncnt(v_i, v_j) + 1)^{\gamma}} \quad (1)$$

where $numEncnt(v_i, v_j)$ is the number of encounters between node v_i and node v_j, $tsNow$ is the current simulation time, $tsLastEncnt(v_i, v_j)$ is the most recent encounter time of node v_i and node v_j, γ is the attenuation factor, an adjustable parameter.

3.3 Routing Mechanism

The fountain-encoded packet is continuously sent until the ACK packet of the destination node is received. This method causes considerable overhead, and the reply of the ACK packet may also be interfered by the interrupt path or long delay. Therefore, the single-hop acknowledgement retransmission mechanism, instead of end-to-end confirmation retransmission mechanism is utilized to achieve efficient data transfer. After receiving the acknowledgment message from the neighbor node, the source node deletes the corresponding message in the cache, otherwise it retransmits after a time.

The routing mechanism of the proposed protocol is based on the above utility value and fountain code. Next, the route initialization, the source node sending process, and the selection of the next-hop node are sequentially explained.

Route Initialization

The route initialization is the process of sending broadcast messages and updating local data. After a period of broadcast message transmission and reception, each node obtains the information of the current one-hop neighbor node, and also accumulates historical encounter information with some nodes of the network, preparing for the selection of the next-hop node.

Sending Process of Source Node

When the source node S sends data to the destination node D, consisting of k original packets, any number of fountain-coded packets can be generated. However, in order to improve end-to-end transmission performance, the amount of fountain-coded packets is controlled at the source node. According to the characteristics of the fountain code, the destination node receives at least $X \geq K = k(1 + \varepsilon)$ coded packets to decode and recover the original data completely, where K is the minimum number of correctly decoded packets, related to the nature of the fountain code used. Due to the existence of the packet loss rate q in the network, consider redundancy at the source node. Taken together, $M \geq K(1 + q) = k(1 + \varepsilon)(1 + q)$ fountain-coded packets are sent by the source node.

Selection of the Next-Hop Node

When the source node and the intermediate node perform message forwarding, n nodes are selected from the current neighbor nodes $NB_j(1 \leq j \leq m)$ as the next-hop nodes, which is denoted as $NB_j(1 \leq i \leq n)$. The selection follows the six criteria below.

a) The utility value of the selected next-hop node with respect to the destination node is greater than the utility value of the current node with respect to the destination node;

$$\forall U_{NH_i}^D > U_M^D \tag{2}$$

b) The utility value of the selected next-hop node with respect to the destination node is the largest among all utility values of neighbor nodes with respect to the destination node;

$$U_{NH_i}^D \geq \max(U_{NB_l(\forall NB_l \in NB \backslash NH)}^D) \tag{3}$$

c) Whether the alternate next hop nodes include the last hop node of the message depends on the reception time. If the interval exceeds the threshold, the last hop node is optional; if the interval is less than the threshold, the last hop node is excluded from the candidate nodes;

d) The amount of data transferred on each path is allocated according to the utility value of the selected next-hop node. The percentage of data sent to the next hop node is proportional to the corresponding utility value;

$$P_i \propto U_{NH_i}^D \tag{4}$$

e) The number of next-hop nodes selected at each intermediate node is not equal, and may be only one;

f) When there is not any next-hop node that meet the above principles, the current node caches the message.

4   Performance Evaluation

4.1   Simulation Scenario and Parameter Settings

This section evaluates and compares the performance of the PFC-DRP protocol through simulation. The evaluation indicators include Delivery Ratio, Average Delay, Average Number of Hops, and Delivery Cost.

The discrete event simulator OMNeT++ is selected to evaluate the performance of routing protocols. The node mobility model is Community-based Mobility Model (CMM) [6]. The simulation scenario is that the terminal devices carried by the staff interact in a large conference. The internal facilities of the venue interfere with or even block the signals of the communication terminals, so the links between the nodes are in a state of intermittent and consistent with the characteristics of the DTNs. Table 2 summarizes the default parameter settings, and Fig. 2 presents the simulation scenario diagram.

Table 2.   Parameters in the PFC-DRP Protocol Simulation

Parameters of simulation scenario	Default Value
Total simulation time	4 h
Simulation area size	1000 m * 1000 m, 2000 m * 2000 m
Number of nodes	100
Communication range of nodes	40 m
Motion speed of nodes	0–6 m/s
Application layer message generation time range	600 s–700 s
Application layer message generation interval	0.5 s
Local state probability of nodes p_l	0.0
Roaming state probability of nodes p_r	1.0
Hello message sending interval	5 s
Retransmission interval of one-hop confirmation	2.5 s
Expiration time of neighbor information	10 s
Expiration time of encounter information	3600 s
Fountain code decoding efficiency ε	5%

Constrain the same application layer raw data in the simulation. For the PFC-DRP protocol, the total amount of data sent is greater than other non-encoded routing protocols. The data redundancy is related to the efficiency of the fountain code used. Set the fountain encoding overhead to 5% in this simulation.

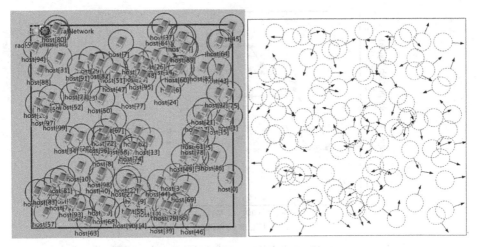

Fig. 2. DTNs Simulation Scenario

4.2 Results

This section first evaluates the performance of the PFC-DRP protocol as the limitation of message TTL (Time To Live) changes, and compares it with other classic routing protocols to examine the validity of the PFC-DRP protocol; then evaluates the PFC-DRP protocol under various network traffic conditions, and determine the operating efficiency of the PFC-DRP protocol through comparison.

Protocols selected for comparison are the proposed protocols, TSRouting, BubbleRap, GreedyAll, Fresh, and Random. Both TSRouting and PFC-DRP use the same utility value, while the PFC-DRP protocol adopts a multipathing mechanism and fountain encoding. The routing metric of BubbleRap is the social centrality [8]. In the Greedy-All protocol [9], messages are forwarded to nodes that have more encounters with other nodes in the network. The Fresh protocol [10] stipulates that the message is forwarded to the node that is closer to the destination node for the last contact. In the Random route, the message is randomly forwarded to the encountering node.

We evaluate the performance of the PFC-DPR protocol as the limitation of message TTL changes, and compare it with other classic routing protocols to examine the validity of the PFC-DRP protocol.

From Fig. 3, the PFC-DRP protocol and the Fresh protocol increase with increasing TTL, the delivery ratio reaches 100%, and other protocols reach 75%–90%.

According to Fig. 4, the average latency of the PFC-DRP protocol is about 10% lower than the Fresh protocol at the same delivery ratio, and is also at a low level in all protocols.

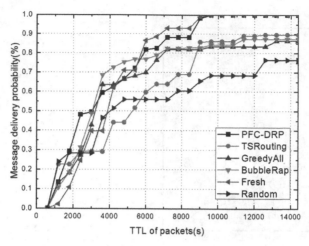

Fig. 3. Message delivery probability of different protocols vs TTL of packets

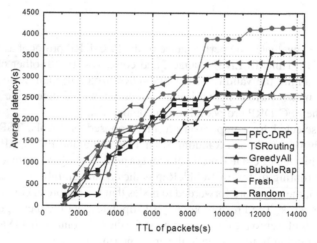

Fig. 4. Message average latency of different protocols vs TTL of packets

As seen in Fig. 5, the average number of hops of the PFC-DRP protocol is the lowest among all protocols.

Figure 6 shows that the message delivery overhead of the PFC-DRP protocol is also lower than other protocols.

In summary, although the PFC-DRP protocol increases the total network transmission traffic due to fountain coding, it can still achieve the highest delivery performance and the lowest delivery overhead. Compared with the TSRouting protocol with the same utility value, the PFC-DRP protocol improves the end-to-end delivery ratio and reduces the delivery cost.

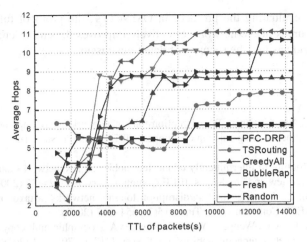

Fig. 5. Average hops vs TTL of packets

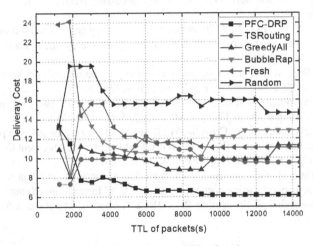

Fig. 6. Delivery Cost vs TTL of packets

As a conclusion, the percolation transmission mechanism in the PFC-DRP protocol is well suited to the network congestion caused by the increase in traffic volume. By distributing the data transmitted to the same destination on the multipath, congestion caused by the excessive pressure of the single node is avoided. It guarantees a higher level of messages delivery in the network.

5 Conclusions

In this paper, from the perspective of efficient transmission and data security, a DTNs routing protocol based on percolation technology and fountain code is proposed. This protocol combines the fountain coding at the source node and multipath transmission techniques. By evaluating the protocol in OMNeT++, the protocol fully utilizes the multi-path resources of the network, effectively improves the end-to-end transmission performance, and ensures the security of data transmission.

References

1. Khabbaz, M., Assi, C., Fawaz, W.: Disruption-tolerant networking: a comprehensive survey on recent developments and persisting challenges. IEEE Commun. Surv. Tutor. **14**(2), 607–640 (2012)
2. Zhang, Z.: Routing in intermittently connected mobile ad hoc networks and delay tolerant networks: Overview and challenges. IEEE Commun. Surv. **8**(1), 24–37 (2006)
3. Cao, Y., Sun, Z.: Routing in delay/disruption tolerant networks: a taxonomy, survey and challenges. IEEE Commun. Surv. Tutor. **15**(2), 654–677 (2013)
4. Cao, Y., Wei, K., Min, Weng, J., Yang, X., Sun, Z.: A geographic multicopy routing scheme for DTNs With heterogeneous mobility. IEEE Syst. J. **12**(1), 790–801 (2018)
5. Le, T., Gerla, M.: Social-Distance based anycast routing in Delay Tolerant Networks. In: Mediterranean Ad Hoc Networking Workshop (Med-Hoc-Net), pp.1–7. IEEE, Vilanova i la Geltru, Spain (2016)
6. Vazintari, A., Cottis, P.G.: Mobility management in energy constrained self-organizing delay tolerant networks: an autonomic scheme based on game theory. IEEE Trans. Mob. Comput. **15**(6), 1401–1411 (2016)
7. Pinto, P.C., Win, M.Z.: Percolation and connectivity in the intrinsically secure communications graph. IEEE Trans. Inf. Theory **58**(3), 1716–1730 (2012)
8. Hui, P., Crowcroft, J., Yoneki, E.: BUBBLE rap: social-based forwarding in delay-tolerant networks. IEEE Trans. Mob. Comput. **10**(11), 1576–1589 (2011)
9. Erramilli, V., Chaintreau, A., Crovella, M.: Diversity of forwarding paths in pocket switched networks. In: Proceedings of the ACM SIGCOMM Internet Measurement Conference, IMC, San Diego, USA, vol. 7, no. 1, pp.161–174. ACM (2007)
10. Dubois-Ferriere, H., Grossglauser, M., Vetterli, M.: Age matters: efficient route discovery in mobile ad hoc networks using encounter ages. In: ACM International Symposium on Mobile Ad Hoc Networking & Computing (MobiHoc), Annapolis, Maryland, USA, pp.257–266. ACM (2003)

Bandwidth Allocation for eMBB and mMTC Slices Based on AI-Aided Traffic Prediction

Xiaoli Zhang[1], Kai Liang[1(✉)], Jen-Jee Chen[2], and Jiaxin Liu[1]

[1] Xidian University, Xi'an 710071, China
kliang@xidian.edu.cn
[2] National Yang Ming Chiao Tung University, Hsinchu 30093, Taiwan

Abstract. Network slicing has emerged as a key enabler to address the diverse requirements of the fast-growing Internet of Things (IoT), such as enhanced Mobile Broad Band (eMBB) and massive Machine Type Communication (mMTC). However, the dynamic nature of service requirements propels challenges for resource allocation of network slicing. This paper proposes a bandwidth allocation method serving eMBB and mMTC slices with the aid of deep learning-based traffic prediction. The problem is formulated as maximizing the number of users served by the mMTC slice while satisfying the rate requirement of users served by the eMBB slice. We adopt traffic prediction by deep learning methods (i.e., ConvLSTM and GRU) to facilitate dynamic allocation of the bandwidth resource, which can be obtained by solving the integer programming problem. Numerical results show that the proposed algorithm outperforms the traditional method in terms of the average number of served mMTC users.

Keywords: Network slicing · Traffic prediction · ConvLSTM · GRU · mMTC · eMBB

1 Introduction

The fast-growing Internet of Things (IoT) leads to various scenarios and applications with increasingly multifarious service requirements [1], such as massive Machine Type Communication (mMTC) with the massive access requirements (e.g., smart cities, intelligent transportation) and enhanced Mobile Broad Band (eMBB) with the high data rate requirement (e.g., immersive games, Augmented Reality) [2]. This brings challenges to serve diverse service requirements under a shared physical infrastructure. Therefore IoT needs to be sliced and tailored to form logically virtual networks, and thus network slicing emerges [3].

This work was supported in part by National Key R&D Program of China (2019YFE0113200), National Natural Science Foundation of China (61901317), Joint Education Project between China and Central-Estern European Countries (202005).

K. Rabie et al. (Eds.): IoTaaS 2022, LNICST 506, pp. 117–126, 2023.
https://doi.org/10.1007/978-3-031-37139-4_11

There has been a lot of research in the field of network slicing. The algorithm UFLOP is proposed to minimize the "over-provisioning rate" by adjusting capacity and traffic allocation with satisfying the latency constraints of users and the service level agreement of the tenant [5]. Alsenwi proposes an algorithm based on deep reinforcement learning to maximize the eMBB data rate under the reliability constraints of ultra-reliable low-latency communication [6]. However, existing researches often reserve resources to prevent busty high data transmission and thereby fail to satisfy on-demand and dynamic resource allocation.

Traffic prediction algorithms can support real-time, on-demand resource allocation [4]. Graves first proposed Long-Short Term Memory (LSTM) which is based on Recurrent Neural Network (RNN), to solve problems such as gradients in long-term memory and backpropagation [7]. The LSTM algorithm performs well on temporal correlation, but it introduces redundancy when dealing with spatial data due to the strong local characteristics of spatial data [8]. To solve this problem, Shi *et al.* proposed the Convolutional LSTM (ConvLSTM) algorithm and experimentally proved that ConvLSTM outperforms LSTM in spatial and temporal data processing [9]. Additionally, Ramakrishnan *et al.* [10] used RNN, LSTM, and Gate Recurrent Unit (GRU) models to predict traffic information, demonstrated that GRU models perform better than RNN and LSTM predictors. While these traffic prediction algorithms are well researched, they are not yet effectively combined with the implementation of real-time on-demand allocation of network resources.

In this paper, we propose a bandwidth allocation algorithm for eMBB and mMTC slices based on AI-aided traffic prediction. The contributions of this paper are summarized as follows. Firstly, we jointly consider service requirements of eMBB slices and mMTC slices, and the problem is formulated as maximizing the number of mMTC users under the eMBB data rate constraint. Then, to dynamically allocate resources, we use the AI-aided traffic prediction to forecast the real-time rate requirement of the served eMBB users and take the prediction result as the boundary to reserve resources, thereby achieving better performance than traditional resource reservation methods.

The rest of this manuscript is organized as follows. Section 2 introduces the system model and the problem formulation. Section 3 discusses our proposed algorithm. In Sect. 4, we present simulation results. Finally, we conclude our discussions in Sect. 5.

2   System Model and Problem Formulation

We consider the uplink transmission of a single cell consisting of one base station(BS) serving an eMBB slice with E users and an mMTC slice with M users, as shown in Fig. 1. The BS and each user are equipped with a single antenna. The uplink channel is shared by all users and is divided into N subchannels with bandwith f, so the total amount of uplink bandwidth is $F = f \times N$. Let $X_{e,n} = 1$ indicate that the subchannel n is allocated to eMBB user e, and $X_{e,n} = 0$, otherwise. Similarly, $X_{m,n} = 1$ denotes that the nth subchannel is allocated to

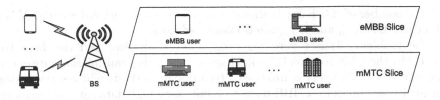

Fig. 1. System model

the mth mMTC user, and $X_{m,n} = 0$, otherwise. Because mMTC services often require massive access with a low data rate, we assume that one subchannel is enough for the data rate requirement of mMTC users. Therefore, the number of mMTC users U served by the mMTC slice is given as follows

$$U = \sum_{m}^{M} \sum_{n}^{N} X_{m,n}. \tag{1}$$

The transmit power of eMBB user e is set to P_e, so the uplink rate of eMBB user e is given by

$$R_e = \sum_{n}^{N} X_{e,n} f \log \left(1 + \frac{P_e |h_{e,n}|^2 \vartheta_{e,n}}{\sigma^2 f} \right), \tag{2}$$

where $h_{e,n} \sim CN(0,1)$ and $\vartheta_{e,n}$ denote Rayleigh fading coefficient and the path loss between the BS and eMBB user e on subchannel n, respectively. σ^2 presents the noise power spectral density.

In this paper, we focus on maximizing the number of users served by the mMTC slice with satisfying the rate requirement of eMBB users. Denote $R_{req}^e(t)$ as the rate requirement in time slot t. The optimal problem can be formulated as follows

$$\max_{X_{e,n}, X_{m,n}} \sum_{m}^{M} \sum_{n}^{N} X_{m,n}(t)$$

$$\text{s.t.} \quad C1 : R_e(t) \geq R_{req}^e(t) \quad e = 1, \cdots, E \quad t = 1, \cdots, T$$

$$C2 : \sum_{e}^{E} X_{e,n}(t) + \sum_{m}^{M} X_{m,n}(t) \leq 1 \quad n = 1, \cdots, N$$

$$C3 : \sum_{n}^{N} \left[\sum_{e}^{E} X_{e,n}(t) + \sum_{m}^{M} X_{m,n}(t) \right] \leq N \tag{3}$$

$$C4 : X_{e,n}(t), X_{m,n}(t) \in \{0,1\}$$

$$n = 1, \cdots, N \quad m = 1, \cdots, M \quad e = 1, \cdots, E.$$

The constraint $C1$ stands for the rate requirements constraints of eMBB users. $C2$ means that subchannel n can be allocated to only one user. $C3$ indicates that the number of subchannels allocated cannot exceed the total amount N, and $C4$ means that $X_{e,n}$ and $X_{m,n}$ are Boolean variables.

The problem (3) is a zero-one programming problem and can be solved directly by the CVX toolbox [12,13]. However, since the transmission rate of each time slot of eMBB users is unknown, traditional methods will reserve enough bandwidth resources for eMBB users to fulfill busty high data rate requirements, leading to low spectral efficiency and thereby serving fewer mMTC users. To deal with this problem, we will introduce a traffic prediction-based algorithm in the next section.

3   Traffic Prediction Based Bandwidth Allocation Algorithm

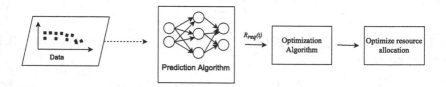

Fig. 2. Traffic Prediction based Bandwidth Allocation Algorithm.

In this section, we first predict the real-time rate of eMBB users based on ConvLSTM and GRU. After obtaining the result, we take it as the boundary of the constraint $C1$ in (3), to dynamically allocate resources, as shown in Fig. 2. Next, we first introduce two deep learning-aided traffic prediction algorithms and then use the prediction results to solve the optimization problem.

3.1   AI-Aided Traffic Predication

ConvLSTM Based Traffic Prediction. In order to improve the accuracy of the prediction, we need to normalize the rate R_t^e of the eMBB user e and turn it into a scalar r_t^e, and the expression is given as follows

$$r_t^e = \frac{R_t^e - \min(R_1^e, \cdots, R_T^e)}{\max(R_1^e, \cdots, R_T^e) - \min(R_1^e, \cdots, R_T^e)} \quad t = 1, \cdots, T, \quad (4)$$

where T is the total time. Then we take the processed data r_t^e as the input which flows to the ConvLSTM layer. The ConvLSTM units use the forget gate, input gate, and output gate to update their cell and hidden states. The forget gate decides how much of the cell state information at the previous time step is to be discarded, and the output of the forget gate is given as follows

$$f_t = \sigma(W_f * [C_{t-1}, h_{t-1}, r_t^e] + b_f), \quad (5)$$

where $*$ denotes the convolution operation and W_f represents the parameter matrix. C_{t-1} and h_{t-1} is the last moment information and b_f is the bias of every neuron. $\sigma(\cdot)$ represents the sigmoid activation function, i.e., $\sigma(x) = 1/(1 + e^{-x})$.

The input gate is used to control the addition of new information, which is given as follows

$$i_t = \sigma(W_i * [C_{t-1}, h_{t-1}, r_t^e] + b_i). \tag{6}$$

Based on the previous memory cell state C_{t-1} and the forget state f_t , the cell state information updates with the formula

$$C_t = f_t \circ C_{t-1} + \tanh(W_c * [h_{t-1}, r_t^e] + b_c), \tag{7}$$

where tanh is the hyperbolic tangent function and $\circ$ is the Hadamard product.

The output gate filters the information achieved by the updated cell state, and the mathematical expression is given as follows

$$o_t = \sigma(W_o * [C_{t-1}, h_{t-1}, r_t^e] + b_o). \tag{8}$$

The hidden state is defined as follows

$$h_t = o_t \circ \tanh(C_t). \tag{9}$$

To alleviate overfitting problems, we add a dropout layer behind the first ConvLSTM layer. Then we reduce the dimension of the output of the dropout layer through flatten function. Finally, we take the output as the input of the next LSTM layer which replaces the convolution operation with matrix multiplication in ConvLSTM.

GRU Based Traffic Prediction. GRU has two gates, namely, the update gate and the reset gate. The update gate determines what information to forget and what new information needs to be added, while the reset gate is used to control how much of the previous information is forgotten. After achieving processed data r_t^e through the formula (4), the update gate z_t is given as follows

$$z_t = \sigma(W_z \times [h_{t-1}, r_t^e] + b_z), \tag{10}$$

and the reset gate s_t is formulated as

$$s_t = \sigma(W_s \times [h_{t-1}, r_t^e] + b_s). \tag{11}$$

Based on the update gate z_t and the reset gate s_t, the hidden state is updated and the formula is given as

$$\hat{h}_t = \tanh(W_h \times [s_t * h_{t-1}, r_t^e]), \tag{12}$$

$$h_t = (1 - z_t) \circ h_{t-1} + z_t * \hat{h}_t. \tag{13}$$

We use the mean square error (MSE) to evaluate the performance of ConvLSTM and GRU prediction algorithms, which is given as follows

$$MSE = \frac{1}{T} \sum_{t}^{T} (\hat{r_t^e} - r_t^e)^2, \tag{14}$$

where $\hat{r_t^e}$ is the predicted result of r_t^e.

3.2   Prediction Based Optimized Algorithm

After the prediction of the above traffic prediction algorithms, we can obtain the predicted scalar $\hat{r_t^e}$ and scale it into the real-time rate requirements $\hat{R}_{req}^e(t)$ of eMBB users. However, since the results obtained by the prediction algorithm may not exactly match the actual requirements, especially in the case of high data transmission rate bursting (see Fig. 3. in Sect. 4), a correction factor η is added to prevent dissatisfying the eMBB data rate requirement $R_{req}^e(t)$. η is the median number of the difference between prediction and actual value when the prediction value is less than the actual value. Therefore, the optimization problem can be formulated as

$$\max_{x_{e,n}(t),x_{m,n}(t)} \sum_{m}^{M} \sum_{n}^{N} X_{m,n}(t)$$
$$\text{s.t.} \quad C1 : R_e(t) \geq \hat{R}_{req}^e(t) + \eta \tag{15}$$
$$C2, \quad C3, \quad C4$$

The new problem is similar to the original one, and can be solved with ease.

4   Numerical Results

We consider a circular network having a radius r = 500 m. The BS is located at the center of the network area. $E = 4$ eMBB users and $M = 20$ mMTC users are uniformly distributed around it. The path loss is computed by $\vartheta(dB) = 32.6 + 36.7log_{10}(d)$ [14], where d(in km) represents the distance between eMBB users and BS and is generated randomly within 500 m. The bandwidth of the subchannel f is 30 kHz and the number of subchannels N is 24. The transmit power P_e of each user is set to be $1W$, and $\sigma^2 = -174\,\text{dBm/Hz}$ [15]. For rate prediction, 4 sets of periodic oscillation signals of eMBB users are taken as the input of the prediction algorithm. We adopt the MSE loss function and the Adam optimizer whose initial learning rate is 0.0001. The window size of both ConvLSTM and GRU equals to 24. The model is trained in batch mode, and the batch size is 32. The training set and testing set contain 70% and 30% of the total dataset, respectively.

Figure 3 shows the prediction results obtained by ConvLSTM and GRU algorithms for each eMBB user. Except for some particularly high data transmission rates required, ConvLSTM and GRU algorithms both profoundly capture the dynamic fluctuations of the oscillating signal, and from Fig. 3 (e) we find that ConvLSTM outperforms GRU, because ConvLSTM introduces convolution operations and has a better grasp of the data features than GRU, e.g., for eMBB user 2, the MSE of ConvLSTM achieves 0.78, 25.7% lower than that of GRU.

We compared the performance of the proposed algorithm with the traditional method which adopts the way of reserving resources to prevent bursty rate requirements of eMBB users. The perfect prediction knows the rate requirements of eMBB users and is considered as a reference standard. To facilitate

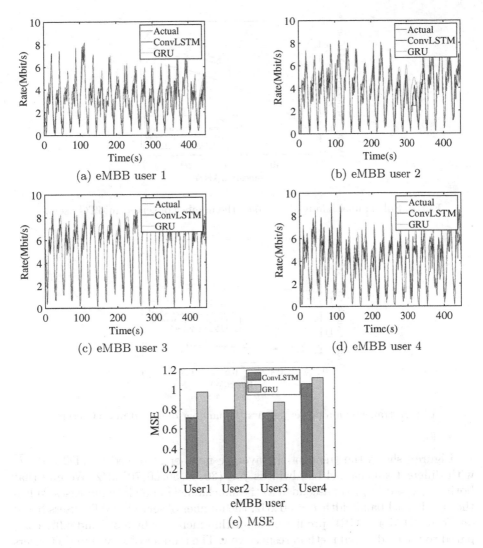

Fig. 3. Prediction results

the analysis of the optimal results, we average the optimized number of served mMTC users over a period T, which is formulated as follows

$$\overline{U} = \frac{1}{T} \sum_{t}^{T} U(t), \tag{16}$$

where $U(t)$ represents the number of served mMTC users at time slot t through the optimized algorithm. Let $\overline{U}_{conv}$ denote the average optimized result of ConvLSTM based optimization algorithm, and $\overline{U}_{gru}$ denotes the counterpart of GRU.

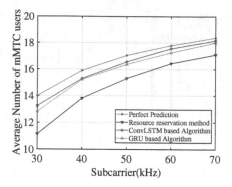

Fig. 4. Subchannel bandwidth versus the number of served mMTC users.

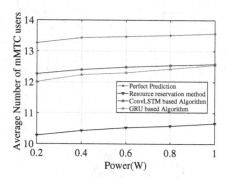

Fig. 5. Transmission power versurs the number of served mMTC users.

Figure 4 shows the trend of the average number of served mMTC users $\overline{U}$ with different subchannel bandwidths $f \in \{30, 40, 50, 60, 70\}$ kHz. We find that both $\overline{U}_{conv}$ and $\overline{U}_{gru}$ are ascended as the subchannel bandwidth increases. When the subchannel bandwidth $f = 50$ kHz, the number of served mMTC users based on ConvLSTM and GRU prediction algorithm increases by 8.3% and 6.9% compared to the traditional method respectively. The number of served mMTC users is almost equal to the result based on perfect prediction when $f = 70$ kHz.

Figure 5 shows the average number of served mMTC users $\overline{U}$ with different values of transmission power $P_e \in \{0.2, 0.4, 0.6, 0.8, 1\}W$ of eMBB users. We find that the proposed algorithms outperform the traditional method in terms of the number of served mMTC users. The algorithm we proposed exhibits an average increase of 18.87%, with a maximum increase of 19.92%.

5   Conclusions

Network slicing technology promotes the diverse requirements of the fast-growing IoT, such as eMBB and mMTC. However, the traditional resource reservation method of network slicing cannot satisfy the dynamic nature of business demands. In this paper, we propose a bandwidth allocation algorithm based on deep learning traffic prediction for eMBB and mMTC slices. Firstly, we maximize the number of served mMTC users with the traditional method. Then, based on the result of the traffic prediction algorithm (i.e., ConvLSTM and GRU), we dynamically allocate bandwidth resources to eMBB and mMTC users by solving an integer programming problem. Finally, the numerical results demonstrate that the proposed method outperforms the traditional method in terms of increasing the number of served mMTC users.

References

1. Shafique, K., Khawaja, B.A., Sabir, F., Qazi, S., Mustaqim, M.: Internet of things (IoT) for next-generation smart systems: a review of current challenges, future trends and prospects for emerging 5G-IoT scenarios. IEEE Access **8**, 23022–23040 (2020)
2. Wijethilaka, S., Liyanage, M.: Survey on network slicing for Internet of Things realization in 5G networks. IEEE Commun. Surv. Tutor. **23**(2), 957–994 (2021)
3. Cao, J., et al.: A survey on security aspects for 3GPP 5G networks. IEEE Commun. Surv. Tutor. **22**(1), 170–195 (2019)
4. Zhang, J., Zheng, Y., Sun, J., Qi, D.: Flow prediction in spatio-temporal networks based on multitask deep learning. IEEE Trans. Knowl. Data Eng. **32**(3), 468–478 (2019)
5. Chien, H.T., Lin, Y.D., Lai, C.L., Wang, C.T.: End-to-end slicing with optimized communication and computing resource allocation in multi-tenant 5G systems. IEEE Trans. Veh. Technol. **69**(2), 2079–2091 (2019)
6. Alsenwi, M., Tran, N.H., Bennis, M., Pandey, S.R., Bairagi, A.K., Hong, C.S.: Intelligent resource slicing for eMBB and URLLC coexistence in 5G and beyond: a deep reinforcement learning based approach. IEEE Trans. Wireless Commun. **20**(7), 4585–4600 (2021)
7. Graves, A.: Long Short-Term Memory. Supervised Sequence Labelling with Recurrent Neural Networks, pp. 37–45 (2012)
8. Essien, A., Giannetti, C.: A deep learning model for smart manufacturing using convolutional LSTM neural network autoencoders. IEEE Trans. Industr. Inf. **16**(9), 6069–6078 (2020)
9. Shi, X., Chen, Z., Wang, H., Yeung, D.Y., Wong, W.K., Woo, W.C.: Convolutional LSTM network: a machine learning approach for precipitation nowcasting. In: Advances in Neural Information Processing Systems, vol. 28 (2015)
10. Ramakrishnan, N., Soni, T.: Network traffic prediction using recurrent neural networks. In: 2018 17th IEEE International Conference on Machine Learning and Applications (ICMLA), pp. 187–193. IEEE (2018)
11. Cho, K., et al.: Learning phrase representations using RNN encoder-decoder for statistical machine translation. arXiv preprint arXiv:1406.1078 (2014)
12. Michael Grant and Stephen Boyd. CVX: Matlab software for disciplined convex programming, version 2.0 beta. https://cvxr.com/cvx (2013)
13. Grant, M., Boyd, S.: Graph implementations for nonsmooth convex programs. In: Blondel, V., Boyd, S., Kimura, H. (eds.) Recent Advances in Learning and Control (a tribute to M. Vidyasagar), pp. 95–110, Lecture Notes in Control and Information Sciences, Springer, London (2008). https://doi.org/10.1007/978-1-84800-155-8_7, https://stanford.edu/~boyd/graph_dcp.html

14. Jiang, T., Cheng, H.V., Yu, W.: Learning to reflect and to beamform for intelligent reflecting surface with implicit channel estimation. IEEE J. Sel. Areas Commun. **39**(7), 1931–1945 (2021)
15. Liang, K., Zhao, L., Yang, K., Chu, X.: Online power and time allocation in MIMO uplink transmissions powered by RF wireless energy transfer. IEEE Trans. Veh. Technol. **66**(8), 6819–6830 (2017)

A Coded Modulation Scheme for IoT System

Yamei Zou[1], Dengsheng Lin[1(✉)], and Zhiyuan Jiang[2]

[1] National Key Laboratory of Science and Technology on Communications, University of Electronic Science and Technology of China, Chengdu, China
1744070461@qq.com, linds@uestc.edu.cn
[2] School of Communication and Information Engineering, Shanghai University, Shanghai, China
jiangzhiyuan@shu.edu.cn

Abstract. The Internet of Things (IoT) gives huge challenges in computation complexity, response latency and transmission reliability. In this paper, we propose a coded modulation scheme for short packet applicable to IoT system. The structure of the proposed scheme is similar to traditional convolutional codes. The states by encoding the information bits are immediately modulated to achieve joint design of coding and modulation. We further theoretically give the optimal generator matrix by maximizing the minimum distance among the branch modulated symbols. Finally, we give some numerical simulations to demonstrate that the proposed scheme is applicable to IoT system.

Keywords: IoT · Channel coding · Coded modulation · Convolutional codes

1 Introduction

The Internet of Things (IoT) has been attracting many attentions from all over the world recently owing to its huge capacity to connect billions of devices and providing wide-range services for them [1,2]. In many application scenarios, the low response latency for IoT services is considerable challenging from system architecture to wireless physical layer technologies [3]. One of them is channel coding that plays an important role on physical layer. It dominates the transmission reliability, the response latency and receiving computation delay [4].

In IoT system, limited by transmission packet size, the codes must be very short, which will critically deteriorate the performance [5,6]. The eligible codes in IoT system should have the capability to support short packet with low computation complexity, low latency and high reliability [7]. Polar codes have successfully applied in commercial communication system, such as 5G cellular communication system [8]. It can achieve the capacity when the length of code is large

This work is supported by the National Key R&D program of China under Grant 2019YFE0196600.

enough [9]. Moreover, it also performs well in finite length regime. The new developed polar codes called polarization-adjustment convolutional (PAC) codes can achieve the bound of finite-length codes at some specific parameters [10]. Both of them are promising codes in application in IoT system [11]. Unfortunately, their performances rely heavily on the constructions, which are usually specific based on various code size and rate [12,13]. It limits the adaptability of codes for various scenarios.

Joint design of coding and modulation can asymptotically achieve high-order discrete memoryless channel (DMC) and additional white Gaussian noise channel (AWGN) [14]. In practical, they are competitive in low signal-to-noise ratio (SNR) channel and strong interference channel as well [15]. They also have advantages in flexible parameter design and construction [16]. However, the traditional coded modulation scheme are usually considered independently for coding and modulation cause they are usually effective for long codes [17]. In this paper, we propose a coded modulation scheme that is similar to traditional convolutional codes. The codeword is recursively generated by encoding the information bits. Different from the traditional convolutional codes, the encoded states are further one-by-one modulated to be modulation symbols. At the receiver, some traditional convolutional suboptimal decoding algorithms [18–20], such as sequential decoding and list decoding, etc., can be efficiently used to decode the code. We further improve the minimum distance of the branch modulated symbols by theoretically give the optimal generator matrix. By numerically comparing with some high-performance short codes, such as polar codes and PAC codes, we finally demonstrate the proposed scheme is promising in application of IoT system.

2   Construction of the Proposed Code

2.1   Encoding and Decoding of the Proposed Code

The diagram of the proposed coding is shown in Fig. 1. The information bits are written in two-dimensional form as $\mathbf{b}_i = \{b_{i,1}, b_{i,2}, \cdots, b_{i,\kappa}\}, i = 1, 2, \cdots, n$. Then a state $\mathbf{s}_i = \{s_{i,1}, s_{i,2}, \cdots, s_{i,n}\}, i = 1, 2, \cdots, n$ can be recursively calculated as

$$\mathbf{s}_i = [\mathbf{s}_{i-1} \ \mathbf{b}_i]\mathbf{G} \tag{1}$$

where $\mathbf{G}$ is the binary generator matrix with dimension $(n+\kappa) \times n$. $\mathbf{s}_0$ is initially set to a random binary vector with length of n. The modulation symbol $c_i, i = 1, 2, \cdots, n$ is calculated as

$$c_i = \frac{\lambda}{2^n}\left(2\sum_{\tau=1}^{n} 2^{\tau-1}s_{i,\tau} - 1\right) \tag{2}$$

So far, we have introduced the basic construction of the proposed code. It is a code with code length n, basic rate $R = \kappa$. The rate can be any adjusted by inserting known bits in $\mathbf{b}_i$.

$\mathbf{G}$ can be further decomposed into the following form:

$$\mathbf{G} = [\mathbf{G}_L \ \mathbf{G}_R]^{\mathrm{T}} \tag{3}$$

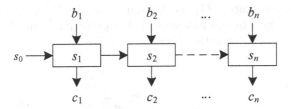

Fig. 1. The diagram of the proposed coding.

where $\mathbf{G}_L$ and $\mathbf{G}_R$ are with dimensions of $n \times n$ and $\kappa \times n$, respectively. Obviously, $\mathbf{G}_L$ is the generator matrix that encodes the information from the previous state $\mathbf{s}_{i-1}$, and $\mathbf{G}_R$ is responsible for encoding the current information bits $\mathbf{b}_i$. Then Eq.(1) can be rewritten as

$$\mathbf{s}_i = \mathbf{s}_{i-1}\mathbf{G}_L \oplus \mathbf{b}_i\mathbf{G}_R = \delta_i \oplus \mathbf{b}_i\mathbf{G}_R \tag{4}$$

where $\delta_i = \mathbf{s}_{i-1}\mathbf{G}_L$ represents the state encoded from all of the past information bits.

We suppose the modulated symbols c_i are transmitted through the AWGN channel as

$$y_i = c_i + n_i \tag{5}$$

where n_i is the noise with mean 0 and variance σ^2. The decoding procedure is similar to the traditional convolutional code. The goal of decoding is to find a minimum global metric from all of the possible transmitting modulated symbols. The global metric formula is calculated as

$$M_{i,j2^\kappa+t} = M_{i-1,j} + m_{i,t} \tag{6}$$

where $M_{i-1,j}$ means the jth, $j = 1, 2, \cdots, \Omega$, global metric related to the $(i-1)$th received symbol and Ω a parameter related to decoding complexity. $m_{i,t}$ represents the tth, $t = 1, 2, \cdots, 2^\kappa$ branch metric related to the ith received symbol. And it is calculated as

$$m_{i,t} = (c_{i,t} - y_i)^2 \tag{7}$$

where $c_{i,t}, t = 1, 2, \cdots, 2^\kappa$ means the possible transmitting symbols related to the ith received symbol. Since Ω grows exponentially along with $n2^\kappa$, we adopt some suboptimal decoding algorithms for convolutional code [18–20], such as sequential decoding and list decoding, etc. to restrict the complexity.

Usually, $\mathbf{G}_L$ is constructed in a random way to randomizing the encoding. However, $\mathbf{G}_R$ with small row size dominating the current modulation symbol c_i performance can be improved by carefully designing.

2.2 Design of $\mathbf{G}_R$

As shown in Fig. 2, while the previous state is randomly transformed to be δ_i by $\mathbf{s}_{i-1}$ times $\mathbf{G}_L$, it outputs 2^κ states $\mathbf{s}_{i,j}, i = 1, 2, \cdots, n, j = 1, 2, \cdots, 2^\kappa$ and 2^κ modulated symbols $c_{i,j}$ corresponding to κ information bits $\mathbf{b}_{i,j}$. Since the designing generator matrix $\mathbf{G}_R$ is the same for all of the encoding stage, we ignore the subscript i in the following. Let superscript $'$ and $''$ means any pair of states, symbols or information bits.

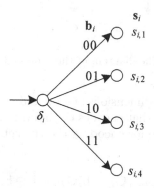

Fig. 2. An example of the branch states.

We define the distance of a pair of current branch modulation symbols (c', c'') as

$$
\begin{aligned}
d(c', c'') &= |c' - c''| \\
&= \left| \frac{\lambda}{2^n} \left(2 \sum_{\tau=1}^{n} 2^{\tau-1} s'_\tau - 1 \right) - \frac{\lambda}{2^n} \left(2 \sum_{\tau=1}^{n} 2^{\tau-1} s''_\tau - 1 \right) \right| \\
&= \frac{\lambda}{2^{n-1}} \left| \sum_{\tau=1}^{n} 2^{\tau-1} (s'_\tau - s''_\tau) \right|
\end{aligned}
\tag{8}
$$

where λ represents the power factor to adjust the average transmission power. When δ and $\mathbf{G}_R$ are given, $d(c', c'')$ is determined by information bits $\mathbf{b}'$ and $\mathbf{b}''$. So for convenience, we use $d(\mathbf{b}', \mathbf{b}'')$ to replace $d(c', c'')$ in the following. The minimum distance of $d(\mathbf{b}', \mathbf{b}'')$ can be written as

$$
d_m = \min_{\mathbf{b}', \mathbf{b}'', \mathbf{b}' \neq \mathbf{b}''} d(\mathbf{b}', \mathbf{b}'')
\tag{9}
$$

We optimize $\mathbf{G}_R$ by maximizing the minimum distance d_m as

$$
D_m = \max_{\mathbf{G}_R} \min_{\mathbf{b}', \mathbf{b}'', \mathbf{b}' \neq \mathbf{b}''} d(\mathbf{b}', \mathbf{b}'')
\tag{10}
$$

In the following, we give two propositions.

Proposition 1. *When* $\mathbf{G}_R = [\mathbf{I}_\kappa \ \mathbf{O}]$, *where* $\mathbf{I}_\kappa$ *is the identity matrix of dimension* κ, $\mathbf{O}$ *is the all-zero matrix of* $\kappa \times (n - \kappa)$, *for any* δ, *the minimum distance of* $d(\mathbf{b}', \mathbf{b}'')$ *is equal to* $\lambda / 2^{\kappa-1}$.

Proof. There are $\mathbf{b}'\mathbf{G}_R = \mathbf{b}'[\mathbf{I}_\kappa \ \mathbf{O}] = [\mathbf{b}' \ \mathbf{O}]$, and $\mathbf{b}''\mathbf{G}_R = \mathbf{b}''[\mathbf{I}_\kappa \ \mathbf{O}] = [\mathbf{b}'' \ \mathbf{O}]$. Then $\mathbf{s}' = \delta \oplus \mathbf{b}'\mathbf{G}_R = \delta \oplus [\mathbf{b}' \ \mathbf{O}]$ and $\mathbf{s}'' = \delta \oplus \mathbf{b}''\mathbf{G}_R = \delta \oplus [\mathbf{b}'' \ \mathbf{O}]$ whose elements are

$$s'_\tau = \begin{cases} \delta_\tau \oplus b'_\tau & , \tau \leq \kappa \\ 0 & , \tau > \kappa \end{cases} \tag{11}$$

and

$$s''_\tau = \begin{cases} \delta_\tau \oplus b''_\tau & , \tau \leq \kappa \\ 0 & , \tau > \kappa \end{cases} \tag{12}$$

Then

$$
\begin{aligned}
d(\mathbf{b}', \mathbf{b}'') &= \frac{\lambda}{2^{n-1}} \left| \sum_{\tau=1}^{n} 2^{\tau-1}(s'_\tau - s''_\tau) \right| \\
&= \frac{\lambda}{2^{n-1}} \left| \sum_{\tau=1}^{\kappa} 2^{n-\kappa-\tau}(\delta_\tau \oplus b'_\tau - \delta_\tau \oplus b''_\tau) \right| \\
&= \frac{\lambda}{2^{\kappa-1}} \left| \sum_{\tau=1}^{\kappa} 2^{\tau-1}(b'_\tau - b''_\tau) \right| \\
&\geq \frac{\lambda}{2^{\kappa-1}}
\end{aligned}
\tag{13}
$$

iff $b_1! = b''_1, b'_\tau = b''_\tau, \tau > 1, d(\mathbf{b}', \mathbf{b}'') = \lambda / 2^{\kappa-1}$.

Proposition 2. *There doesn't exist* $\mathbf{G}_R$ *for any* δ *such that* $d_m > \lambda / 2^{\kappa-1}$.

Proof. Assuming that there is a $\mathbf{G}_R$ such that $d_m > \lambda / 2^{\kappa-1}$, since the elementary transformation of matrices will not reduce the minimum distance, we can carry out the elementary transformation $\mathbf{G}_R$ to the systematic code form as $\mathbf{G}_R = [\mathbf{I}_k \ \varepsilon]$ where ε is a binary matrix of $\kappa \times (n-\kappa)$. Obviously, according to Proposition 1, ε must be a nonzero matrix. Otherwise, its minimum distance is equal to $\lambda / 2^{\kappa-1}$, then $[\mathbf{b}' \ \mathbf{G}_R] = [\mathbf{b}' \ \varphi']$, and $[\mathbf{b}'' \ \mathbf{G}_R] = [\mathbf{b}'' \ \varphi'']$, φ' and φ'' are a nonzero vector of length $n - \kappa$, and they are not equal, then

$$
d(\mathbf{b}', \mathbf{b}'') =
$$

$$
\frac{\lambda}{2^{n-1}} \left| \sum_{\tau=1}^{\kappa} 2^{n-\kappa+\tau-1}(b'_\tau - b_\tau'') + \sum_{\tau=1}^{n-\kappa} 2^{\tau-1}(\delta_\tau \oplus \varphi'_\tau - \delta_\tau \oplus \varphi_\tau'') \right| \tag{14}
$$

$$
= \frac{\lambda}{2^{n-1}} |\Delta_1 + \Delta_2|
$$

Clearly, $|\Delta_1| \leq 2^{n-\kappa}$. In order to make the minimum distance of $d(\mathbf{b}', \mathbf{b}'')$ greater than $\lambda / 2^{\kappa-1}$, it means that when Δ_1 taking the minimum value, Δ_2 must be greater than 0. Assuming that there is a vector δ such that Δ_2 is greater than 0, then with the negation of δ, we have

$$
\begin{aligned}
\bar{\Delta}_2 &= \sum_{\tau=1}^{n-\kappa} 2^{\tau-1}(\bar{\delta} \oplus \varphi' - \bar{\delta} \oplus \varphi'') \\
&= -\sum_{\tau=1}^{n-\kappa} 2^{\tau-1}(\delta \oplus \varphi' - \delta \oplus \varphi'') \\
&= -\Delta_2
\end{aligned}
\tag{15}
$$

In this case, $\bar{\Delta}_2$ is less than 0. So there is no $\mathbf{G}_R$ for any δ such that $d_m > \lambda/2^{\kappa-1}$.

It concludes that the maximum distance equaling $\lambda/2^{\kappa-1}$ can be achieved by simply setting $\mathbf{G}_R = [\mathbf{I}_\kappa \ \mathbf{O}]$.

3   Numerical Results

In this section, we will give some simulations to show the advantage of the proposed code. We choose a polar code and a PAC code for the comparison. The basic simulation parameters including the length of the codeword and the length of the information bits are 128 and 40 for the three codes. The channel we choose is AWGN channel. In particular, the construction methods of the polar code and the PAC code are Gaussian approximation and Reed-Muller Gaussian approximation, respectively. For the polar code, we use 4-bit CRC aided to improve the performance. Correspondingly, a CRC-aided list successive cancellation algorithm with list length of 32 is used to decode the code. For the PAC code, the decoding algorithm is list successive cancellation. For the proposed code, to keep the same of code length and rate, we let $\kappa = 1$ and set 40 zeros by equal interval among the first 80 information bits and append 48 zeros at the end of information bits as tail bits. The decoding algorithm we choose is list decoding algorithm. The final simulation results in terms of block error rate (BLER) are shown in Fig. 3. From this figure, we can see that the three codes show very close performance in the low SNR regime. But in high SNR regime, say, 0.5dB $\sim$ 1dB, the polar code performs slightly worse than the others. And the proposed code has almost the same performance with the PAC code. But the proposed code is with advantage in flexible construction and parameter design. Any codes with various lengths and rates can be constructed in real time, which is very competitive in IoT system.

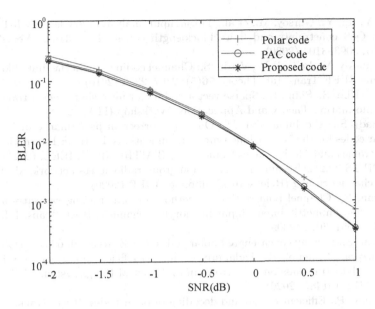

Fig. 3. BLER performance comparison among the polar code, the PAC code and the proposed code.

4 Conclusions

To meet the requirement of channel coding in IoT system, we study a coded modulation scheme for short packet with high reliability and flexible construction. Different from the traditional coded modulation schemes, the modulated symbols are generated one-by-one directly from the encoded states. The state is generated similar to the traditional convolutional codes. Accordingly, some traditional convolutional suboptimal decoding algorithms, such as sequential decoding and list decoding, etc., can be used to decode the code. By theoretically design the optimal generator matrix, we further improve the minimum distance among the branch modulated symbols. Finally, we give some numerical results to compare BLER performance with some high-performance short codes, such as polar code and PAC code and demonstrate the applicability of the proposed scheme in IoT system.

References

1. 3GPP TR 38.913: Study on scenarios and requirements for next generation access technologies (Release 14) (2016)
2. Vaezi, M., et al.: Cellular, Wide-Area, and Non-Terrestrial IoT: a survey on 5G advances and the road toward 6G. IEEE Commun. Surv. Tutorials **24**(2), 1117–1174 (2022)
3. ITU-R M.2410-0: Minimum requirements related to technical performance for IMT-2020 radio interface(s) (2017)

 4. Hu, Y., Li, Y., Gursoy, M., et al.: Throughput analysis of low-latency IoT systems with QoS constraints and finite blocklength codes. IEEE Trans. Veh. Technol. **69**(3), 3093–3104 (2020)
 5. Polyanskiy, Y., Poor, H.V., Verdu, S.: Channel coding rate in the finite blocklength regime. IEEE Trans. Inf. Theory **56**(5), 2307–2359 (2010)
 6. Ji, H., Kim, S., Shim, B.: Sparse vector coding for ultra short packet transmission. In: Information Theory and Applications Workshop (ITA) (2018)
 7. Belhadj, S., Abdelmounaim, M.: On error correction performance of LDPC and Polar codes for the 5G machine type communications. In: IEEE International IOT, Electronics and Mechatronics Conference (IEMTRONICS). IEEE, (2021)
 8. 3GPP TS 38.212: Technical specification group radio access network; Multiplexing and channel coding (Release16). Valbonne: 3GPP (2020)
 9. Arıkan, E.: Channel polarization: a method for constructing capacity- achieving codes for symmetric binary-input memoryless channels. IEEE Trans. Inf. Theory **55**(7), 3051–3073 (2009)
10. Arikan, E.: Serially concatenated polar codes. IEEE Access **6**, 64549–64555 (2018)
11. Zakariyya, R., Jewel, K., Fadamiro, et al.: An efficient polar coding scheme for uplink data transmission in narrowband internet of things systems. IEEE Access **8**, 191472–191481 (2020)
12. Trifonov, P.: Efficient design and decoding of polar codes. IEEE Trans. Commun. **60**(11), 3221–3227 (2012)
13. Rowshan, M., Viterbo, E.: On convolutional precoding in PAC codes. In: IEEE Globecom Workshops, pp. 1–6. IEEE, (2021)
14. Shannon, C.: Probability of error for optimal codes in a Gaussian channel. Bell Syst. Tech. J. **38**, 611–656 (1959)
15. Ungerboeck, G.: Channel coding with multilevel phase signals. IEEE Trans. Inf. Theory IT **28**(1), 55–67 (1982)
16. Perry, J., Balakrishnan, H., Shah, D.: Rateless spinal codes. In: Proceedings of the 10th ACM Workshop on Hot Topics in Networks. ACM, (2011)
17. Li, P., Tong, J., Yuan, X., Guo, Q.: Superposition coded modulation and iterative linear MMSE detection. IEEE J. Selected Areas in Comm. **27**(6), 995–1004 (2009)
18. Fano, R.: A heuristic discussion of probabilistic decoding. IEEE Trans. Inf. Theory **9**(2), 64–74 (1963)
19. Tal, I., A. Vardy, A.: List decoding of polar codes. IEEE Trans. Inf. Theory **61**(5), 2213–2226 (2015)
20. Rowshan, M., Burg, A., Viterbo, E.: Polarization-adjusted convolutional (PAC) codes: sequential decoding vs list decoding. IEEE Trans. Veh. Tech. **70**(2), 1434–1447 (2021)

A Resource- and Power-Efficient Implementation of PSS Synchronization on FPGA in Vehicular Networks

Chengxiang Ge[1], Fei Peng[1], Shan Cao[1], Zhiyuan Jiang[1(✉)], and Terng-Yin Hsu[2]

[1] School of Communication and Information Engineering, Shanghai University, Shanghai 200444, China
jiangzhiyuan@shu.edu.cn
[2] Department of Computer Science, National Chiao Tung University, Hsinchu, Taiwan

Abstract. This paper proposes a resource- and power-efficient implementation of primary synchronization signal (PSS) synchronization on FPGA in vehicular networks. Firstly, the received signal is preprocessed. Secondly, the synchronization signal is detected and its timing position is calculated. Thirdly, a sequence is extracted for frequency offset estimation. Finally, the received original signal is marked with the frame header and compensated with proper frequency offset. The hardware implementation scheme is based on FPGA and uses the advantages of FPGA high-speed pipeline computing to realize real-time sampling and synchronization of transmitter and receiver, the consumption of Slice Look-Up-Table (LUT) is 9545 and the total on-chip power is 1.213 w.

Keywords: Synchronization · FPGA · Primary Synchronization Signal(PSS)

1 Introduction

Long term evolution vehicle (LTE-V) is an emerging vehicular communication technology that is widely-adopted by many countries. LTE-V (Release 14) [1] which often referred to Cellular V2X (C-V2X) technology is defined in the 3rd Generation Partnership Project (3GPP) community. V2X means that it can realize vehicle to everything communication including vehicle to vehicle, vehicle to pedestrian, vehicle to network, vehicle to cloud, and vehicle to infrastructure. LTE based C-V2X allows vehicles to communicate with each other directly without the need for base station infrastructures and is expected to be a critical enabler for connected and autonomous vehicles [5]. Through the wireless network, vehicle shares basic information such as position and vehicle speed with the surrounding vehicles, so that driver can know the vehicle's position and status around [3]. LTE-V technology is based on OFDM technology, which requires the use of synchronization technology in the design of the receiver to ensure the strict orthogonality of the transmitted signal and the received signal.

K. Rabie et al. (Eds.): IoTaaS 2022, LNICST 506, pp. 135–147, 2023.
https://doi.org/10.1007/978-3-031-37139-4_13

This paper proposes a resource- and power-efficient implementation of Primary Synchronization Signal (PSS) synchronization on FPGA in vehicular networks. Firstly, the received signal is preprocessed. Second, the synchronization signal is detected and its position in the time domain is calculated. Thirdly, a sequence is extracted for frequency offset estimation. Finally, the received original signal is marked with frame header and proper frequency offset compensation is carried out to prepare for subsequent decoding operations. The hardware implementation scheme is based on FPGA, which uses the advantages of FPGA high-speed pipeline computing to achieve real-time sampling and synchronization of transmitter and receiver. The consumption of Slice Look-Up-Table (LUT) is 9545 and the total on-chip power is 1.213 w.

2   Physical Layer of LTE-V

In this section, a brief introduction of LTE-V frame structure and Synchronous signal structure are provided.

2.1   LTE-V Frame Structure

The frame structure of LTE-V is shown in Fig. 1. T_f is the period of a wireless frame, T_s is the period of each signal sampling point. A wireless frame consists of 20 slots with a total length of 10 ms. Every two slots form a subframe with a length of $30720T_s$, which is 1 ms. Each subframe consists of 14 Single-carrier Frequency-Division Multiple Access (SC-FDMA) symbols where 9 symbols are available for data transmission [2]. The synchronization technique is used to mark the frame header of the frame to ensure that the receiver can determine the starting point of each received signal subframe.

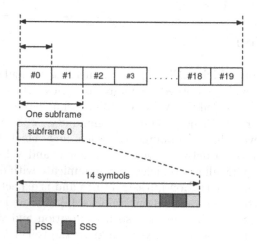

Fig. 1. LTE-V frame structure and position of synchronization signal.

2.2   Synchronization Sequence

This paper studies the detection of PSS. As shown in Fig. 1, the signal is transmitted on the second and third SC-FDMA symbols of subframe 0, which are adjacent to each other. PSS sequence is generated in frequency domain by using Zadoff Chu sequence [6], which has good mutual property and can resist certain noise and frequency offset. The expression generated by PSS sequence is defined as

$$d_u(n) = \begin{cases} e^{-j\frac{\pi u n(n+1)}{63}} & n = 0, 1, 2, \ldots, 30 \\ e^{-j\frac{\pi u n(n+1)(n+1)}{63}} & n = 31, 32, 33, \ldots, 61 \end{cases} , \tag{1}$$

where u is the root index of different Zadoff Chu sequence, and n is the index of each point of the sequence, this paper choose two sequences, which respectively corresponding to the sequence generated by $u = 26$ and $u = 37$.

2.3   Frequency Offset

In the process of signal transmission, due to Doppler effect and clock source error between transmitter and receiver, the received signal will have frequency offset relative to the signal sent by transmitter. It can be judged intuitively by analyzing the spectrum diagram. Frequency offset will cause Cyclic Redundancy Check (CRC) failure at the receiver, and the packet cannot be solved correctly. Therefore, in synchronization technology, frequency offset estimation is necessary for the received signal at the receiver, and original signal need to be compensated with proper frequency offset.

3   Proposed Synchronization Method

3.1   Traditional Synchronization Methods

The traditional synchronization method mainly includes correlation calculation and traversing the calculation results to find the maximum value, in which correlation calculation includes cross-correlation, auto-correlation and partial cross-correlation [4], such as (2), (3), (4).

$$R = \max_n \left[\left| \sum_{i=0}^{N_{FFT}-1} Y(i)X^*(i+n) \right|^2 \right], \tag{2}$$

$$R = \max_n \left[\left| \sum_{i=0}^{N_{FFT}/2-1} Y(i+n)Y^* \left[(N_{FFT} - i) + n \right] \right|^2 \right], \tag{3}$$

$$R = \max_{n} \left[\sum_{m=0}^{N_{PB}-1} \left| \sum_{i=m(N_{FFT}/N_{PB})}^{\frac{(m+1)N_{FFT}}{N_{PB}}-1} Y(i)X^*(i+n) \right|^2 \right], \qquad (4)$$

where R is the calculated correlation peak value result, $X(i)$ is the local reference PSS signal, and $Y(i)$ is the received signal containing PSS information. The first cross-correlation algorithm cross correlates the received signal containing PSS information with the local PSS sequence, and then traverses all the results to get the maximum value. The second auto-correlation method is to auto correlate the received signal containing PSS information, and also to traverse all results to find the maximum value. The third kind of partial correlation splits the first kind of cross-correlation algorithm into multiple segments for cross correlation, then sums each result up, and finally traverses to get the maximum value.

The above three methods can calculate the location of the PSS, however, if use FPGA to achieve these methods directly, the resource consumption is large. Therefore, a new synchronization method is proposed in this paper, which uses cross-correlation to resist the interference of frequency offset and noise, and uses the characteristics of PSS cross-correlation peak to determine the peak only by local traversal, and it is convenient for hardware implementation.

3.2 Proposed Correlation Method

The cross correlation algorithm selects two segments of signals in time domain for cross correlation and then sum the results up, which can resist the influence of frequency offset. The receiver performs real-time cross-correlation between the received signal and the locally stored PSS sequence, and calculates the energy of the signal. By comparing the peak value of the cross-correlation result and the result of energy calculation, the location of the PSS is realized. The calculation formula is as follows

$$R_{pss128}(n) = \left| \sum_{i=0}^{127} d_{pre}(n+i) \cdot S_{pss128*}(i) \right|^2 +$$

$$\left| \sum_{i=0}^{127} d_{pre}\left(n + \frac{2048+144}{16} + i\right) \cdot S_{pss128*}^{*}(i) \right|^2, \qquad (5)$$

where n is the index of each cross correlation calculation result, i is the serial number of 128 sampling points selected for calculation, $d_{pre}(i)$ is the signal generated by low-pass filtering and down sampling of the original signal received by the receiver, $S_{pss128}(i)^*$ is the reference primary synchronous sequence generated according to the protocol and stored locally.

The pre-processed received signal is cross-correlated with the local reference PSS sequence to determine whether there is PSS in the corresponding original signal. Since two PSS reference sequences with different root indexes are selected when designing the physical layer protocol, two synchronization sequences are used for parallel calculation. The expression of the energy calculation of the received signal is as follows as

$$E(n) = \sum_{i=0}^{127} |d_{pre}(n + i)|^2$$

$$+ \sum_{i=0}^{127} |d_{pre}(n + (2048 + 144)/16 + i)|^2. \tag{6}$$

where n is the index of the sample points. In order to compare with the cross-correlation results, 128 sampling points are selected for calculation. The energy result is obtained after the auto-correlation calculation of the received signal d_{pre}. Two sequences in the time domain is taken here. If the real-time cross-correlation result and the energy calculation result meet (7) and (8), it is considered that the peak value of the synchronization signal has been detected.

$$R_{pss128}(r) > \varepsilon \cdot E(r). \tag{7}$$

$$R_{result}(r) = \max_{n} [(R_{pss128}(r)]. \tag{8}$$

Where r is the index of corresponding position, ε is the energy threshold coefficient, which will be fine-tuned according to the specific hardware implementation results, n is the number of sampling points. The starting position of the synchronization signal can be obtained by selecting the maximum peak value within the length of half subframe $15360T_s$ in the time domain, as shown in (8).

3.3   Frequency Offset Estimation and Compensation Algorithm

The frequency offset compensation of the signal needs to be implemented to avoid the subsequent decoding affected by the frequency offset of the received signal in the actual transmission process. Therefore, after the synchronization correlation is completed, it is necessary to estimate the frequency offset of a sequence corresponding to the peak's position in the original input signal, and the calculation formula is shown as

$$C_{pss} = \sum_{i=0}^{63} (d_{new}(i) \cdot S_{pss128}{}^*(i))^* \cdot$$

$$(d_{new}(i + 64) \cdot S_{pss128}{}^*(i + 64)). \tag{9}$$

$$FFO_1 = \frac{1}{\pi} \operatorname{angle}(C_{pss}). \tag{10}$$

where $d_{new}(i)$ is the signal after the input signal is filtered and 16 times down sampled. The starting position is the position of the PSS. $S_{pss128}{}^*(i)$ is the conjugate of the primary synchronization sequence stored locally in Read-Only

Memory (ROM). C_{pss} is the cumulative value of frequency offset calculation. The frequency offset value FFO_1 of decimal times can be calculated by calculating the arc-tangent of C_{pss}. After the frequency offset estimation is completed, the original signal is compensated for the frequency offset according to the value of the frequency offset estimation. The compensation formula is as follows

$$d_{out}(n) = d_{in}(n)e^{-j2\pi\varepsilon\frac{n}{N}}, \tag{11}$$

where $d_{in}(n)$ is the input of frequency offset compensation and $d_{out}(n)$ is the output, ε is the normalized frequency offset. N is the number of Fast Fourier Transform (FFT) points, and n is the index.

3.4   Simulation Result

The implementation of the proposed algorithm is on MATLAB R2019a. In this paper, two PSS sequences generated by the different root index are adopted, and one of them is detected in Fig. 2. It can be seen that a main peak value and two secondary peaks are detected. If no synchronization signal is detected, the cross-correlation result is shown in Fig. 3.

Compared with the three methods mentioned above, the algorithm used in this paper only uses 128 points, taking into account the frequency offset resistance and the complexity of hardware implementation. Figure 4 shows the cross-correlation results of 128 points without segmentation (M = 1), with two segments (M = 2) and with four segments (M = 4), respectively. Where M is the number of segments. When M = 2, the signal with length of 128 points is divided into two data with length of 64 points for cross-correlation calculation. Theoretically, the more the number of segments, the stronger the anti-noise ability of cross-correlation. However, given the complexity of the hardware implementation, the non-segmented (M = 1) approach is chosen here.

4   Hardware Implementation Structure

4.1   Proposed Hardware Implementation Method

Hardware implementation is based on the proposed synchronization algorithm, and the implementation block diagram is shown in Fig. 5. Divided by function, there are three main modules: synchronization module, frequency offset estimation and compensation module, and timing mark module. In the synchronization module, signal preprocessing, cross-correlation calculation, energy calculation and peak value comparison functions are completed. In the frequency offset estimation and compensation module, a segment of signal is extracted according to the position of the PSS to estimate the frequency offset and compensate the frequency offset of the original signal. Finally, the frame header is marked in the timing marking module to facilitate subsequent processing.

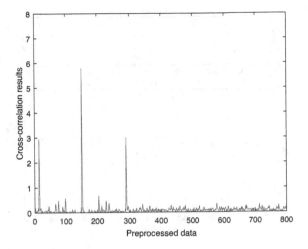

Fig. 2. Cross correlation results when PSS is detected.

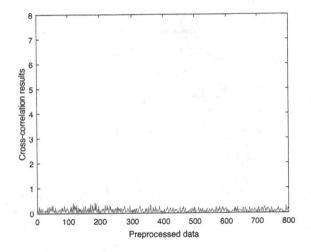

Fig. 3. Cross correlation results when no PSS is detected.

4.2 Implementation of Cross-Correlation

The calculation of Finite Impulse Response (FIR) is shown in (12) as

$$y(k) = \sum_{n=0}^{N-1} a(n)x(k-n) \quad k = 0, 1, \ldots. \tag{12}$$

where $x(k-n)$ is the input data, $y(k)$ is the output of FIR IP, $a(n)$ is the tap coefficients, and N is the filter order.

Since the calculation method of cross correlation is very similar to that of FIR, this paper uses FIR IP core to complete the calculation of cross correlation.

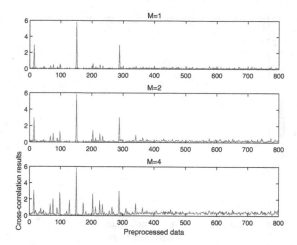

Fig. 4. Cross correlation results with different number of segments.

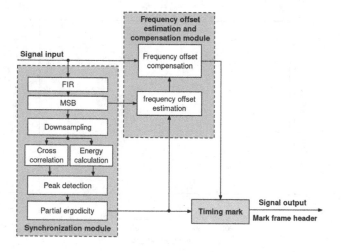

Fig. 5. Hardware implementation structure.

Figure 6 is the implementation structure of FIR. In the actual FPGA design, the FIR IP core will adopt a more optimized structure to realize the automatic selection of the smallest time-sharing multiplication and accumulation unit according to the user-specified throughput, and then optimize the use of the final hardware resources. Since the form of the input data is a complex number, the original algorithm needs to be processed accordingly to facilitate the implementation of FPGA. Assume that $X(k)$ and $Y(k)$ are two complex numbers, according to the multiplication association law, the complex multiplication of each point can be split to calculate the real part and imaginary part of the complex multiplication result, which can be expressed as

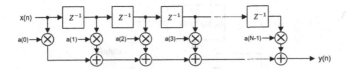

Fig. 6. Implementation of FIR.

$$Y(k) \cdot X^*(k) = [Y_r(k) + Y_i(k) \cdot j] \cdot [X_r(k) - X_i(k) \cdot j]$$
$$= [Y_r(k) \cdot X_i(k) + Y_i(k) \cdot X_i(k)]$$
$$+ [Y_i(k) \cdot X_r(k) - Y_r(k) \cdot X_i(k)] \cdot j. \qquad (13)$$

The real and imaginary parts of the local reference PSS sequence are respectively imported into two FIR IP cores as the tap coefficients of FIR. Each FIR IP core is configured as two channels with the same tap coefficients, so that the real and imaginary parts of the final cross-correlation results can be calculated, as shown in Fig. 7.

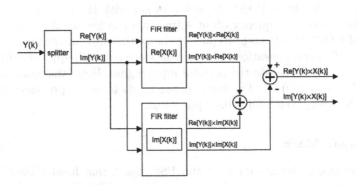

Fig. 7. Cross correlation implementation architecture using FIR IP core.

4.3   Energy Calculation

According to (6), the implementation structure of energy calculation is shown in Fig. 8. Two segments of signals are selected for calculation in the time domain. The final energy calculation result is obtained by adding the calculation results of the first segment of signals and the second segment of signals in the Random Access Memory (RAM) buffer.

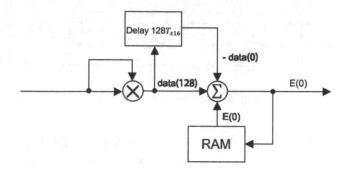

Fig. 8. Energy calculation architecture.

4.4 Frequency Offset Estimation and Compensation

Refer to (9) (10), the architecture of frequency offset estimation is shown in Fig. 9. Use RAM to buffer the preprocessed signal. When the location of the synchronization signal is detected, the 128 point data at the corresponding location are extracted from RAM and dot product with the local reference PSS in ROM. The result of frequency offset estimation can be calculated by ARCTAN module of CORDIC IP core. Figure 10 shows the implementation structure of frequency offset compensation. The calculation result of frequency offset estimation is used to compensate the original input signal. Here, the rotation mode of CORDIC IP core is used. The input phase needs to be preprocessed to $(-\pi, \pi)$ to meet the configured CORDIC input range.

4.5 Timing Mark

After completing the detection of the PSS, the frame header position of the next subframe can be deduced according to the LTE-V frame structure and the position of the synchronization signal. As shown in Fig. 11, point A is the position of the PSS, and point B is the moment when the synchronization signal is detected. The frame header of the next subframe is after the delay t, which is the position of point C. The relative positions of A, B and C are fixed, and the delay parameter t is a fixed number that can be calculated. As shown in Fig. 3 above, cross correlation may calculate multiple peaks, including the main peak and the secondary peak, and the correct location is the location of the main peak. Traditional methods determine the maximum peak value by traversing all the results, but consume too much hardware resources. The method proposed in this paper makes use of the characteristics of synchronous signals. The distance between the first sub peak and the last peak is within the length of half sub frame, therefore, only half the length of the sub frame after the first sub peak need to be selected for traversal.

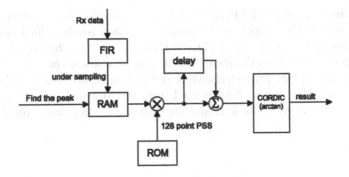

Fig. 9. Architecture of frequency offset estimation.

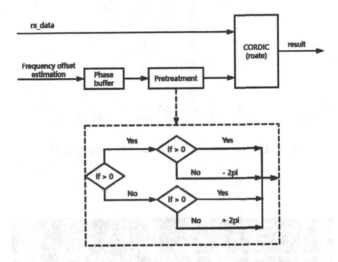

Fig. 10. Architecture of frequency offset compensation.

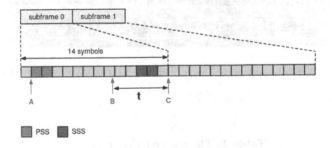

Fig. 11. Timing mark.

5 FPGA Implementation Results

FPGA implementation includes Register Transfer Level (RTL) coding, the simulation and comprehensive implementation on VIVADO 2019.1, and the test on a Xilinx Virtex-7 XC7Z035FFG676-2 FPGA. The simulation results are shown in Fig. 12, where the output is the cross-correlation result, which is consistent with the simulation results of MATLAB R2019a. The final test result on FPGA is shown in Fig. 13, where the frame header can be marked correctly. The overall test in the subsequent project shows that the two boards is correctly synchronized and the video can be transmitted from transmitter to receiver. Resource consumption is shown in Table 1, and the energy consumption analysis is shown in Fig. 14.

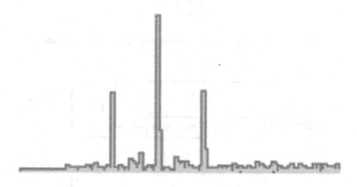

Fig. 12. Simulation result on VIVADO 2019.1.

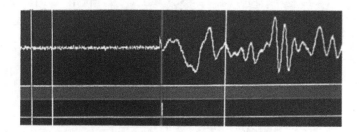

Fig. 13. Test result on a Xilinx Virtex-7 XC7Z035FFG676-2 FPGA.

Table 1. The resource consumption

TYPE	Slice LUTs	Slice Registers	Block RAM Tile
number	9545	11549	14

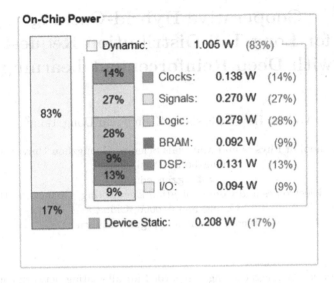

Fig. 14. Energy consumption analysis.

6   Conclusion

Based on the structure of LTE-V physical layer and the characteristics of the synchronization signal, a resource- and power-efficient implementation of PSS synchronization on FPGA in vehicular networks is proposed. Referring to traditional algorithm, an optimized method has been developed, which is suitable for implementation for FPGA. After completing comprehensive simulation analysis on MATLAB R2019a and digital Design on VIVADO 2019.1, this method is finally tested on a Xilinx Virtex-7 XC7Z035FFG676-2 FPGA. Evaluations based on test results show that the proposed design work well in LTE-V system.

References

1. Study on lte-based v2x services (v14.0.0 release 14) 3gpp (2016)
2. Physical channels and modulation (release 14) (2018)
3. et al, Z.Y.: Implementing its applications by lte-v2x equipment-challenges and opportunities, pp. 120–124 (2018)
4. M. J. Shim, J. S. Han, H.J.R., Choi, H.J.: A frequency synchronization method for 3gpp lte ofdma system in tdd mode, pp. 864–868 (2009)
5. Saifuddin, M., Zaman, M., Toghi, B., Fallah, Y.P., Rao, J.: Performance analysis of cellular-v2x with adaptive & selective power control, pp. 1–7 (2020)
6. Popovic, B.M., Berggren, F.: Primary synchronization signal in e-utra. In: 2008 IEEE 10th International Symposium on Spread Spectrum Techniques and Applications, pp. 426–430 (2008)

Cooperative Hybrid-Caching for Long-Tail Distribution Request with Deep Reinforcement Learning

Weibao He[1][✉], Fasheng Zhou[2], and Dong Tang[2]

[1] School of Physics and Materials Science, Guangzhou University,
Guangzhou 510006, China
`hwb@e.gzhu.edu.cn`
[2] School of Electronics and Communication Engineering, Guangzhou University,
Guangzhou 510006, China
`{zhoufs,tangdong}@gzhu.edu.cn`

Abstract. Wireless caching is regarded for alleviating network congestion in next-generation communications. In this work, we focus on the impact of input data non-uniformity on neural network training when using deep learning to solve the wireless cache strategy. In particular, in wireless caching, the assumed user request is generally a classical long-tailed distribution: Zipf law. We address this problem from cache models and deep reinforcement learning models. On the one hand, base station will prefetch partial most popular contents on the user side to reduce the partiality of caching strategies. On the other hand, the trick of deep long-tail learning is added to prevent the neural network from been over-fitting caused by inputs are concentrated in the most popular files. The performance for different reinforcement learning methods is analyzed, which show that our method can achieve better performance and latency than the existing content caching.

Keywords: Edge caching · Deep reinforcement learning · Deep long-tail learning

1 Introduction

Wireless network devices and traffic will expand exponentially over the next generation of mobile communications. Specifically, the proportion of streaming media in cellular network traffic is growing rapidly [1]. Wireless caching is promised as a technique to improve network resource utilization because it can cache popular contents with off-peak traffic and make cache strategy. When users ask for popular content, the base station(BS) sends it directly via the wireless link, which reduces the peak connecting traffic. What's more, the neighboring BS may share the cached content via wired or wireless links to expand the service's capacity and coverage.

© ICST Institute for Computer Sciences, Social Informatics and Telecommunications Engineering 2023
Published by Springer Nature Switzerland AG 2023. All Rights Reserved
K. Rabie et al. (Eds.): IoTaaS 2022, LNICST 506, pp. 148–160, 2023.
https://doi.org/10.1007/978-3-031-37139-4_14

In general, caching strategy depends not only on the content popularity, but also on the BS-user channel, BS capacity, wireless cooperative network topology, etc. At the same time, the content of the Internet changes rapidly, and it is necessary to redesign the caching strategy between BSs periodically to suit the environment. Deep reinforcement learning (DRL) has strong adaptability to the environment, and it will be effective to solve the wireless cache strategy [2]. In [3], the authors use long short term memory (LSTM) and supervised deep deterministic policy gradient (SDDPG) to learn the caching strategy based on time-variant content popularity.

However, since the distribution of popular contents is non-uniform, taking user requests as observations may make the neural network too dependent on the most popular contents [4]. Referring to Deep long-tail learning for visual recognition [5], commonly used solutions include meta reinforcement learning [6], weight balance [7], etc. However, not all methods can be applied to DRL. Motivated by this, we strive to balance the contribution between the most popular content and the less popular content, which includes the innovations in cache model and proposed DRL method. In this work, we reconsider the reward, state and action design in DRL and based on the deep deterministic policy gradient [8] (DDPG) algorithm, transform anti-longtail techniques to obtain the proposed method. The main components of our contributions includes:

1) Considering a hybrid-caching model, which the BS can prefetch the most popular contents to users. In this way, wireless caching can further reduce the delay caused by the most popular contents and cut down the weight of the most popular contents.
2) A DDPG-based DRL method is proposed to solve the formulated problem, which can achieve advanced low-latency performance compared to tradition DRL method.
3) For popular streaming media data, the user's request delay for the most popular contents will be zero, and the dependence of the BS on the most popular contents in proposed method will be reduced.

Notations: $A >> B$ denotes that A is far greater than B; while $<<$ is far smaller than. $\mathbb{E}$ is the expectation operator. ∇_θ denotes the gradient with respect to θ, and $A|B$ denotes the event A conditioned on B.

2   System Model

2.1   Wireless Model

The considered centralized wireless hybrid-caching model contains M base stations(BSs) and U users, denoted by $\Phi_M = \{1, 2, \ldots, M\}$ and $\Phi_U = \{1, 2, \ldots, U\}$, respectively. The service distance of each BS is limited within l_p. Assuming that the distance between BS m and user u is l_{mu}. Therefore, the user served by m-th BS is denoted by U_m, which the set is defined by $\Phi_U^{(m)} \triangleq \{l_{um} < l_p, u \in \Phi_U\}$. Consider the achievable radio data rate between BS m and user u with transmission bandwidth B is denoted by:

$$R_{mu} = B \log(1 + \frac{P_t l_{mu}^{-\alpha}}{\sigma^2}), \tag{1}$$

where P_t is transmit power, α is path-loss factor and σ^2 is the power of noise. For BSs cooperative cache scenario, assume that the BSs cooperate over a wireless link. The achievable radio data rate with bandwidth of B_{co} and the distance between neighboring BSs l_{co} is denoted by

$$R_{co} = B_{co} \log(1 + \frac{P_t l_{co}^{-\alpha}}{\sigma^2}). \tag{2}$$

Assuming that users are randomly spread across the service area of the BS, and the distance between neighboring BSs will not change. Depending on the different distances between users, the BS should adopt a reasonable cache strategy to minimize the transmission delay.

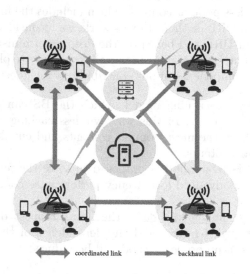

coordinated link   backhaul link

Fig. 1. A centralized coordinated hybrid-caching network.

2.2   Caching Model

As shown in Fig. 1, we show the centralized wireless hybrid-caching model. Assuming that BSs can collaborate to serve users, meanwhile users also have extremely limited cache space for BS prefetch popular contents to reduce delay. The user cache can effectively reduce the rely of the learning algorithm to the most popular contents. The capacity of BS and user m are denoted by C_{BS} and C_u. In particular, there is a central control unit (CU) in the model, which estimate the caching strategies of each BS through global channel information and user requests. Assuming that the total number of content and the set of content are denoted by F and $\mathcal{F}$. To simplify analysis, assume that each content size is Z bits. Practically, the capacity of BS is generally smaller than the content number and the capacity of user is much smaller than BS *i.e.*, $F > C_{BS} \gg C_u \geq 0$.

Since user cache capacity is extremely limited, we divide a content into K parts and the user only cache the first part of each content. Assuming that the physical capacity of user is C_{user}, then, the capacity of user is denoted by $C_u = KC_{real}$. In this way, on the one hand, the partial cache will expanded the cache range. On the other hand, the stored contents can also reduce the user delay to 0 for streaming video or audio.

The BS cache strategy in time slot t in denoted by $\mathbb{A}^t = \{0,1\}^{M \times F}$, with each of element $a^t_{m,f} = 1$ indicating content f is cached in BS m in time slot t if $a^t_{m,f} = 1$ or otherwise not if $a^t_{m,f} = 0$. The user request in time slot t can be similarly defined by $\mathbb{B}^t = \{0,1\}^{U \times F}$ where each element $b^t_{u,f} = 1$ or 0 indicating that the g-th content is requested by user u in time slot t or not. The user cache in time slot t can be similarly defined by $\mathbb{G}^t = \{0,1\}^{U \times F}$ where each element $g^t_{u,f} = 1$ or 0 indicating that the g-th content cached by user u in time slot t or not. The contents are sorted in descending order by their popularity, and obey the classic long-tailed distribution : Zipf distribution, which can be expressed by:

$$P_i = \frac{i^{-\gamma}}{\sum_{j=1}^{F} j^{-\gamma}} \forall i \in \mathcal{F}, \tag{3}$$

where γ is Zipf factor. The larger γ is, the more request probability will concentrate on the most popular contents.

When contents are cached in a nearby BS instead of a service BS, the service BS will fetch the contents through a cooperative BS-BS link. Therefore, the CU can jointly design the cache strategies for each BS.

3   Problem Analysis and Formulation

As stated in system model, we aim to design a global cache strategy to minimize the overall transmission delay.

The wireless link delay for content transmission between BS m and user u can be defined as:

$$d^{dir}_{u,m} = \frac{Z}{R_{mu}} = \frac{Z}{B \log(1 + \frac{P_t l_{um}^{-\alpha}}{\sigma^2})}, \tag{4}$$

Considering the user u cache, when the user requests content f in time slot t, the wireless link delay is:

$$d^{dir}_{m,u,f} = \begin{cases} d^{dir}_{u,m} & g^t_{u,f} = 0 \\ \frac{K-1}{K} d^{dir}_{u,m} & g^t_{u,f} = 1. \end{cases} \tag{5}$$

Meanwhile, the set of wireless link delay between BSs and users can be defined as: $\zeta = \{\frac{Z}{R_{mu}} | \forall u \in \Phi_U^{(m)}, \forall m \in \Phi_M\}$. The cooperation delay of user u through the cooperation request content f between BSs can also be similarly expressed as:

$$d_{u,f}^{co} = \begin{cases} \dfrac{Z}{R_{co}} & g_{u,f}^t = 0 \\ \dfrac{K-1}{K}\dfrac{Z}{R_{co}} & g_{u,f}^t = 1. \end{cases} \tag{6}$$

Assuming that there are two processes to fetch a content from the cloud server: fetch and download delay is correspondingly defined with d^{fetch} and d^{down}, respectively. In particularly, the download time will be much larger than the wireless latency $i.e.$, $d^{down} \gg \frac{Z}{R_{mu}}$. d_{fetch} will be inevitable unless the user caches the entire content ($i.e.$, $K = 1$). Therefore, the backhaul delay for user m to download content f from the cloud server through the BS is:

$$d_{u,f}^{backhaul} = \begin{cases} d^{fetch} + d^{down} & g_{u,f}^t = 0, K \geq 1 \\ d^{fetch} + \dfrac{K-1}{K}d^{down} & g_{u,f}^t = 1, K > 1 \\ 0 & g_{u,f}^t = 1, K = 1 \end{cases} \tag{7}$$

Based on (Eqs. 5, 6, 7) and caching model, in time slot t, the transmission delay for user u to request a content f through its serving BS m is:

$$d_{m,u,f}^t = \begin{cases} d_{m,u,f}^{dir} & a_{m,f}^t = 1 \\ d_{m,u,f}^{dir} + d_{u,f}^{co} & \exists a_{m_{co},f}^t = 1, m_{co} \in \Phi_M \\ d_{m,u,f}^{dir} + d_{u,f}^{backhaul} & others. \end{cases} \tag{8}$$

Therefore, the overall transmission delay in time slot t can be expressed by:

$$\mathbb{D}^t(\mathbb{A}^t, \mathbb{B}^t, \mathbb{G}^t) = \sum_m^M \sum_u^{U_m} \sum_f^F d_{m,u,f}^t b_{u,f}^t. \tag{9}$$

In order to minimize the long-term network transmission delay $\mathbb{D}^t(\mathbb{A}^t, \mathbb{B}^t, \mathbb{G}^t)$, the hybrid-cache centralize problem can be formulated as:

$$\mathbf{P1}: \min_{\mathbb{A}^t} \quad \sum_{t=1}^T \mathbb{D}^t(\mathbb{A}^t, \mathbb{B}^t, \mathbb{G}^t) \tag{10}$$
$$\text{s.t.} \quad \sum_{f=1}^F a_{m,f}^t \leq C_{BS}/Z, t = 1, 2, \cdots, T \forall m \in \Phi_M.$$
$$a_{m,f}^t \in \{0,1\}, t = 1, 2, \cdots, T \quad \forall f \in \mathcal{F}, \forall s \in \Phi_S.$$

Obviously, $\mathbb{A}^t$ in $\mathbf{P1}$ is a high-dimensional discrete variable, and the delay in $D^t(\mathbb{A}^t, \mathbb{B}^t, \mathbb{G}^t)$ is continuous. Therefore, $\mathbf{P1}$ is a NP-hard problem and complexity of solving non-convex $\mathbf{P1}$ with traditional optimization algorithms will be extremely high. To achieve the design goal in (10), the CU should improve the caching hit-ratio ($i.e.$, the ratio of the number of request contents that are cached over the total number of request contents) for each BS and reduce delays by designing coordination strategy among BSs.

4 Proposed Method and Algorithm

Reinforcement learning has a strong ability to adapt to the environment, but when the input data has a longtail distribution, the neural network responsible for the policy will still rely the most popular contents.

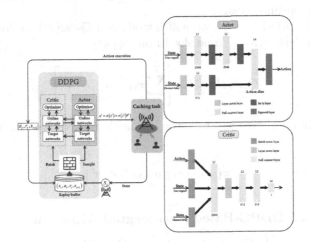

Fig. 2. Proposed DDPG-based Anti-longtail Algorithm.

In this work, we use DDPG as the baseline model, and by referring to deep long-tail learning, we propose a reinforcement learning algorithm dedicated to wireless caching. As illustrated in Fig. 2, is the algorithm architecture of DDPG. DDPG consists of two parts, actor and critic, both of which are composed of deep neural networks.

4.1 Reinforcement Learning

Reinforcement learning framework is generally defined based on Markov decision process(MDP). MDP is usually including three base components: (S, A, R), which is define as state space, action space and rewards respectively. Correspondingly, the system state and action in time slot t can be defined as $s^t \in S$ and $a^t \in A$. To be precise, the agent will observe the environment state s^t in each time slot t and make an action with policy function $\pi^t(a|s)$ to maximum the reward r^t.

The state, action and reward are accordingly formulated in our proposed DRL and introduced as follows: **System state**: According to optimization problem (**P1**), in order to further reduce the transmission delay in this work, the BS cache strategy needs to be designed according to user requests and the channel conditions of different users. Since users request the same set of contents, $\mathbb{B}^t$ can be reduced to $\mathbb{H}^t = \left\{ \sum_u^U b_{u,f}^t \right\}^{1 \times F}$: The system state is defined as user request and current BS - User channel state: $s^t = (\mathbb{H}^t, \mathbb{G}^t)$. **Action space**: In propose

DRL, the action is defined as the optimization variable in (**P1**). So the system action: $a^t = \mathbb{A}^t$. **Reward**: We normalize the total delay value in a time slot t as reward: $r(s^t, a^t) = e^{-\mathbb{D}^t(\mathbb{A}^t, \mathbb{B}^t, \mathbb{G}^t)}$. Latency caused by the most popular contents is further reduced due to the presence of user caches. Less popular contents will be an important factor influencing further declines in latency. Therefore, some of the most popular contents and the less popular contents will become the primary goals of agent optimization.

To further optimize (**P1**), we will introduce a Q-value function to optimize the long-term delay with T time slot in one epoch:

$$Q(s^t, a^t) = \mathbb{E}_\pi \left[\sum_{t'}^{T} r(s^{t'}, a^{t'}) | s^t, a^t \right] \tag{11}$$

So the policy function will take the action that maximizes the Q-value function:

$$\pi(s^t) = \arg\max_{a^t} Q(s^t, a^t). \tag{12}$$

4.2   Proposed DDPG-Based Anti-longtail Algorithm

The architecture of DDPG is shown in Fig. 2(a). There are five components in DDPG: actor network, actor target network, critic network, critic target network and replay buffer. The replay buffer will record each step of the reinforcement learning algorithm in the form of (s^t, a^t, r^t, s^{t+1}).

The action selection is given by the actor network. Assuming that the parameter of the actor network is θ^π, then: $a^t = \pi(s^t) = \pi(s^t|\theta^\pi)$, the actor target network extracts the state s' from the replay buffer and gets the action a', assuming its parameter is $\theta^{\pi'}$ then $a' = \pi'(s') = \pi(s'|\theta^{\pi'})$.

The role of the critic is to evaluate the actor network, and the critic is to fit and implement the Q-value function. Assuming that the parameter of the critic network is θ^Q, then the Q-value function is: $Q(s^t, a^t) = Q(s^t, a^t|\theta^Q)$. The critic target network evaluates the target Q-value Q' from the next state extracted from the replay buffer and the output of the actor target network. Assuming that its parameter is $\theta^{Q'}$, there is $Q'(s', a')) = Q'(s', a'|\theta^{Q'})$. So the loss function of critic network is the mean squared error(MSE) between Q' output by the critic target network plus reward and the output of the critic network:

$$\mathcal{L}_{critic} = \frac{1}{N} \sum_t (r^t + \delta Q'(s^{t+1}, \pi'(s^{t+1}|\theta^{\pi'})|\theta^{Q'}) - Q(s^t, a^t|\theta^Q))^2, \tag{13}$$

where N is the size of the mini-batch extracted from the replay buffer, and δ is the discount factor, whose function is to make the Q-value pay more attention to the current environmental state. Therefore, the critic network can be updated as:

$$\theta^Q = \theta^Q - \beta_{critic}\mathcal{L}_{critic},\tag{14}$$

where β_{critic} is the learning rate of critic. The loss function of actor network will be given by critic network:

$$\mathcal{L}_{actor} = \frac{1}{N}\sum_t \nabla_a Q(s^t, a^t|\theta^Q) \times \nabla_{\theta^\pi}\pi(s^t|\theta^\pi).\tag{15}$$

The network parameters of the actor network can be updated as:

$$\theta^\pi = \theta^\pi - \beta_{actor}\mathcal{L}_{actor}.\tag{16}$$

The parameter of actor target network and critic target network are sync with actor and critic, respectively. Assuming that the soft update factor is τ, the update process can be express as:

$$\begin{aligned}\theta^{\pi'} &= \tau\theta^\pi + (1-\tau)\theta^{\pi'}\\ \theta^{Q'} &= \tau\theta^Q + (1-\tau)\theta^{Q'}.\end{aligned}\tag{17}$$

Actor network architecture is shown in Fig. 2(b). Since the state contains discrete user requests and continuous wireless channels, it is isolated at the entrance of the network, and then a layer of layer normalize is passed to normalize the parameters. At the output end of the network, the network output is discrete by the sigmoid function, and the caching strategy of each BS is obtained.

The critical network architecture is shown in Fig. 2(c). Since the state contains discrete user requests, the BS caching strategy is associated with continuous wireless channels. Therefore, batch normalize is also done at the entrance, and after passing through independent fully connected layers, they are concentrate together. What's more, in order to prevent over-fitting when there are too many most popular contents, we add L2 regularization to make a new loss function $\mathcal{L}'_{critic}$:

$$\mathcal{L}'_{critic} = \mathcal{L}_{critic} + \lambda||\theta^Q||^2,\tag{18}$$

where λ is the penalty factor. So far, the algorithm flow of our proposal is:

Algorithm 1. Proposed DDPG-base anti-longtail algorithm
___

Require:

β_{actor}, β_{critic}: learning rate for actor and critic; BS set Φ_S, User set Φ_U, $\Phi_U^{(s)}$;

randomly Initialize θ^π and θ^Q

Initialize target network $\theta^{\pi'} = \theta^\pi$ and $\theta^{Q'} = \theta^Q$

Create an empty replay buffer $\mathbb{D}$

Initialize a random system state $s^0 = (\mathbb{H}^0, \mathbb{G}^0)$

for each epoch **do**

    for t=0,T **do**

        Select action $a^t = \pi(s^t|\theta^\pi)$ and transfer to caching strategy $\mathbb{A}^t$ with limited capacity of BS.

        According to the caching strategy $\mathbb{A}^t$, and system state $s^t = (\mathbb{H}^t, \mathbb{G}^t)$, calculate the overall delay using (9) to observe the reward $r^t = r(s^t, a^t) = e^{-\mathbb{D}^t(\mathbb{A}^t, \mathbb{B}^t, \mathbb{G}^t)}$.

        Observe new state s^{t+1}.

        Store trajectory (s^t, a^t, r^t, s^{t+1}) in $\mathbb{D}$

        $\theta^{\pi'}$, θ^π, $\theta^{Q'}$, θ^Q = DDPG-LEARNING($\mathbb{D}, \theta^{\pi'}, \theta^\pi, \theta^{Q'}, \theta^Q$)

    end for

end for

procedure DDPG-LEARNING($\mathbb{D}$, $\theta^{\pi'}$, θ^π, $\theta^{Q'}$, θ^Q)

    Sample a random mini-batch of N trajectories from $\mathbb{D}$

    Minimize the critic loss $\mathcal{L}_{critic}$ using (13) or (18)

    Update critic network θ^Q using (14)

    Minimize the critic loss $\mathcal{L}_{actor}$ using (15)

    Update critic network θ^π using (16)

    Soft update the target network using (17):

    $\theta^{\pi'} = \tau\theta^\pi + (1 - \tau)\theta^{\pi'}$

    $\theta^{Q'} = \tau\theta^Q + (1 - \tau)\theta^{Q'}$

    return $\theta^{\pi'}, \theta^\pi, \theta^{Q'}, \theta^Q$

end procedure
___

5   Performance Evaluation

In this part, the numerical simulations are performed to demonstrate the performance of propose method. In order to facilitate discussion purposes, the cache hit rate is divided into two parts: direct hits indicate that user requests can be served by the serving BS and coordinated hits indicate that user requests can be served by coordinated BSs with extra delay. In this way, the user's cache does not directly affect the cache hit rate.

The bandwidth is set as 40 MHz, while the path-loss exponent α is set as 2.5, transmit power and noise power are set as 40 dBm and -120 dBm/Hz, respectively. To verify its effectiveness, we use the commonly adopted deep Q-learning (DQN) algorithm as a comparison benchmark while ensuring that the data is consistent in the comparison. The In DQN method, the neural network in DQN use MLP and Adam optimizer. The structure and parameter of DQN neural network keep the same with propose actor network, without normalize layer (Batch-normalize Layer and Layer-normalize Layer). In order to verify the promotion effect of the hybrid-caching model on method, there are a group DQN will use the normal cache model (without user partial cache).

Assume that distance between adjacent BS is set as 500 m and the BS serving distance l_p is set as 250 m. The remaining parameters are given in Table 1.

Table 1. Simulation settings.

Attribute	Value
Number of BSs	4
Number of users	120
F (number of content set)	400
C (Capacity of each BS)	50
γ (Zipf parameter)	1
Batch size	2048
β_{actor} (Actor learning rate)	0.01
β_{critic} (Critic learning rate)	0.02
Z (size of content)	5×10^8 bits
d_0 (backhaul delay)	4 s
d_{fetch} (fetch contents delay)	0.4 s
δ (discount factor)	0.96
τ (soft update parameter)	0.02
C_{real} (user physical capacity)	5
K	2
λ	10^{-4}

First, we consider the delay and caching hit rate comparison between proposed method and compared algorithms for different Zipf parameter γ, where $F = 400$ is set. As seen in Fig. 3, the propose method consistently maintains the lowest latency. Specially, as the γ increases, the delay gap increases, which show the influence of Normalize Layer and L2 regularization in proposed method on long-tail distribution. In the cache hit rate, DQN has a weak advantage over the no user cache case, which indicates that user cache does not affect the cache hit rate in method comparison. This proves the algorithmic advantage of the propose method on DRL.

Then, we consider the impact of the content-set size on the compared algorithms. As can be seen in Fig. 4, as the content set becomes larger, the request probability of popular contents leaks slowly (from 200 to 1000, the request probability of the top 100 contents decreases by 18.9%). So the less popular contents allocation will greatly affect the latency performance. In addition, the unpopular contents will interfere with the convergence of the algorithm. The propose one, the delay is slowly increasing as the contents set gets larger. In contrast, DQN appears unstable and falls into a local optimum, especially when $F = 500$. In fact, when $F = 200$, through the cooperation between BSs, the algorithm has the theoretical possibility of caching the entire content set. It can be seen that only the propose method has a high overall cache hit ratio.

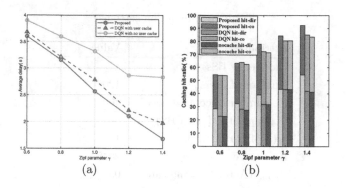

Fig. 3. Delay and caching hit rate comparison with different γ where $l_{\max} = 500\,\text{m}$.

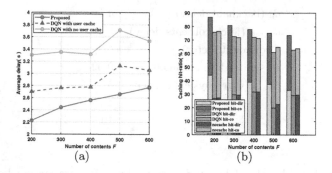

Fig. 4. Delay and caching hit rate comparison for different F.

In Fig. 5, we present the comparison of average delays between the proposed and DDPG with different transmit power, where $F = 400$ and $\gamma = 1$. It can be seen that, each of the three algorithms has a slight delay drop and is relatively stable. On the one hand, it shows the strong adaptability of reinforcement learning to the environment and the generalization ability of the algorithm. On the other hand, it shows that in the wireless cache, backhaul traffic is still the major cause of delay. In fact, the overall delay of the wireless link is also significantly reduced (the number of users is 120).

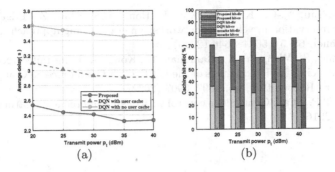

Fig. 5. Delay and caching hit rate comparison for different p_t.

6   Conclusion

We studied the edge caching design under the multi-BS cooperate hybrid-cache model. A DDPG-based Anti-longtail method is proposed to cope with the impact on DRL with longtail input. Particularly, the long-tail request distribution will make the neural network depend on the most popular content after gradient descent, which will affect the deployment and training of the less popular content. Through the transformation of the algorithm and the proposed hybrid cache model, we further reduce the transmission delay in the wireless cache. Numerical simulations show that this method outperforms commonly used DRL methods in terms of cache hit rate and overall transmission delay.

Acknowledgement. The work was supported in part by National Key Research and Development Program of China (No. 2021YFB2012403), in part by the Science and Technology Program of Guangzhou (No. 202201020182) and in part by the Guangdong Basic and Applied Basic Research Foundation (No. 2021A1515011812).

References

1. Barnett, T., Jain, S., Andra, U., Khurana, T.: Cisco visual networking index (VNI) complete forecast update, 2017–2022. Americas/EMEAR Cisco Knowledge Network (CKN) Presentation, pp. 1–30 (2018)
2. Sheraz, M., et al.: Artificial intelligence for wireless caching: schemes, performance, and challenges. IEEE Commun. Surv. Tutorials **23**(1), 631–661 (2021)
3. Zhang, Z., Tao, M.: Deep learning for wireless coded caching with unknown and time-variant content popularity. IEEE Trans. Wireless Commun. **20**(2), 1152–1163 (2021)
4. Chaudhary, A., Gupta, H.P., Shukla, K.K.: Real-time activities of daily living recognition under long-tailed class distribution. IEEE Trans. Emerging Top. Comput. Intell. **6**(4), 740–750 (2022)
5. Zhang, Y., Kang, B., Hooi, B., Yan, S., Feng, J.: Deep long-tailed learning: a survey. arXiv preprint arXiv:2110.04596 (2021)

6. Chen, D., Liu, Y.-C., Kim, B., Xie, J., Hong, C.S., Han, Z.: Edge computing resources reservation in vehicular networks: a meta-learning approach. IEEE Trans. Veh. Technol. **69**(5), 5634–5646 (2020)
7. Alshammari, S., Wang, Y.-X., Ramanan, D., Kong, S.: Long-tailed recognition via weight balancing. In: Proceedings of the IEEE/CVF Conference on Computer Vision and Pattern Recognition, pp. 6897–6907 (2022)
8. Lillicrap, T.P., et al.: Continuous control with deep reinforcement learning. In: ICLR (Poster) (2016)

Distributed Routing Algorithm for LEO Satellite Network Based on Deep Reinforcement Learning

Yudie Chen[1,2,3], Lan Wang[1], Houze Liang[2], Dong Lv[4], Weizhi Wu[4], Xiang Chen[2(✉)], and Terngyin Hsu[5]

[1] College of Electronics and Information Engineering, Shenzhen University, Shenzhen, China
[2] School of Electronics and Information Technology, Sun Yat-sen University, Guangzhou, China
chenxiang@mail.sysu.edu.cn
[3] Research Institute of Tsinghua University in Shenzhen (RITS), Shenzhen, China
[4] IPLOOK Technologies Co. Ltd., Guangzhou, China
[5] Department of Computer Science, National Chiao Tung University, Hsinchu, Taiwan

Abstract. Low earth orbit (LEO) satellites have the advantages of low transmission delay and wide coverage, which are widely used in current and future satellite communication systems. However, the large-scale and unevenly distributed traffic will easily cause severe inter-satellite-link (ISL) congestion. Therefore, the inter-satellite routing design of the LEO satellite networks is of vital importance. Traditional shortest path-based routing algorithms in LEO networks might cause overlapped loops that aggravate network delay. In this paper, by introducing the deep Q-network (DQN) into routing design, a distributed routing algorithm is proposed to reduce the delay and relieve congestion. Particularly, a reward function, considering routing loop as restriction to identify the best pathways, is designed to prevent the agent from getting stuck in a loop owing to duplicate paths. Meanwhile, instead of simply select-ing a fixed shortest path, the proposed DQN model selects the next hop with a certain random probability, which helps to avoid overlapped paths and efficiently relieve congestion. A hybrid OPNET-STK simula-tion platform is built up for a typical LEO constellation with more than 200 satellites. Simulation results reveal that, compared with the tradi-tional algorithms, the proposed approach can effectively relieve the ISL congestion and brings higher throughput for the LEO networks.

Keywords: low earth orbit satellite · deep Q networks · routing algorithm

This research is supported in part by the State's Key Project of Research and Devel-opment Plan under Grants (2019YFE0196400), and in part by the Shenzhen Natural Science Foundation under Grant JCYJ20200109143016563.

K. Rabie et al. (Eds.): IoTaaS 2022, LNICST 506, pp. 161–173, 2023.
https://doi.org/10.1007/978-3-031-37139-4_15

1   Introduction

Satellite communication technologies are developing continuously, and LEO satellite communication networks with the advantages of global coverage and on-demand services have been re-injected with new vitality [1]. However, with the rapid development of LEO satellite communication networks, the user traffic is also growing dramatically and the distribution is very uneven, making the ISLs prone to congestion. Then the Quality of Service (QoS) of satellite networks is greatly reduced [2]. Therefore, how to design a load balancing routing strategy with regional distribution is particularly imperative in the construction of LEO satellite communication networks [3].

A number of routing algorithms have been proposed for LEO satellite networks. Dijkstra Shortest Path (DSP) algorithm utilizes a greedy algorithm strategy to traverse all nodes until a shortest path is found between the source node and destination node. However, DSP algorithm cannot adjust routing strategy when the LEO satellite network topology changes dynamically, which will cause severe packet loss when the traffic is enormous and uneven. On this basis, several algorithms for dealing with network congestion are proposed. Tarik et al. [4] proposed an Explicit Load Balancing (ELB) algorithm that can exchange congestion information of neighboring satellites. When a node is congested, it requests to reduce the packet transmission rate by sending self-congestion notifications to its neighboring nodes, so that the neighboring nodes can bypass this congested node to choose a more suitable path. Besides, by differentiating the services and guaranteeing the service rates of different QoS, ELB can reduce the packet loss rate via better traffic scheduling. Nevertheless, ELB does not consider the next-hop delay and hence cannot ensure the efficiency and speed of routing. The Distributed Hierarchical Routing Protocol (DHRP) [5] assigns a speaker in each orbit. The speaker periodically collects queuing delay information and sends it to other satellites in the same orbit to assist in updating the whole network topology. However, it is a challenge for DHRP to determine a proper period of delay information broadcasting and then balance the real time of optimal routes and communication load. Song et al. [6] proposed a Traffic Light-based intelligent Routing (TLR) algorithm for satellite networks. A set of traffic light signals is used in this algorithm to indicate the congestion status of the current node and the next node. An approximately optimal transmission path for each packet can be obtained by combining initial planning and real-time adjustment. The public waiting queue scheme of TLR can fully use the free space in the cache queue and reduce the packet loss rate. However, the TLR algorithm defaults the transmission delay to a fixed value. It simplifies the time-varying transmission delay model to a static model, so the next hop of the TLR algorithm is not always the best choice. In summary, the above traditional algorithms all select a fixed shortest path, so that there will be a large quantity of repeated paths in different routes, which will aggravate congestion of ISLs and degrade the QoS of users.

In recent years, the introduction of deep learning has brought new room for improvements in routing algorithms. Bomin Mao et al. [7] used the deep belief network to extract the deep dimension features in the routing information. Taking the current routing information tensor as input, the deep belief network can automatically give the optimal next hop. However, the statistics of network link states are hysteretic, and the modeling and implementation of the tensor are relatively complex for all networks. Peiliang Zuo et al. [8] proposed an intelligent distributed routing algorithm in dynamic LEO satellite networks, which integrates the spatial location of nodes, mutual distance, queuing delay and available bandwidth to select routing paths. Despite the fact that the above routing algorithms have has good convergence and lower latency, these methods do not constrain the duplicate paths when training the model, resulting in relatively more loops.

In this paper, we propose a distributed routing algorithm based on deep reinforcement learning. Our contributions can be summarized as:

- The routing algorithm selects the next hop with a certain random probability instead of the minimum delay. It avoids the problem of path overlap in different routing paths, effectively alleviates the congestion caused by using a single optimal path and increases the network's overall link utilization as well.
- In the training of the Deep Q Network (DQN) model, the queuing delay and propagation delay between nodes are also embedded into the reward function to help to select the optimal path in the LEO satellite networks. Furthermore, the reward function constraint on the agent is used to prevent from getting into loops by choosing duplicate paths.

The rest of this article is outlined below. Section 2 briefly introduces the system model and optimization problem construction based on the DQN architecture. Section 3 presents the implementation of the proposed method in the OPNET platform. Simulation results and analysis are performed in Sect. 4. Finally, Sect. 5 draws some conclusions.

2   System Model

2.1   System Model

The inter-satellite link routing algorithm proposed in this paper is based on a LEO constellation composed of 228 satellites and 6 ground stations(GS), as shown in Fig. 1. The constellation has 12 evenly distributed inclined orbits and in each orbit there are 19 satellites, which are also evenly distributed. We utilize the STK software to generate the corresponding parameters such as orbit number, orbit inclination, geocentric coordinates. All of the these parameters are then imported to the OPNET platform to build a simulation environment of this constellation. Besides, each satellite has 4 inter-satellite links (2 inter-orbital links and 2 intra-orbital links) for communicating with neighboring satellites.Two adjacent satellites can only communicate when their transmitters and receivers oriented towards each other are using the same frequency band. The processing capacity and load capacity of different satellite nodes in the constellation are significantly different. In addition, 6 ground stations are distributed in densely populated or vast cities.

Packets are generated in a uniform distribution at ground station and forwarded to the closest satellite that the source ground station can access. Then they are routed to the satellite covering the destination ground station. Finally, they are delivered to the destination ground station. When the networks are bearing great service traffic, the satellites in a specific region might be overloaded, while the ones in other regions can be idle. In this case, the queuing delay and available bandwidth of different nodes and even different directions of the same node can be completely different. To realize traffic scheduling, we suppose each LEO satellite are equipped with a performance monitor, which can record the packet sending rate and calculate the current waiting time of the queues in four directions.

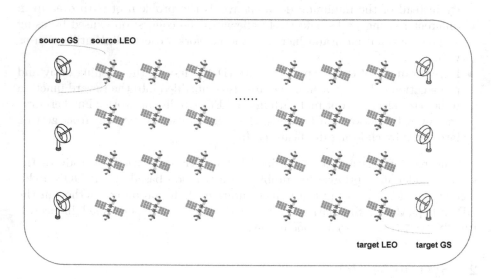

Fig. 1. Topology of LEO satellite networks.

2.2 Problem Formulation

The end-to-end(E2E) delay of ISLs routing is usually composed of propagation delay and queuing delay. The propagation delay is associated with the distance between two satellites. Additionally, the queuing delay is related to the congestion level of the satellite link. This paper defines the queuing delay of the links as:

$$D_q = l/r_q, \tag{1}$$

where l is the total length of the data packets in the queue and r_q is the data transmission rate of the queue. The propagation delay is determined by the distance s between satellite nodes and the light speed c, denoted as:

$$D_p = s/c. \tag{2}$$

Therefore, the E2E delay of the inter-satellite link can be expressed as:

$$D = D_p + D_q. \tag{3}$$

The packet loss rate in the LEO network is also an important concern of the routing algorithm. The packet loss rate is defined as:

$$P = N_r/N_s, \tag{4}$$

where N_s represents the number of packets forwarded from the satellite covering the source ground station, meanwhile, N_r represents the number of packets received by the satellite covering the target ground station.

In addition, loops in the network will performance of the routing algorithm, such as E2E delay and packet loss rate, etc. The loop rate is defined as following:

$$R = R_l/R_w. \tag{5}$$

In order to save computing resources, we only calculate the routing paths between the satellites visible to the ground station. We denote the number of routing paths between these visible satellites as R_w, and denote the routing paths with loops as R_l. R is used as a metric to analyze the impact of routing loops on delay and packet loss rate.

3 The Proposed DQN-Based Routing Algorithm

Agents in reinforcement learning (RL) can interact with the environment to search for the best path without knowing the environment. The value of a state and an action under a given policy is usually referred to as Q value. Traditional RL algorithms use a Q-table to record the Q values. However, when the combination of states and actions is complex, the Q-table is required to have a large storage space, so using traditional RL algorithms is not the best choice. In contrast, DQN uses a deep neural network as a function that takes the state and action as inputs and output the corresponding Q value. This avoids maintaining a large table. Therefore, this paper introduces a routing algorithm based on DQN, which is suitable for the above-mentioned LEO satellite network. The routing algorithm aims to find the optimal path under the constraint of packet loss rate and minimize the end-to-end delay.

3.1 Markov Decision Process Formulation

As depicted in Fig. 2, in reinforcement learning, the agent explores the environment in a trial-and-error manner, earning rewards through interacting with the environment. The purpose of training the model is to maximize the reward obtained by the agent. In the initial stage of model training, the agent takes the current node as the input of DQN, and selects the next hop with random probability and gets feedback from the environment, that is, the reward of this hop. The four-tuple information, including state, action, next state and reward, generated by each interaction between the agent and the environment will be saved into the experience pool. When the training episodes reach a certain number, i.e., the *BatchSize*, the model will be updated. The proposed method combines the routing in the LEO constellations with RL, and the state, action, and reward are defined as follows:

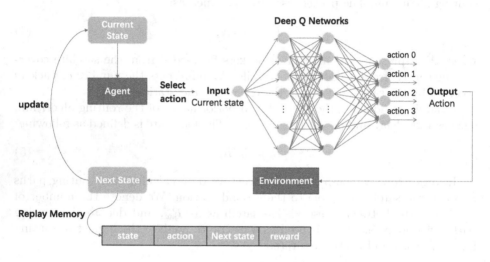

Fig. 2. DQN model of the proposed algorithm.

State: The state of satellite node i at moment t can be expressed as:

$$s_t^i = \{P_{i,j}, Q_{i,j}, D_{i,j}, T_i\}, j = 1, 2, 3 \cdots, \tag{6}$$

where $P_{i,j}$ denotes the propagation delay between nodes i and j, which is proportional to their distance. $Q_{i,j}$ is the queue delay between node i and node j. The queue delay grows as the packet generating rate and volume increase, and the queue delay is usually related to the packet loss rate. $D_{i,j}$ denotes the Euclidean distance between node i and node j. T_i is the identification of the target node, which equals 1 if the current node is the target node and equals 0 otherwise.

Action: The action of the satellite can be expressed as:

$$a \in \{node_{i1}, node_{i2}, \cdots, node_{ij}\}, \tag{7}$$

where a a represents the action taken at the current node, that is, selecting one of the four neighbor nodes, and $node_{ij}$ indicates that the next hop of node i is node j. The agent uses a greedy strategy based on exploration-exploitation for each action selection. At the early stage of training, the agent randomly selects the action with a higher probability and judges the correctness of the selection based on the long-term reward obtained. The agent records the training parameters periodically through replay memory. In the later stage of training, the agent selects the action with a higher probability of obtaining the largest long-term reward. The strategy is denoted as:

$$a = \begin{cases} random\ action\ with\ probability & \epsilon \\ \arg\max_{a \in A} Q^\pi(s, a)\ with\ probability & 1 - \epsilon \end{cases} \tag{8}$$

Reward: The reward function is:

$$R = k_1(D_{i,target} - D_{i-1,target}) + k_2 H_i + k_3 Rep_i. \tag{9}$$

$D_{i,target}$ is the distance from node i to the target node, $D_{i-1,target}$ is the distance from the previous hop to the target node. If $D_{i,target} - D_{i-1,target}$ is negative, which indicates that the currently selected node is closer to the target node than the previous node, the coefficient k_1 is positive, and the reward value is positive. H_i indicates the number of steps from the source node to the current node. If the number of steps exceeds the given threshold, the exploration is terminated by k_2 to prevent the agent from making multiple repetitions of meaningless exploration in the environment and falling into a dead loop. Besides, Rep_i is the duplicate path flag. We set k_3 to be negative, when the next hop has been marked, $k_3 Rep_i$ will be negative to impose a penalty on this choice.

3.2   Distributed Satellite Routing Algorithm Design

In the network topology shown in Fig. 3, the routing process is as follows:

Step 1: The LEO satellite detects the number of the communicative adjacent nodes by sending hello packets to its four neighbors, and constructs a network topology map based on the spatial location information, queue delay, and propagation delay of the corresponding neighbor nodes.

Step 2: The ground station calculates the visibility with the LEO satellites at the current moment and fills in the visibility table. The source ground station randomly generates packets and requests transmission to the destination ground station at a certain time interval. It then sends the packets to the satellite (source satellite) that covers the ground station and has the shortest distance from the ground station.

Step 3: The network topology map is used as a environment to train the DQN model.

Step 4: The source satellite transmits the packets to the node selected based on the action given by the DQN. The selected node is then regarded as a new source satellite, and the above process repeats until the data is finally transmitted to the destination node.

The workflow of the proposed DQN based routing algorithm is given in Algorithm 1.

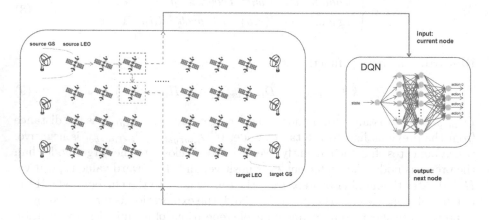

Fig. 3. Illustration of path selection based on DQN.

4 Simulation Results and Analysis

4.1 Parameters

In this paper, the network topology map generated on the OPNET platform is used as the environment for DQN training, and we verify the capability of the trained model in determining inter-satellite routing paths through three metrics, i.e., E2E delay, packet loss rate and throughput. The simulation parameters of the OPNET platform and the DQN model are summarized in Table 1.

4.2 Comparison of Experimental Results

Since this paper only studies the transmission characteristics of inter-satellite routing, the transmission time from the coverage satellite of the source earth station (source satellite node) to the coverage satellite of the target earth station (target satellite node) is referred to as the E2E delay, and the packet loss in this path is calculated by Eq. (4).

Algorithm 1. The proposed DQN-based routing algorithm

Input: State S, action A, discount factor γ, learning rate α, target network update frequency T, source satellite node and target satellite node.

Output: the next-hop node.

1: **Initialize** replay memory RM, prediction network $Q(s, a|\theta)$ with random weights θ, target network $Q(s, a|\theta')$ with weights $\theta' = \theta$, eps, eps_threshold, R_s, R_i, Path

2: **for** each episode **do**

3:     Initialize the beginning state s_0

4:     **for** each decision step t **do**

5:         Generate a random number samp
            from 0 to 1

6:         **if** $samp \leq eps\_threshold$ **then**

7:             select a random action a

8:         **else**

9:             arg max$_{a \in A}$ $Q^\pi(s, a)$

10:        Save a into path; take action a and make
           state transition $s \to s'$; and calculate R

11:        Store transition(s_t, a_t, r_t, S_{t+1}) to RM

12:        Randomly extract mine-batch of transitions(s_j, a_j, r_j, S_{j+1})
           from RM

13:        Update target network $Q(s, a|\theta')$

14:        Set $s_t = s_{t+1}$

15:        Update the weights of Target Net
           periodically with $\theta'_i = \theta_i$

16:     **end for**

17: **end for**

18: **return** Path

E2E Delay. First, as shown in Fig. 4, we compare the delay performance of the algorithm proposed in this paper with the traditional DSP routing algorithm, the Speaker routing algorithm and the traditional DQN routing algorithm in the case of different traffic volume. When the packet rate is below 125 pkts/sec, the end-to-end delay of the three routing algorithms is lower because the queue's processing rate is relatively high, and the packets in the queue can be sent through the transmitter in time for the next hop. The delay of the DSP routing algorithm and the Speaker routing algorithm gradually increases as the packet sending rate increases above 125 pkt/sec. And the end-to-end delay of the routing algorithm proposed in this paper decreases significantly compared with the former because the path selected by Dijkstra has a large number of duplicate paths locally such that the queuing delay between queues increases. And the proposed algorithm in this paper has randomness in selecting the next hop, which can alleviate the packet queuing wait due to the same path. The traditional DQN algorithm has a higher end-to-end delay because it does not restrict the agent from choosing repeated paths and makes the agent fall into loops. These loops also raise the queue delay of associated links, lowering the overall network's end-to-end latency performance. Through a well-designed reward function, the distributed

Table 1. Simulation Parameters

Hyper-parameter	Value
Packet capacity(pks)	50
Bit capacity(bits)	102400
Queue service rate(Kbps)	200
Packet Size(bits)	1024
γ, lr	0.999, 0.01
ϵ_{start}, ϵ_{end}, ϵ_{decay}	1, 0, 1000
Experience-replay memory capacity	4000
Target network update frequency C	100
Experience-replay batch size	640

DQN routing algorithm suggested in this research prevents the agent from falling into the loop, resulting in a lower delay.

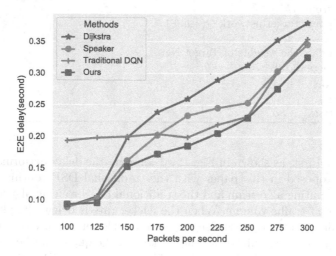

Fig. 4. Comparison of average end-to-end latency between different algorithms.

Packets Loss Rate. As illustrated in Fig. 5, the packet loss rates of the four routing strategies are compared. When the packet rate is low, the queue is less congested, the traditional DQN algorithm cannot reach the target satellite due to the influence of the loops, causing a certain amount of packet loss. The other three algorithms do not lose data packets. As the packet rate increases, the queuing delay of packets increases, and the traditional DSP routing algorithm ignores this dynamic change and still transmits packets in the original path,

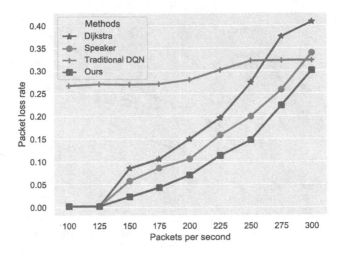

Fig. 5. Comparison of packet loss rates between different algorithms.

resulting in a large number of packet losses. Although the Speaker algorithm periodically updates the queuing delay information in the network, there is a lag, which still causes certain packet losses. However, the algorithm proposed in this paper randomly selects the next hop based on a greedy strategy, which avoids the duplication of local paths and the queuing delay is lower than the other two algorithms. Hence the packet loss rate is generally reduced by 5% - 10%.

Table 2. Comparison of hops between different algorithms.

Algorithms \ Packets/sec	100	125	175	200	250	300
Dijkstra	6.350059	6.350853	6.307295	6.172909	5.840352	5.539334
Speaker	6.350059	6.351141	6.235041	6.238398	6.191605	6.215915
traditional DQN	6.305049	6.268570	6.318532	6.217788	6.261644	6.260731
Ours	6.681810	6.680046	6.704537	6.555520	6.448777	6.496003

Throughput. Figure 6 shows a comparison of the throughput of the four routing strategies. The throughput of the traditional DQN algorithm is the lowest due to packet loss caused by the loops. The traditional DSP algorithm's throughput grows slowly as the number of packets sent increases. In contrast, the Speaker routing algorithm's throughput fluctuates more, owing to the Speaker mechanism's need to update the network topology on a regular basis by sending information packets, which add to the network's load. The algorithm suggested in this paper's throughput grows quicker than the previous algorithm' throughput.

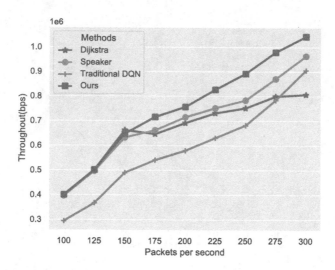

Fig. 6. Comparison of network throughput between different algorithms.

Compared with other algorithms, the algorithm proposed in this paper significantly improves the routing performance in delay, packet loss rate, and throughput. However, it is accompanied by a slight increase in the number of hops, as shown in Table 2. This is because the algorithm proposed in this paper does not choose a fixed shortest path when selecting a path but randomly selects the next hop with a certain probability, so it does not make the best decision regarding the number of hops.

5   Conclusion

In order to alleviate the problem of congestion in inter-satellite links caused by the growth of user traffic and uneven distribution, this paper proposes a distributed routing algorithm based on deep reinforcement learning. The randomness of selecting the next hop avoids local path overlap in different routing paths and effectively relieves the congestion caused by the fixed shortest path. The DQN mdoel is trained with a reward function that constrains the occur of path loops. Then, the optimal path is selected in the LEO satellite networks based on the queue delay and propagation delay between nodes. The simulation results of OPNET in this scenario show that the algorithm can effectively alleviate congestion and has lower packet loss rate, lower latency and higher throughput compared with existing algorithms, improving network throughput while ensuring low latency.

References

1. Liu, C., Xu, M., Geng, N., Zhang, X.: A survey on machine learning based routing algorithms. J. Comput. Res. Develop. **57**(4), 671–687 (2020)

2. Wang, F., Jiang, D., Qi, S.: An adaptive routing algorithm for integrated information networks. China Commun. **16**(7), 195–206 (2019)
3. Zhou, W., Zhu, Y.F., Li, Y.Y., Li, Q., Yu, Q.Z.: Research on hierarchical architecture and routing of satellite constellation with IGSO-GEO-MEO network. Int. J. Satellite Commun. Netw. **38**(2), 162–176 (2020)
4. Taleb, T., Mashimo, D., Jamalipour, A., Kato, N., Nemoto, Y.: Explicit load balancing technique for NGEO satellite IP networks with on-board processing capabilities. IEEE/ACM Trans. Networking **17**(1), 281–293 (2008)
5. Bai, J., Lu, X., Lu, Z., Peng, W.: A distributed hierarchical routing protocol for non-GEO satellite networks. In: Workshops on Mobile and Wireless Networking/High Performance Scientific, Engineering Computing/Network Design and Architecture/Optical Networks Control and Management/Ad Hoc and Sensor Networks/Compil, pp. 148–154. IEEE (2004)
6. Song, G., Chao, M., Yang, B., Zheng, Y.: TLR: a traffic-light-based intelligent routing strategy for NGEO satellite IP networks. IEEE Trans. Wireless Commun. **13**(6), 3380–3393 (2014)
7. Mao, B., et al.: A tensor based deep learning technique for intelligent packet routing. In: GLOBECOM 2017–2017 IEEE Global Communications Conference, pp. 1–6. IEEE (2017)
8. Zuo, P., Wang, C., Yao, Z., Hou, S., Jiang, H.: An intelligent routing algorithm for LEO satellites based on deep reinforcement learning. In: 2021 IEEE 94th Vehicular Technology Conference (VTC2021-Fall), pp. 1–5. IEEE (2021)

An Intelligent Wireless Signal Detection and Recognition Platform

Haoyu Zhao, Yan Zhang, Wancheng Zhang(✉), Guangchuan Cao, Jiupeng Song, and Shanping Yu

School of Information and Electronics, Beijing Institute of Technology, Beijing 100081, People's Republic of China
{zhaohaoyu,zhangy,zhangwancheng,caoguangchuan,3220220694,ysp}@bit.edu.cn

Abstract. The detection and recognition of wireless signals play an essential role in the communications security of the Internet of Things (IoT). In order to monitor wireless signals, a platform that can detect and recognize wireless signals in real time is needed. This paper describes an intelligent wireless signal detection and recognition platform. The platform can monitor the presence or absence of wireless signals in real time and perform parameter analysis and modulation classification of wireless signals. We design and implement an integrated detection and recognition scheme based on the You Only Look Once for Signal Detection (YOLO-SD) and the Convolutional Neural Networks (CNN). The YOLO-SD algorithm has a fast running speed, thus the platform can work in real-time. The platform is designed and implemented on Field Programmable Gate Array (FPGA) platform. The result shows that our proposed platform achieves a detection accuracy of 80% and recognition accuracy of 93%, thus demonstrating the significant potential for analyzing RF spectral activity with high accuracy.

Keywords: Radio frequency (RF) signal acquisition · time-frequency map analysis · signal detection and recognition · deep learning · YOLO target detection

1 Introduction

Nowadays, billions of IoT devices arise around us. IoT systems are becoming more widespread in various areas of applications, namely in industry, power engineering, systems of implantable medical devices for monitoring vital characteristics of the human body, transport systems, and mobile operational control systems in emergency situations [1], etc. Thus, it is important to ensure the safety of the communication system by detecting the signals in real-time [2–4].

Due to the low response latency for IoT services, the wireless signals need to be detected in real-time. Nowadays, the most commonly used equipment for wireless signal analysis is the spectrum analyzer. The primary role of a spectrum

© ICST Institute for Computer Sciences, Social Informatics and Telecommunications Engineering 2023
Published by Springer Nature Switzerland AG 2023. All Rights Reserved
K. Rabie et al. (Eds.): IoTaaS 2022, LNICST 506, pp. 174–183, 2023.
https://doi.org/10.1007/978-3-031-37139-4_16

analyzer is the measurement of signal power versus frequency [5]. A method used for spectrum analyzer is the Discrete Fourier Transform (DFT). The classical general-purpose swept spectrum analyzer has the disadvantage of having less access to information about the wireless signals. In addition, it is not suitable for real-time detecting [6]. In [7], the authors proposed Passive IoT Radar (PIoTR) to perform RF sensing. PIoTR is designed based on passive radar technology, with a generic architecture to utilize various signal sources including the WiFi signal and wireless energy at the Industrial, Scientific and Medical (ISM) band. The PIoTR systems typically make use of relative narrowband signals for detecting large targets at long distances. However, variations in bandwidth, signal strength and data rate can significantly affect the sensing performance of PIoTR systems.

Traditionally, non-cooperative signal detection tasks are accomplished through energy detection [8]. The authors detect the signal by comparing the output of the energy detector with a threshold which depends on the noise floor. The energy detection method obtain the signal bandwidth and center frequency. However, at low signal-to-noise ratios (SNR), the accuracy of the energy detection method greatly reduced. In [9], the authors detected and recognized signals by converting them to pictures and using the YOLO algorithm, which reduce the effect of noise on detection accuracy. However, this method requires a more demanding window length for the short-time Fourier transform [10], which is difficult to determine.

In this paper, we describe an intelligent platform for wireless signal detection and recognition. To the best of our knowledge, this is the first work to integrate signal acquisition, signal detection, and signal recognition in an FPGA-based platform. The hardware model is implemented inside the FPGA that addresses the development of complex applications for continuous data acquisition and processing. Moreover, We propose YOLO-SD algorithm to detect wireless signal in real-time, which substantially improves the signal detection results in the case of low SNR.

The rest of the paper is structured as follows. Section 2 presents the overview of the platform. Section 3 explains the theoretical description of the platform, including the detection algorithm and the recognition alogrithm. Section 4 presents the FPGA real-time implementation. Section 5 presents the performance evaluation. The conclusion is drawn in Sect. 6.

2   Overview of the Platform

The platform automatically detects and analyses wireless signals. The wireless signal collected by the antenna is sufficient.

Output parameters of the platform are the following.

1) Bandwidth of all received signals $B <= 2f_s$. Where f_s is the sampling rate. Limited by Nyquist's sampling theorem, the platform can only correctly acquire and analyze wireless signals with a bandwidth no greater than twice the sampling rate.

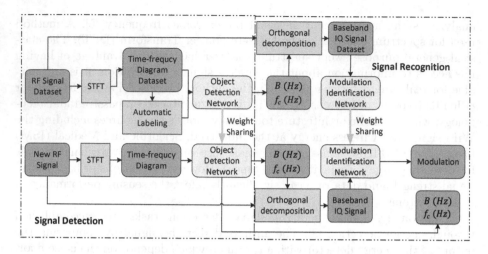

Fig. 1. RF signal detection and recognition algorithm block diagram.

2) Center frequency of all received signals f_c. To be transmitted in the channel, the signal usually needs to be upconverted. f_c is the frequency of the center of the signal after upconversion.
3) Modulation of all received signals such as Binary Phase Shift Keying (BPSK), Quadrature Phase Shift Keying (QPSK), 16-Quadrature Amplitude Modulation (16QAM), 2-Amplitude Shift Keying (2ASK), 2-Frequency Shift Keying (2FSK) etc.

Due to the high sampling rate of the acquisition module and the high processing rate of the signal processing algorithm, the platform can monitor and analyze the parameters of all signals received in real-time.

The proposed solution consists of an FPGA-based RF signal acquisition module and deep learning based signal processing module. The signal processing module consists of two steps: signal detection and signal recognition.

3   Deep-Learning-Based Wireless Signal Processing Method

The integrated wireless signal processing is divided into two phases as shown in Fig. 1. Firstly, the valid signals are detected and located. The bandwidth and center frequency of the valid signals are obtained. Afterwards, the signal recognition module downconverts and filters the signals according to the bandwidth and center frequency to extract the valid signals as baseband IQ signals. The CNN is used for recognition. The specific schemes are as follows.

Signal Detection. This phase detects if one or more wireless signals are received. If a signal is detected, this phase will output the bandwidth and center frequency of the signal.

a) The short-time Fourier transform (STFT) can convert the RF signal into a two-dimensional time-frequency map. RF signal shows a banded geometry on the time-frequency diagram. Therefore, the signal detection task can be converted into an image target detection task.
b) As a one-stage detection algorithm, YOLO has a high detection speed. In consideration of the real-time requirements of the platform, YOLO v3 is selected as the target detection network for the time-frequency map. And we have improved YOLO to fit the banded geometry characteristics of RF signals on the time-frequency diagram.

Signal Recognition. This phase recognizes the modulation of the signal. The modulation recognition algorithm is a two-step process: orthogonal decomposition then CNN completes signal feature extraction and modulation recognition.

a) This phase downconvert every valid signal with f_c and filter with a low-pass filter of bandwidth B (orthogonal decomposition). This phase will output N baseband IQ signals. Where N is the number of valid signals.
b) The baseband IQ signals can be used as input to the CNN for modulation type classification.

3.1   YOLO-SD Object Detection Network

YOLO is a state-of-the-art object detection algorithm, which is divided into two parts: a backbone feature extraction network and a feature prediction network. The backbone feature extraction network uses a residual network for extracting the main features of the target in the image. This backbone feature extraction network uses only convolutional layers and is a fully convolutional network. The feature prediction network constructs an Feature Pyramid Networks (FPN) feature pyramid for feature enhancement extraction [11]. Using the feature pyramid, three feature matrices of the enhanced features can be obtained. Each cell inside each feature matrix can predict three bounding boxes. The input image is equally divided into $S \times S$ grid, and each cell predicts B bounding boxes. This allows multiple targets to be detected and located on a single image.

Improving the Priori Bounding Box. The common YOLO v3 network is mainly used for the target detection of objects in images, and its prior bounding box is usually more similar to the objects in life. The signal target in the RF signal time-frequency diagram is in the shape of bars, and the prior bounding box of YOLO v3 cannot fit the characteristics of the RF signal time-frequency diagram well. To solve this problem, this paper adopts the K-means clustering algorithm to statistically cluster the signal borders in the constructed time-frequency map data set. The results that can fit the bars in the time-frequency diagram of the RF signal are used as the prior bounding box.

Detection Accuracy Metric. The metric is called generalized Intersection over Union (gIoU), which is defined as:

$$\text{gIoU} = \text{IoU} - \frac{C - (A \cup B)}{C}, \tag{1}$$

where A is the predicted box and B is the actual box. C is the smallest box that can enclose both A and B boxes. The Intersection over Union (IoU) is $(A \cap B)/(A \cup B)$. Compared with the IoU metrics, gIoU applies to the case of the bounding boxes do not overlap each other. In this case, IoU is 0, which does not reflect any information about the proximity of the bounding boxes. The gIoU is the lower bound of IoU, in the case of infinite overlap of two boxes, IoU=gIoU=1. IoU takes values in the range $[0, 1]$ and gIoU takes values in the range $(-1, 1]$. The gIoU converges to -1 when $(A \cup B)/C \approx 0$ and there is no intersection between A and B. For the problem of signal detection, this property of gIoU can be helpful in high noise scenarios where the network is expected to predict many error detections and bounding boxes that do not overlap with any signal. The gIoU-based loss for error detection can be high, thus forcing the network to gradually penalize such false predictions during training. Based on the above, we replace IoU with gIoU in the general YOLO algorithm and thus propose the YOLO-SD algorithm to adapt to the signal detection task.

3.2 Deep Learning Based Wireless Signal Modulation Recognition Method

To facilitate the recognition of the signal by the convolutional neural network, we decompose the signal orthogonally and thus downconvert the signal from RF to baseband. The process of quadrature decomposition is to multiply the received signal by the cosine signal and pass it through a low-pass filter so that the I-way and Q-way baseband signals can be obtained. The process of orthogonal decomposition to obtain the I-way baseband signal can be described as

$$y_I(t) = [r(t) \cos 2\pi f_c t] * h(t) = \tfrac{1}{2} x_I(t) + n_I(t), \tag{2}$$

where $r(t)$ is the signal, $h(t)$ is the low-pass filter, $x_I(t)$ is the I-way baseband signal and $n_I(t)$ is the I-way noise. Similarly, the Q-way baseband signal can be obtained by

$$y_Q(t) = [r(t) \sin 2\pi f_c t] * h(t) = \tfrac{1}{2} x_Q(t) + n_Q(t), \tag{3}$$

where $x_Q(t)$ is the Q-way baseband signal and $n_Q(t)$ is the Q-way noise.

The CNN uses four convolutional layers with different sizes of convolutional kernels for feature extraction, including shallow features with a perceptual field slightly larger than the symbol rate, and deep features with a global field of view. This is a network structure designed to address the characteristics of modulated signals. The IQ signal can be viewed as two channels, each of which is one-dimensional sampled data. Both channels use a one-dimensional convolutional layer and convolutional kernel at the same time.

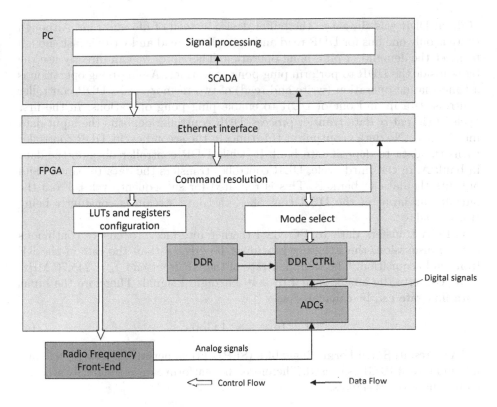

Fig. 2. Block diagram of the platform.

4   Platform Implementation

The key to hardware implementation is to pipeline the acquired signals to the signal processing module. The architecture of the platform is shown in Fig. 2. The PC sends commands to the FPGA via Supervisory Control and Data Acquisition (SCADA). SCADA controls the RF parameters of the platform (RF frequency point, receive gain, etc.) by configuring the through look-up tables (LUTs) and registers of the FPGA. The RF front-end reads RF parameters to complete the setup of the acquisition module and starts to acquire signals.

The analog signals are converted to digital signals by ADC. The ADC is included in the ADRV9009. The ADRV9009 RF transceiver uses the JESD204B protocol and communicates via a GTX high-speed serial transceiver. The ADC continuously transmit digital signals to Double Data Rate Synchronous Dynamic Random Access Memory (DDR) via Advanced eXtensible Interface (AXI) bus. Due to the advanced RF front-end, the platform supports frequencies from 123 MHz to 6000 MHz MHz with a bandwidth of up to 200 MHz.

The input data is continuous. The rate of acquisition and the rate of transmission to the PC are different. To achieve continuous data transfer, a ping-pong storage structure is used. Due to the fast acquisition rate and a large amount of data, DDR was chosen as the buffer device instead of fifo and ram. Although there is only one bus for DDR read and write, DDR read and write is fast enough to meet the demand of ping pong operation. Therefore, we can directly use the bank inside the DDR to perform ping pong operations. A ping-pong operation is a time-sharing operation (write and read) of two memory cells. DDR controller controls data in and out of DDR to enable ping pong operations. In the first cycle of the entire data transfer process, DDR controller deposits the input data into bank A. No data is output at this time. In the second cycle, DDR controller turns the data to deposit into bank B, while DDR controller outputs the data in bank A. In the third cycle, DDR controller transfers the data to bank A and outputs the data in bank B. This is repeated for subsequent cycles. From the output and input of the DDR controller, the data stream is constantly being transferred.

FPGA transfers data to PC via Ethernet interface. To ensure continuous data transmission, the Ethernet rate must be greater than the rate of the RF front-end acquisition. The sampling rate of the RF front-end $f_s = 245.76$ MHz. ADC converts the analog signal to a 16 bit digital signal. Therefore the input data flow rate can be calculated as

$$R = 16 \times f_s = 4 \text{ Gbps.} \tag{4}$$

As a result, Small Form Pluggables (SFP) optical network port with a transmission rate of 10 Gbps is used. Therefore, the platform can continuously acquire, store, and process signals.

5   Performance Evaluation

5.1   Dataset Generation

Signal detection and signal recognition algorithms are both based on deep learning. So it is necessary to build an efficient and comprehensive RF signal dataset. The centre frequency of the signal is set in the range of 10 MHz to 110 MHz. The signal bandwidth is set from 3 MHz to 10 MHz. The RF signal data is modulated by choosing digital modulation methods such as 2FSK, 16QAM, QPSK, BPSK, 2ASK, etc.

5.2   Results

Figure 3 shows the detection accuracy of YOLO-SD, YOLO-general, and energy Detection at 0–20 dB SNR. The detection accuracy is characterized by the IoU metric. We choose YOLO-general [10] and energy detection [12] as the baselines. The energy detection method detect the signal by comparing the output of the energy detector with a threshold which depends on the noise floor. So the energy detection method will mistakenly detect noise lines as signals. At the same time, due to the existence of intraband splitting of signals (e.g. FSK), the energy detection method misclassify a signal as multiple signals. In addition,

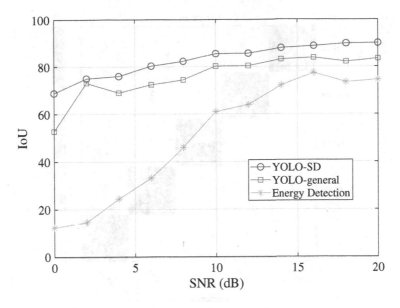

Fig. 3. IoU with different schemes and SNR.

The detection accuracy of the energy detection method decreases rapidly as the SNR decreases. This is mainly due to the fact that the signal in the experiment will have some random noise lines in the spectrum at low SNR with similar or even stronger amplitude than the signal. The YOLO-general algorithm, compared to the energy detection method, is no longer affected by the random noise spectrum. However, it sometimes appears that the accuracy in the high SNR case is lower than that in the neighboring low SNR case. This is mainly due to the poor fit of the box and signal identified by the algorithm when using IoU as the metric, and this error exceeds the effect of 2–4 dB noise. It is also found that when IoU is used as the metric, the accuracy drops abruptly at low SNR. This is mainly because the IoU is 0 when there is no intersection between the prediction box and the actual box, and the loss function is also 0 at this time. So it is impossible to perform gradient calculation and training. Therefore, the algorithm using IoU as a metric has a poor learning ability for low SNR data, which leads to a weak detection ability for low SNR signals.

YOLO-SD uses a computer vision approach to reduce the effect of noise on signal detection. In addition, the priori bounding box and accuracy metric are improved. So it can be seen that Compared with the other two detection methods, the YOLO-SD algorithm shows a significant improvement in detection accuracy at each SNR.

To analyze the modulation classification performance, Fig. 4 shows the confusion matrix of all detections and recognition in the dataset acquired with hardware. The data set was collected in an environment with SNR = 34.7 dB. From the experimental results, it can be seen that the intelligent wireless signal

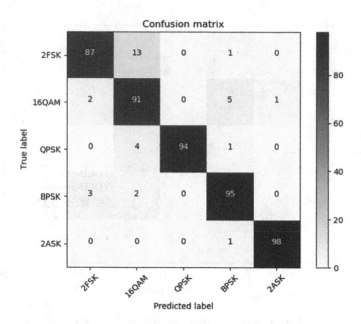

Fig. 4. Acquisition and analysis platform experimental results with SNR = 34.7 dB.

detection and recognition platform achieves an average recognition accuracy of 93% for six modulation types of RF signals.

6   Conclusions

This paper designed and implemented an intelligent IoT signal Monitoring platform, which could automatically detect the wireless signals and output the bandwidth, center frequency, and modulation of the signals. The YOLO-SD algorithm is adopted as the detection algorithm, which has improved the detection accuracy and the performance in terms of low SNR compared with YOLO-general. Adopting the method of orthogonal decomposition followed by a neural network for recognition, the modulation mode can be recognized for signals of any frequency. Due to the hardware sampling frequency of up to 245.76 MHz, the platform can detect and recognize signals with a wide bandwidth (no larger than 245.76 MHz). In addition, due to the ping-pong structure of the hardware part, the data can be continuously collected, transmitted, and processed, thus realizing the function of collecting signals and processing them in real-time.

Acknowledgement. This work was supported by the National Key Research and Development Program of China (No. 2019YFE0196400) and the National Natural Science Foundation of China (No. 62271051 and No. 61871035).

References

1. Meneghello, F., et al.: IoT: internet of threats? a survey of practical security vulnerabilities in real IoT devices. IEEE Internet Things J. **6**(5), 8182–8201 (2019)
2. Yadav, E.P., Mittal, E.A., Yadav, H.: IoT: challenges and issues in Indian perspective. In: Proceedings International Conference Internet Things: Smart Innovation Usages (IoT-SIU), pp. 1–5 (2018)
3. Cao, Z., Yang, S.: A security communication device based on narrowband internet of things. In: Proc. IEEE 5th Int. Conf. Comput. Commun. (ICCC), pp. 2141–2145 (2019)
4. Tokuda, H., Yonezawa, T., Nakazawa, J.: Monitoring dependability of city-scale IoT using D-case. In: Proc. IEEE World Forum Int. Things (WF-IoT), pp. 371–372 (2014)
5. Hunter, M.T., Kourtellis, A.G., Ziomek, C.D., Mikhael, W.B.: Fundamentals of modern spectral analysis. IEEE Instrum. Meas. Mag. **14**(4), 12–16 (2011)
6. Tektronix. Fundamentals of Real-Time Spectrum Analysis. http://info.tek.com/Fundamentals-of-Real-Time-SpectrumAnalysis-LP.html. Accessed 2009. http://info.tek.com/Fundamentals-of-Real-Time-SpectrumAnalysis-LP.html. Accessed 2009. http://info.tek.com/Fundamentals-of-Real-Time-SpectrumAnalysis-LP.htmlAccessed 2009.
7. Li, W., Vishwakarma, S., Tang, C., Woodbridge, K., Piechocki, R.J., Chetty, K.: Using RF transmissions from IoT devices for occupancy detection and activity recognition. IEEE Sensors J. **22**(3), 2484–2495 (2022)
8. Suseela, B., Sivakumar, D.: Non-cooperative spectrum sensing techniques in cognitive radio-a survey. In: Proceedings IEEE Technological Innovation in ICT for Agriculture and Rural Development (TIAR), pp. 127–133 (2015)
9. Vagollari, A., et al.: Joint detection and classification of RF signals using deep learning. In: Proceedings of IEEE 93rd Veh. Technol. Conf. (VTC2021-Spring), pp. 1–7 (2021)
10. Basak, S., Rajendran, S., Pollin, S., Scheers, B.: Combined RF-based drone detection and classification. IEEE Trans. Cogn. Commun. Netw. **8**(1), 111–120 (2022)
11. Redmon, J., Divvala, S., Girshick, R., Farhadi, A.: You Only Look Once: unified, real-time object detection. In: Proc. IEEE Conf. Comput. Vis. Pattern Recognit. (CVPR), pp. 779–788 (2016)
12. Salt, J.E., Nguyen, H.H.: Performance prediction for energy detection of unknown signals. IEEE Trans. Veh. Technol. **57**(6), 3900–3904 (2008)

Network Security

A Novel Approach to Transmit Audio Content Over a Secure Communication Channel by Using Light Optics Under the Acousto-Optic Premise

Vijay A. Kanade[✉]

Pune, India
kanade.science@gmail.com

Abstract. This research paper discloses a novel method to transmit audio content over a secure communication channel by using light optics. The proposal uses Light-based Doppler Interferometry (LDI) to measure sound-field in the room. The measured sound-field values are used to create silence bubbles at the sender and recipient side by using hybrid active noise-cancellation to ensure effective communication. An audio signal is picked up from the speaker placed at the sender's side and is used to modulate the current source that drives a light emitting diode (LED). Upon audio-to-light conversion, the output optical signal is transmitted through the air to the intended recipient present at the other end of the room, who is some distance away from the sender. The experiments were performed using the LED light and a laser diode separately to explore different options available for indoor communication. According to the experimental results, LED light could transmit 12 dB more power than the laser diode across different audio frequencies for both setups of no air gap (i.e. 0 cm) and an air gap of 4 cm between the light source and photodetector. Also, it was identified that the laser diode transmitted consistent power for a known distance as compared to LED light. The attenuation for LED light and laser diode with respect to distance was found to be ≈5.5 dB/cm and ≈4.9 dB/cm respectively.

Keywords: LED Light · Audio Content Transmission · Light-based Doppler Interferometry (LDI) · Sound-Field Measurements · Hybrid Active Noise Cancellation · Photodetector

1 Introduction

In today's digital world, cyberattacks have been rising at an alarming rate. Malware attack, Man-in-the-middle (MitM) attack, Phishing attack, Denial-of-service attack, and so on are putting individuals and enterprises data at risk. Irrespective of the encryption layers added over the communication channel, no communication can be regarded as 100% safe in today's day and age.

V. A. Kanade—Researcher.

© ICST Institute for Computer Sciences, Social Informatics and Telecommunications Engineering 2023
Published by Springer Nature Switzerland AG 2023. All Rights Reserved
K. Rabie et al. (Eds.): IoTaaS 2022, LNICST 506, pp. 187–198, 2023.
https://doi.org/10.1007/978-3-031-37139-4_17

With the growing market for Internet-of-Things (IoT) devices, such cyberattacks are only expected to shoot up. According to a Jan 2022 report 'Global Cybersecurity Outlook 2022' by World Economic Forum, each successful cyberattack incident in 2021 cost an enterprise a whopping $3.6 million. Moreover, COVID19 added fuel to fire as the cybercrimes only grew exponentially during this period with each organization reporting to have faced 270 cyberattacks. Also, in 2021 the ransomware attacks saw a steep rise of 151% [1].

Moreover, attacks like MitM facilitate eavesdropping, which is a common problem experienced by corporate professionals where confidential data is on the line. With eavesdropping, the attacker can intercept, delete, or modify data that travels between two or more devices. Eavesdropping, which is also known as sniffing or snooping, primarily occurs in an unsecured network environment. However, with increased sophistication of Machine Learning (ML) and Artificial Intelligence (AI) algorithms, even secured networks are open to such attacks [2].

Looking at the current trend of cybercrimes, it has become inevitable to develop innovative solutions that make the data in transit more secure and safe. Various end-to-end encryption methods are already being employed to safeguard data in motion. Companies like Apple use it for their iMessage and FaceTime services along with Microsoft that uses it for Skype services [3]. However, such encryption methods are only making eavesdropping difficult, but not impossible. Moreover, as all of today's devices are internet enabled, hence ensuring the safety of personal and confidential data has become even more crucial.

Recently, researchers from MIT Lincoln Laboratory developed a method for sending audible messages directly to an individual's ear from a distance by using lasers [4]. Although the implemented technology is said to be safe from eavesdropping, lasers can be dangerous. Delivering a laser directly to a human's ear can cause injury to a person's skin, damage skin tissues due to high temperature of lasers, lead to skin burns, and plenty other problems [5].

Another option to leverage safe communication is by using the high frequency RF (i.e. radio frequency) signal. However, as the RF signal is widely used across devices, one disadvantage here is that it is difficult to determine whether the RF signal is detected by an unknown party. Hence, there seems to be a long standing need to develop a secure communication system that is free from eavesdropping while two or more individuals communicate.

2 Theory

In this paper we present an implementation of using an optical signal to transmit audio content between two communicators sitting in a room, typically in an office setting. The deployment can be enabled via a uniquely designed IoT device similar to a simple Bluetooth device that has multiple modules embedded in it. However, the present research focuses on the development of an innovative approach for audio message communication using light which can be incorporated in any IoT device in future.

2.1 Sound-Field Measurements Using LDI

In step-I, Light-based Doppler Interferometry (LDI) is used for sound-field measurement [6]. It senses, captures, and analyzes the spatial properties of the sound-field in a room arising from sound sources like people having discussions or points like walls, windows, floors, equipment, and so on. Conventionally, laser driven equipment is used for such measurements (i.e. Laser Doppler Interferometry) [7]. However, we use LEDs that showcase higher brightness and have the ability to act like tiny lasers but are safe to use [8]. Thus, we use this measured sound data for further optical light modulation. The LDI setup is shown in Fig. 1 below.

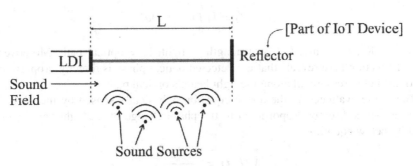

Fig. 1. Sound-field measurement setup

In our case, LDI is the part of the IoT device that transmits audio signals. Fundamentally, the LDI transmits focused light towards the intended user wearing a similar IoT device that has the reflector to reflect the light received from the sender. Thus, the reflected light is used to analyze the sound-field aspects. The light undergoes optical path change as it traverses the air gap between the sender and receiver due to the change in the refractive index occurring because of the surrounding sound-field or sound and light interaction.

For a transparent medium like air, the refractive index n varies with respect to density ρ which is given by equation n = ρK + 1, where K is the Gladstone-Dale constant [9]. Now, with the presence of sound waves in the air medium, its density varies based on the acoustic pressure. This relation is given by the below equation:

$$\left(\frac{p+p_0}{p_0}\right) = \left(\frac{\rho}{\rho_0}\right)^{\gamma}$$

where, p_0 = undisturbed pressure, ρ_0 = density, and γ is the specific-heat ratio. Moreover, p and ρ_0 highlight the acoustic contribution to the overall pressure and density fields under static conditions.

This causes a change in the refractive index of the medium given by below equation:

$$n = n_0 + \frac{n_0 - 1}{\gamma p_0} p$$

where, n_0 = refractive index and the term $(n_0 - 1) / (\gamma p_0)$ represents the acousto-optic coefficient. Also, for sound-field measurement in air, the standard coefficient values are $\gamma = 1.40$ and $p_0 = 101325$ [10].

Let's consider a real life scenario of a corporate office room where sound-fields exist all around. In our approach, the light beam from LDI traverses the room by following a straight path L to the intended recipient. The LDI emits light in the direction of the receiver which gets scattered and is eventually reflected back to LDI by the reflector at the receiver's end as seen in the Fig. 1. As a result, the phase of the light beam ϕ emitted by LDI is determined based on its optical path. The phase is given by following equation:

$$\phi(L, t) = k_l \int_0^L n(r, t, l) dl$$

where $r \in R^3$, t = time, k = wavelength of light, L = optical path. Moreover, the integral function here reveals that the detected optical phase is directly proportional to the sound-field pressure all along the light beam's optical path.

The phase evaluated in the above equation is basically sensed by the LDI. Thus, LDI's output is directly proportional to the phase change of the light beam which is given by below equation:

$$V(L, t) = \frac{1}{k_l n_0} \frac{d\phi}{dt},$$

Evaluating it all, the eventual vibration measured by the LDI is given by below equation:

$$V = U_w + \frac{n_0 - 1}{\gamma p_0 n_0} j\omega \int_0^L P(l) dl.$$

where, U_w = vibration of hard surfaces like walls, second term arises due to the acousto-optic effect. When the room where the users reside has hard walls and floors, then the term U_w can be neglected at mid and high frequencies. Thus the output signal V recorded by LDI is only the result of the acousto-optic effect [7, 10].

In summary, the above equation indicates that the measured signal V is proportional to the sound-field that's projected along the path of the light beam.

2.2 Hybrid Active Noise Cancellation

In step-II, the measured signal or vibrational values V are used for generating active noise cancellation signals at the communicating parties. In our case, we use hybrid active noise cancellation that combines both feedforward and feedback technology for generating noise-free silence bubbles around the device wearer's ear [11]. Feedforward typically cancels the ambient noise while the feedback monitors what the user hears and cancels the internal noise if any. This illustration is shown in Fig. 2.

The entire procedure basically creates a silence bubble around the communicating users which is similar to a virtual silence zone. The functionality benefits the users as the surrounding noise or sounds within the room are negated entirely to enable noise-free focused audio communication.

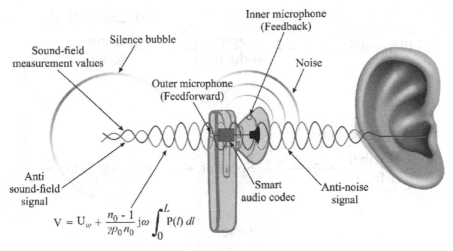

Fig. 2. Hybrid active noise cancellation

2.3 Modulate LED Power to Transmit Audio

In step-III, the sender speaks over the speaker to transmit the audio content. The speaker is connected to the light modulating unit that modulates the optical current source providing power to the LED. Note that the LED light used to transmit audio content is different from LEDs used in the LDI.

The modulated light is then allowed to propagate through the air gap between the sender and receiver. Upon being emitted, it is received by the photodetector at the recipient's end. This photodetector is further connected to the output speaker to produce the audio content sent by the sender.

3 Experimental Design

In our experiments, the audio messages to be transmitted do not exceed 5Vpp. The current source for the LED / laser diode is of 10V, thereby making the audio range permissible. Also, the input current to the current source does not exceed the limit of 5 mA/V. As the current source is in the low bandwidth mode, the input it takes is around 14–15 kHz. Since the input frequency range for music lies between 20 Hz to 10 kHz, 14–15 kHz is acceptable. Moreover, the gain of the photodetector should not exceed a limit as the output signal should not go beyond 5Vpp. Also, at 2 cm from the speaker, we placed a smartphone decibel meter that uses a sound level meter app (Decibel X) to measure the audio level of the received signal.

We have used a 5 mm green LED as light source and two 8 Ω 0.5W speakers for our experiments. The experimental layout is disclosed in Fig. 3 below:

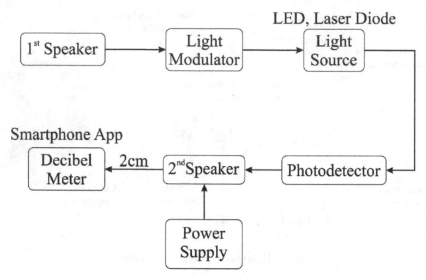

Fig. 3. Experimental layout

The portable testbed for LED light that validates the propositions of our research is represented in the below image. A similar setup was used with a laser diode which is not shown here. Also, please note that the power supply unit used to supply power to the circuit and voltage meter used to measure voltages at different points in the circuit is not shown in the captured image (Fig. 4):

To determine the results, the testbed shown in Fig. 4 was used where we supplied music as an input audio signal to the first speaker (8 Ω 0.5 W). The music was chosen in a manner which ensured that the notes within the song were made up of multiple frequencies. We also used an indigenously made light modulating unit that controlled the power to the LED/laser diode. The photodetector we used for experimental purposes is a light sensor that is placed at 0 cm and 4 cm from the LED/laser diode in the initial and final settings respectively. Moreover, the light sensor is further connected to the second speaker that reproduces the original audio signal. The smartphone sound meter is placed at a distance of 2 cm from the second speaker (8 Ω 0.5 W). The sound meter not only records the sound decibels but also shows the fluctuations in the output frequencies of the received audio signal.

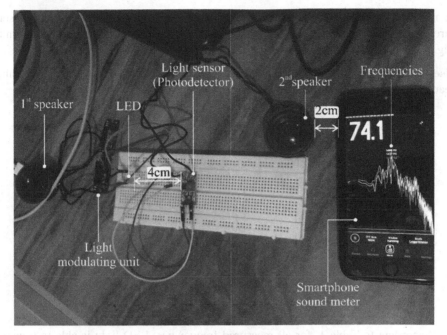

Fig. 4. Testbed for audio transmission using LED placed at 4 cm from the photodetector

4 Testing

To test the experimental setup, the voltage output at each signal processing juncture was measured. Moreover, to ensure that the voltage fluctuations were consistent for all measurements, the data was measured while the music was being played at the first speaker. It was identified that the voltage measured at the output of the first speaker did not exceed 2 Vpp. Also, the voltage of the photodetector placed on the opposite side of the LED light/laser diode with gain on turned out to be less than 1Vpp. Also, the output of the second speaker connected to the power supply was about 2.5 Vpp. All the measured voltages showcased an acceptable range.

In the initial iteration, the experimental setup did not produce the audible sound as required. When music with high frequency notes was played, the speakers produced a crashing noise. When verified, it was found that the LED had a current source that was set to 45 mA. In the following iteration, when the current source was reduced to 35 mA, music was clearly heard.

5 Results

As stated earlier, we used the LED and laser diode separately as optical sources and measured decibel readings for different settings. Initially, the audio content transmission for zero air gap between LED and photodetector was measured, followed by audio transmission with the air gap of 4cm. Moreover, we used a free, open source audio software named Audacity to record and measure attenuation of different sound frequencies sent through the developed system [12]. All the results evaluated using the testbed shown in Fig. 4 are outlined in the below tables.

Use case-I: No gap between the LED/laser diode and the photodetector. The decibel reading for this use case are as follows:

Table 1. Decibel Readings for No Air Gap Configuration

Sr. No	f(Hz)	LED (dB)	Laser diode (dB)
1	80	91	79
2	500	109	100
3	1000	108	98
4	2500	103	92
5	5000	104	95

According to Table 1, for all measured frequencies, LED light is able to transmit sound with more decibel level as compared to laser diode. The attenuation for each light source with zero air gap is tabulated below:

Table 2. Attenuation for LED and Laser Diode with No Air Gap

Sr. No	f(Hz)	LED loss (dB)	Laser diode loss (dB)
1	80	−3	7
2	500	2	9
3	1000	0	7
4	2500	−5	3
5	5000	−11	−3

According to Table 2, the laser diode shows a gain of 7 to 9 dB on average for all measured frequencies in a no air gap setup as compared to LED.

Use case-II: Upon testing the no air gap scenario, we increased the distance between the LED/laser diode and the photodetector to 4 cm and recorded the decibel reading and corresponding attenuation. The readings are given in the Tables 3 and 4:

Table 3. Decibel Reading for Air Gap of 4cm

Sr. No	f(Hz)	LED (dB)	Laser diode (dB)
1	80	69	66
2	500	94	83
3	1000	95	82
4	2500	87	76
5	5000	89	77

Further, the attenuation for LED and laser diode was determined with an air gap of 4 cm. The readings are as given below:

Table 4. Attenuation for LED and Laser Diode with 4cm Air Gap

Sr. No	f(Hz)	LED loss (dB)	Laser diode loss (dB)
1	80	17	20
2	500	17	26
3	1000	15	24
4	2500	11	19
5	5000	6	15

On observing the two configurations, it was identified that the average attenuation for LED and laser diode with respect to distance was ≈5.5 dB/cm and ≈4.9 dB/cm respectively.

It is worth noting that we have successfully implemented optical light-based audio data transmission as desired. Since the developed prototype uses LED light instead of harmful lasers, it seems to have an edge over the laser-based audio message transmission method designed by MIT Lincoln Laboratory researchers in 2019 [4, 5]. We are currently working on the practical implementation of the remaining two modules of 'LDI based sound-field measurements' and 'hybrid active noise cancellation.' Upon realization, we will integrate these modules with the already developed light-based audio transmission module.

6 Advantages and Applications

Today, one can say that any kind of wireless communication is inevitably vulnerable to external attacks. Our research tries to isolate one such communication that does not involve the usage of the internet or any other external network. The communication

method is restricted to living rooms in households, corporate office rooms, and audi-
toriums where the enclosed space is without any obstacles or partitions such as glass
partition, wooden partition, and so on. Implying, the open room space allows barrier-free
passage of optical light. With such room configuration and novel communication method
the chances of eavesdropping and other cyberattacks are potentially brought down to
zero. Thereby, establishing a unique communication channel for user interaction.

Corporate professionals can use the technology for meetings, conferences, or group
discussions while physically staying in the same office space. For example, let's say a
manager in an IT firm wishes to have a physical meeting with two of his subordinates.
In a general scenario, the manager has to either call the individuals at his desk or take
them to a conference room where other company employees are not present while they
discuss project related matters.

However, with the proposed technology, the manager can do it seamlessly by sitting
at his own desk. In this case, let's assume that all the intended users are wearing the IoT
device that enables light-based audio communication. Initially the manager identifies the
employees with whom he wants to have a collaborative discussion. Once identified, the
target employees are notified about it on their respective IoT devices. Upon notifying, the
manager's IoT device then performs sound-field measurement of that very room. Once
that's done, the sound-field measurement values are communicated to the participating
user devices. Then, the devices used by all three users' initiate noise cancellation to create
silence zones for each of them based on the sound-field values. These virtual silence
bubbles that are noise-free then allow communication between participating users. Thus,
a group meeting of three is conducted in the same office arena without having the users
move to another isolated conference room or space.

Figure 5 is a representation of the proposed light-based audio transmission approach in an office setting by establishing a secure communication channel between the
communicating users.

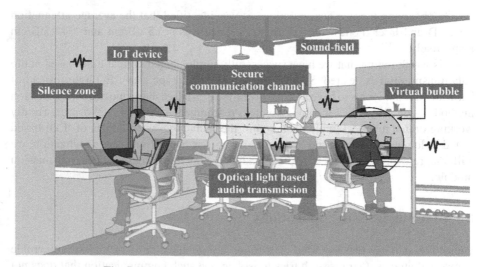

Fig. 5. Light-based audio transmission in an office setting

7 Conclusion

This research proposes a unique approach for sending audio content to intended users in a room by harnessing the properties of light. The method employs a three step process for audio transmission: sound-field measurement using LDI, hybrid active noise cancellation, and audio files transmission by manipulating LED power. Moreover, sound-field parameters enable noise cancellation phenomena, thereby highlighting a novel process for creating silence zones at the sender and receiver end while communicating.

On the experimental front, our research revealed that one can use LED light instead of lasers for audio content transmission. It is a safer approach for point-to-point communication. The results revealed that LED light could transmit 12 dB more power than the laser diode across different audio frequencies for configurations of 0cm and 4cm air gap between the light source and photodetector. Lasers had lower attenuation of $\approx$4.9 dB/cm over distance as compared to LED light attenuation of $\approx$5.5 dB/cm. Since lasers use polarized light, they use less power for transmission as compared to LED light, thereby justifying the attenuation values. However, in a room setting, since the distance is not much of a concern, LED light beams can be a go-to choice for delivering audio messages from one corner of the room to another.

8 Future Work

In future, we intend to use a lens (e.g. bi-convex lens) between the audio transmitter and receiver to increase the intensity of light at the photodetector. Such an arrangement would inevitably increase the power received at the photodetector, thereby lowering the loss for used light sources.

Secondly, we also intend to use an amplifier (e.g. a non-inverting amplifier) between the speaker and photodetector. This is because, without the amplifier, although the music is distinguishable, there is an element of noise that still persists in the audio signals produced by the second speaker. Thus, by adding the amplifier, we would be adding gain to the speakers which would reduce the 'noise variable' from the speaker that reproduces audio signal at the receiver end. This would make the audio messages more clear to the intended user.

We also intend to work on adding security layers to the developed model to ensure that it is resistant to any form of external penetration or attack. Moreover, we intend to test the developed prototype under different lighting conditions. This will give us key insights into whether our model can withstand interference from external lights whilst still maintaining a secure communication.

Acknowledgement. I would like to extend my sincere gratitude to Dr. A. S. Kanade for his relentless support during my research work.

Confict of Interest. The authors declare that they have no conflict of interest.

References

1. World Economic Forum, Global Cybersecurity Outlook 2022, 18 January 2022
2. Miao, Y., Chen, C., Pan, L., Han, Q.-L., Zhang, J., Xiang, Y.: Machine learning based cyber attacks targeting on controlled information: a survey, ACM Comput. Surv. **54**(7), Article No. 139, 1–36 (2022). https://doi.org/10.1145/3465171, 18 July 2021
3. Greenemeier, L.: Fact or Fiction: encryption prevents digital eavesdropping, Scientific American, 15 July (2013)
4. Foy, K.: A laser can deliver messages directly to your ear from across the room, Communications & Community Outreach Office, Lincoln Laboratory, Massachusetts Institute of Technology, 4 November (2019)
5. Laser Hazards-General, Environmental Health and Safety, Oregon State University
6. Olsson, E.: Doctoral thesis on sound source localization from laser vibrometry recordings. Luleå University of Technology, Department of Applied Physics and Mechanical Engineering, Division of Experimental Mechanics **23**|ISSN: 1402–1544 (2007)
7. Fernandez-Grande, E., Verburg, S., Hahmann, M.: Acousto-optic capture of the sound field in a room based on sparse measurement data. In: Proceedings of the International Symposium on Room Acoustics, Amsterdam, Netherlands, 15 to 17 September (2019)
8. National Institute of Standards and Technology (NIST). A light bright and tiny: Scientists build a better nanoscale LED: New design overcomes long-standing LED efficiency problem -- and can transform into a laser to boot. ScienceDaily. ScienceDaily, 14 August (2020)
9. Tatar, K.: Doctoral Thesis on Machine tool vibrations and violin sound fields studied using laser vibrometry. Luleå University of Technology, Department of Applied Physics and Mechanical Engineering, Division of Experimental Mechanics **27**|ISSN: 1402-1757 (2006)
10. Ishikawa, K., Shiraki, Y., Moriya, T., et al.: Low-noise optical measurement of sound using midfringe locked interferometer with differential detection. Acoustical Soc. Am., J. Acoustical Soc. Am. **150**(1514), 1523 (2021). https://doi.org/10.1121/10.0005939
11. Triggs, R.: SoundGuys, Active noise cancelling (ANC) technology types explained, 29 October (2021)
12. Audacity (2022). https://www.audacityteam.org/download/

Author Index

A

Abdugapbar, Kozhakhmet 38
Al-Ali, Reem 58
Amanbek, Yerasyl 3
Arora, Mireya 58

B

Bechtsis, Dimitrios 12
Bendoukha, Sidi Ahmed. 58

C

Cao, Guangchuan 174
Cao, Shan 135
Chen, Hao 82
Chen, Jen-Jee 117
Chen, Whai-En 82
Chen, Xiang 94, 161
Chen, Yudie 161

D

Dautov, Kassen 38, 48
Dong, Yuhan 94

G

Ge, Chengxiang 135
Geng, Jiaxiang 82
Georgakidis, Konstantinos 12
Ghaoud, Tareg 58
Guan, Lele 73
Guo, Yinan 82

H

Haitaamar, Zineddine N. 58
Hashmi, Mohammad 38, 48
He, Weibao 148
Hou, Yanzhao 82
Hsu, Terng-Yin 135
Hsu, Terngyin 161
Hsu, Terng-Yin 94

J

Jiang, Zhiyuan 127, 135

K

Kalakova, Aidana 3
Kanade, Vijay A. 187
Karunamurthy, Jayakumar V. 58

L

Liang, Houze 161
Liang, Kai 117
Lin, Dengsheng 127
Liu, Jiaxin 117
Liu, Jing 94
Lv, Dong 161

N

Nauryzbayev, Galymzhan 38, 48

P

Papapanagiotakis, Georgios 12
Papaspyropoulou, Maria 12
Peng, Fei 135

S

Sfitis, Nikolaos 12
Shalpeneyeva, Kamila 48
Shi, Chenrui 73
Shi, Yuming 73
Song, Jiupeng 174
Syrmos, Evangelos 12

T

Tang, Dong 148
Tian, Lu 73
Tian, Zhigang 106
Todi, Theodora 12

V

Vlachos, Dimitrios 12

K. Rabie et al. (Eds.): IoTaaS 2022, LNICST 506, pp. 199–200, 2023.
https://doi.org/10.1007/978-3-031-37139-4

W
Wang, Lan   161
Wu, Weizhi   161

X
Xiao, Jianxiong   94
Xu, Zhan   73

Y
Yedilkhan, Didar   3
Yu, Shanping   174

Z
Zakariya Saleh, Zahraa   23
Zhakiyev, Nurkhat   3
Zhang, Wancheng   174
Zhang, Xiaoli   117
Zhang, Yan   174
Zhao, Haoyu   174
Zhi, Ruxin   106
Zhou, Bilei   106
Zhou, Fasheng   148
Zou, Yamei   127

Printed in the United States
by Baker & Taylor Publisher Services

Printed in the United States
by Baker & Taylor Publisher Services